The Cosmos In Becoming

Edited by

Theresa Wong Yai-Chow
Wen Hsiang Chen
Frank Budenholzer

The Fu Jen Series on Religion, Science and Culture is published by Fu Jen Catholic University in Taiwan in collaboration with the Australasian Theological Forum Ltd. Volumes may consist of monographs, lecture series or conference proceedings. Each volume seeks to engage questions of religion, science and culture within the framework of Chinese and Taiwanese culture in dialogue with world culture.

Series Editor: Frank E Budenholzer SVD, is Professor of Chemistry at Fu Jen Catholic University and Academic Coordinator of the Center for the Study of Science and Religion and Fu Jen.

1. *The Palace Of Glory: God's World And Science*, by Arthur Peacocke, 2005.
2. *Religion And Science In The Context Of Chinese Culture*, edited by Chan, Tak-Kwong, Tsai, Yi-Jia, 2006.

The Cosmos In Becoming
Perspectives of Christianity and Chinese Religions

Edited by

Theresa Wong Yai-Chow
Wen Hsiang Chen
Frank Budenholzer

ATF Press

Adelaide

Text copyright © 2008 by the authors for their individual papers and to ATF Press for the introduction and the collection.

All rights reserved. Except for any fair dealing permitted under the Copyright Act, no part of this book may be reproduced by any means without prior permission. Inquiries should be made to the publisher.

The moral right of the authors have been asserted

First published 2008

ISBN 9781920691943

Published by ATF Press
An imprint of the Australasian Theological Forum Ltd
PO Box 504 Hindmarsh
SA 5007
ABN 90 116 359 963
www.atfpress.com

cover design by Astrid Sengkey

Contents

Introduction — vii

Acknowledgments — xiii

Part One

1. Is Nature All There Is?
   John F Haught — 3

2. Science, Religion And The Quest For Cosmic Purpose
   John F Haught — 21

3. Darwin And Divine Providence
   John F Haught — 39

4. Theology, Ecology And Cosmology
   John F Haught — 61

Part Two

5. Myths Of Origination In Early Chinese Thought
   Cheng, Chih-Ming — 91

6. One Universe, Two Perspectives: Cosmology, Epistemology and Science-Religion Dialogue
   Kang Phee-Seng — 135

Part Three

7. Living Creatures: The Buddhist Perspective
   Shih Chao-Hwei — 155

8. What Is Life—Current Scientific And Philosophical Perspectives
   Frank Budenholzer   201

Part Four

9. Matter And Spirit In Taoism
   John Chuang   229

10. Considerations Of The 'Soul' In Western Thought
    Thomas Berg   255

Contributors   285

Glossary   287

Introduction

Teresa Wong Yai-Chow, Wen Hsiang Chen and Frank Budenholzer

'And God saw everything that he had made, and behold, it was very good. And there was evening and there was morning on the sixth day. And thus the heavens were finished and all the host of them.' (Genesis 1:31 – 2:1) Thus the Hebrew Scriptures, the basis of the faith of the three great monotheistic traditions, describe a process in which the cosmos came to be. However, the fact of process in the becoming of the cosmos was also a bedrock of traditional Chinese thought and now has become the central tenet of the scientific picture of the cosmos. In November of 2004, the Department of Religious Studies and the Center for the Study of Science and Religion, of Fu Jen Catholic University, sponsored a three day conference: 'The Cosmos in Becoming: Religion and Science in Dialogue'. The conference was held from Friday, November 26, 2004 through Sunday noon, November 28, 2004. During these three days there were eleven formal lectures and two panel discussions.

At least from the point of view of the human species, we can indentify three key stages in this process of becoming—the beginning of the universe with the big bang, the origin of life on the planet earth and the emergence of consciousness and rationality in *homo sapiens*. These thee stages, became the organising subthemes of the conference.

The keynote address was given by Professor John Haught, a Catholic theologian and Professor Emeritus in the Department Theology of Georgetown University in Washington, DC: 'Science and the Quest for Cosmic

Purpose'. In many quarters, the discoveries of science have been thought to imply a mindless, meaningless cosmos. Taking his clue from Whitehead, Professor Haught argues for an 'aesthetic cosmological principle', He 'suggests that the universe has apparently been "set up" from the very beginning in such a manner as to allow for the ongoing creation of manifold forms of beauty'.

While in Taiwan Professor Haught was invited to give lectures at several other universities and these have also been included in this volume, a total of four lectures. They provide both the background and a follow-up to the keynote address. 'Is Nature All There Is?' was delivered at the Department of Philosophy of Taiwan National University the day after the conference. Haught argues, against the evolutionary naturalism of thinkers like Richard Dawkins and Carl Sagan. There are layers of explanation and Darwinian evolutionary explanations, while presumably true, need to be supplemented by a deeper theological explanation.

But does not Darwinian science bring into disrepute traditional understanding of Divine Providence? Professor Haught sought to deal with the objection in a lecture given at Fu Jen's College of Theology and later at the Department of Religious Studies of National Chengchr University in Taipei. Haught argues that after Darwin can we still have a plausible understanding of God that is both consistent with traditional belief and adequate to the reality of evolution.

Professor Haught's final lecture considered not only the history of human kind, but also our future: 'Theology, Ecology and Cosmology'. This lecture was given at Fu Jen's Department of Philosophy and at Wenzao College of Modern Languages, a Sister Catholic College of Fu Jen, located in southern Taiwan's port city of Kaohsiung. 'A Christian vision will lead us to strive not to get out of the world but to do what we can to shepherd this still unfinished universe toward the fulfillment of the promise that underlies and impels it toward the future'.

Haught's four papers lay the foundation for a consideration of the evolving universe as seen from both traditional Chinese religions and Christianity. These six papers deal with the three main sub-themes of the conference: cosmology, life and human life. The original conference format also included three papers that focused exclusively on recent scientific advances— 'Cosmology and the Big Bang', by Dr Frank Shu, a well known astrophysicist and at the time president of the National Tsing Hua University in Hsinchu, Taiwan; 'The Origen of Life: Chemical Evolution' by Dr Lee Wei-Chia, Director of the National Science Museum in Taichung and professor in the College of Life Sciences of National Tsing Hua University and 'Contemporary Accounts of Human Evolution' by the physical anthropologist Dr Chen Shau-Feng of the Graduate Institute of Anthropology of Tzu-Chi University in Hualien, Taiwan. In keeping with the theme of the conference, these papers set the stage for religious and philosophical papers on the beginnings of the universe, the emergence of life and the emergence of the human being. The material in these papers is readily available in English and so the decision was made not to translate the papers into English and include them in this volume. While understandable, the decision does change the dynamics of the volume. Readers are encouraged to explore the science in other sources.

The first of the sub-themes was cosmology—the origin of the material universe. From the perspective of traditional Chinese religions, Professor Cheng, Chi-ming, Professor in the Department of Religious Studies of Fu Jen Catholic University, considered 'Myths of Origin in Early Chinese Thought'. The second paper, by Professor Kang, Phee-Seng, Professor in the Department of Religion and Philosophy of Hong Kong Baptist College, considered the 'Christian Understanding of the Origin of the Universe and the Christian Dialogue with Contemporary Science'.

The cosmos as we know it is filled with life, and so the second sub-theme was the origin and nature of life. The first paper of this section considered life from a Buddhist perspective. Master Shih Chao-Hwei Shih spoke on the topic, 'Life's Creatures: The Buddhist Perspective'. She explained the common characteristics of all life in Buddhist thought and the ethical implications with regard to the destruction of human embryos. This was followed by a more philosophical contribution by Frank Budenholzer, Professor of Chemistry and part-time lecturer in the Department of Philosophy at Fu Jen Catholic University, 'What is Life?' Using the thought of the Canadian philosopher-theologian Bernard Lonergan, he argued that living things are emergent unities, integrating previously random chemical processes.

The final sub-theme was human life. Again the first paper addressed the issue from the perspective of early Chinese thought. Dr. John Chuang, Associate Professor in the Department of Religious Studies at Fu Jen, talked on 'Matter and Spirit in Taoism'. He considered the human body and spirit in Taoist thought, their origin and their destination after death. Thomas Berg of the Center for Higher Studies of the Legion of Christ in Thornwood, New York brought this session to a close with a philosophical consideration of the nature of the human person, 'Considerations of the Soul in Western Thought'. His basic question was whether science can dialogue with Aristotle and Aquinas. He argued that the 'soul-body communion constitutes one reality: the human person'.

The final two sessions of the conference are not reproduced in this volume. They were two panel discussions: 'Consciousness and Mind' and 'The Human

Person and Human Dignity: Scientific and Religious Perspectives'.

The work of translation, both from Chinese to English and English to Chinese, is a difficult and often insufficiently recognized work. The names of the translators, when the original was in Chinese, are given for each of the chapters. We are grateful for their services. For the spelling of Chinese terms, we have in general used the standard *Hanyu Pinyin*. For the convenience of those who know Chinese characters, a glossary of the main Chinese terms used has been provided.

We here at Fu Jen Catholic University, Department of Religious Studies and the Center for the Study of Religion and Science, are thankful to those who worked to make the conference the success it was. Finally, our thanks to Hilary Regan and the editorial staff of ATF Press who guided us in the tedious process of bringing this material to an English audience.

Teresa Wong Yai-Chow Chair, Department of Religious Studies, Fu Jen Catholic University

Wen Hsiang Chen Post-doctoral fellow, Center for the Study of Science and Religion, Fu Jen Catholic University

Frank Budenholzer Professor, Department of Chemistry, Academic Coordinator, Center for the Study of Science and Religion, Fu Jen Catholic University

April 2008

Acknowledgments

Many of the papers in the volume have been published elsewhere and we are grateful to the publishers for their kind permission to include these papers in the present volume.

Of the four papers of John Haught, 'Darwin and Divine Providence' was especially prepared for presentation in Taiwan.

Professor Haught's paper 'Is Nature All There Is?' was adapted from 'Is Nature Enough? No', which appeared in *Zygon: Journal of Science and Religion* 38 (December, 2003): 769–82

'Science and the Quest for Cosmic Purpose', the keynote address at the Fu Jen Conference, was in part adapted from an earlier book chapter, 'Science and the Quest for Cosmic Purpose', in *The Future of Religion: Perspectives from the Engelsberg Seminar 2001*, edited by Kurt Almqvist and Erik Wallrup (Stockholm: Axel and Margaret Ax: Son Johnson Foundation, 2005), 199–210.

Dr Haught's lecture 'Theology, Ecology and Cosmology', was adapted in part from: 'Theology and Ecology in an Unfinished Universe', in *Religion and the New Ecology: Environmental Responsibility in a World in Flux,* edited by David M Lodge and Christopher Hamlin (Notre Dame: University of Notre Dame Press, 2006), pp. 226-45.

Many of the papers presented at the Conference 'Cosmology: Religion and Science in Dialogue' have been published in the journal of the Department of Religious Studies of Fu Jen Catholic University. The keynote address of John Haught as well as the papers of Thomas Berg, Kang Phee-Seng and Shih Chao-hwei were published in the winter 2004 number of *Fu Jen Religious Studies*. The summer 2005 number of *Fu Jen Religious Studies* carried the contributions of Kang Phee-Seng (in Chinese), Frank Budenholzer (Chinese) and Chen, Chi-ming (Chinese).

Finally, the English version of 'What is Life?' will be published in *Method: Journal of Lonergan Studies*, published by the Lonergan Institute of Boston College.

Teresa Wong Yai-Chow
Wen Hsiang Chen
Frank Budenholzer   April 2008

Part One

Is Nature All There Is?

John F Haught

Abstract

After briefly reviewing the tenets of 'naturalism', this lecture will raise questions about naturalism's sufficiency as a worldview from the point of view of rational coherence, explanatory adequacy and spiritual resourcefulness. Is nature enough, in other words, to satisfy the human longing for ultimate intelligibility, explanation and meaning? Or is it possible that in the pursuit of these goals we are still rightly guided by many of the religious traditions of the world to extend our reach beyond 'nature' especially as the latter notion is understood in an age of science? I will approach these questions by asking specifically whether there is a legitimate place for theological explanation in our accounting for life, intelligence, ethics and religion.

The famous scientist and writer Carl Sagan began his popular *Cosmos* TV series by stating that 'the universe is all there is, all there ever was and all there ever will be'. Sagan was a proponent of naturalism, the belief that 'nature is all there is'. According to naturalism, there is no need to look beyond the physical world for a divine creator or source of meaning. Nature is quite enough all by itself, and science is the best way to understand it. Even when we look at the marvel of living beings through the eyes of science it seems now that nature alone is the creator and designer. Random genetic changes, plus natural selection, plus an enormous depth of time—isn't this Darwinian recipe enough to cook up for all the diversity and complexity of life, including beings endowed with minds? Why would rational persons want to look beyond science in order to make sense of the universe?

In *Climbing Mount Improbable* the well-known evolutionist Richard Dawkins pictures life on earth as making its way up a mountain. On one side the mountain rises straight up from the plain below, while on the other side it slopes gently from bottom to top. It is on the sloped side that life makes its long journey. If life had only the biblical period of several thousand years to climb up the vertical side, then a miraculous boost may have been essential to explain how something as complex as the human brain could have emerged so quickly. Natural, scientific explanations would not be enough. But if the story of life in fact takes place very gradually, on a path moving back and fourth up the gentler slope, over a period of four billion years, then no supernatural help is needed. Minute incremental changes, together with the relentless weeding out of nonadaptive variations by natural selection in the course of *deep time,* are enough to account for all the extraordinary variety and complexity of life. Nature, it would appear, is quite enough.

In this essay I shall raising several questions about the claim that nature is enough. Today naturalism usually assumes that only the scientifically knowable universe is real. But isn't this a worldview or belief rather than verifiable knowledge? Most naturalists will concede that it is, but they would add that it is a reasonable belief. For many inquirers naturalism is the undebatable starting point for all their reflections on the universe. But does it hold up under careful scrutiny?

I shall not be challenging scientific naturalism as a *method* of investigating the universe. As far as science itself is concerned, nature is indeed all there is. One should never introduce the idea of God or the miraculous into scientific work itself. As a theologian, I am happy to accept methodological naturalism as essential to science. But suppose there are dimensions of reality that science cannot reach. If there are, then *metaphysical* naturalism—the assumption that scientifically knowable nature alone is real, is an irrational belief. I will argue below that this is indeed the case. By implication, I shall conclude that the universe is not all there is, all there ever was, or all there ever will be.

There are several strains of naturalism. For example, there is hard naturalism and soft naturalism.[1] The former is equivalent to mechanism or reductionist materialism, whereas the latter thinks of physical reality as much subtler than the older mechanistic models allowed. Soft naturalists emphasise that nature consists of systems or organic wholes that cannot be reduced to their physical antecedents or atomic components. Emergent rules come into play spontaneously as the universe evolves in complexity. But these new ordering principles are not in any way mystical or in need of theological explanation. They are simply part of nature.

Among soft naturalists there are some who call themselves religious naturalists. Religious naturalists do not believe there is anything beyond nature, but they often use religious terminology—words such as 'mystery' and 'the sacred'—to express their sense that nature by itself is worthy of our reverent submission.[2]

In all its various shapes, however, naturalism embraces the following core doctrines (adapted in part from Hardwick):

1. Outside of nature, which includes humans and their cultural creations, there is nothing.
2. It follows then that nature is self-originating.

3. Since there is nothing beyond nature, there can be no overarching purpose or goal that would give any lasting meaning to the universe.
4. Since there is no divine cause, all causes are purely natural causes. This means that every natural event is itself a product of other natural events.
5. The various features of living beings, including humans, can be explained ultimately in evolutionary and specifically Darwinian terms (evolutionary naturalism).
6. There is no possibility of conscious human survival or resurrection beyond death.

Is naturalism spiritually adequate?

With this outline of naturalism's creed before us, I want to ask especially about its reasonableness. Before doing so, however, I would like to look at two other questions that also demand a response from the naturalist. The first concerns naturalism's *spiritual* adequacy. By this I mean: can naturalism respond fully to the human quest for meaning and fulfillment? I raise this question because religious naturalists themselves claim that nature is quite enough to give our lives meaning as well as intellectual satisfaction (see Goodenough). Even some of the most entrenched naturalists now admit that we humans possess ineradicably religious instincts as part of our genetic endowment. But can naturalism, as a belief system, really satisfy our native religious craving for meaning? Can it bring coherence, happiness and ultimate satisfaction to our brief life-spans?

The answers that naturalists themselves give to this question range from sunny to sober. Sunny naturalists say something like this:

> Nature's mystery and beauty, human love and goodness, the joy of creativity, the gratification of scientific discovery—these are enough to fill a person's life. There is no need to look toward any meaning beyond nature. Likewise, our moral inclinations don't require that we postulate, as Immanuel Kant did, the existence of God or immortality. Our ethical and religious tendencies, which are imprinted in our genes, are purely adaptive features that can be accounted for without appealing to the illusion of God. Nature is quite enough.

Sober naturalists, on the other hand, are not so buoyant. Nature is *not* enough to satisfy our hunger for meaning, they attest. In fact, our religious appetites will never be satisfied, since the universe ultimately makes no sense. A representative of sober naturalism is the French writer Albert Camus (1955). Camus admits that we humans have insatiable desires for ultimate meaning and eternal happiness. It would be dishonest, he says, to deny this. The hard fact, however, is that the universe can never satisfy such craving. Eventually the universe leads all life toward annihilation. If God and immortality do not exist—and for Camus they do not—then reality is absurd. Hence the hero of the human condition is Sisyphus, the exemplar of all striving in the face of futility.[3]

Another representative of sober naturalism is the physicist Steven Weinberg. In *Dreams of a Final Theory* (1992), he writes:

> It would be wonderful to find in the laws of nature a plan prepared by a concerned creator in which human beings played some

special role. I find sadness in doubting that we will. There are some among my scientific colleagues who say that the contemplation of nature gives them all the spiritual satisfaction that others have found in a belief in an interested God. Some of them may even feel that way. I do not.[4]

Like Camus, Weinberg takes seriously the question of God, and he regrets that science has made atheism the only reasonable option today. Science provides no evidence that we live in a purposeful universe, and so the most we can salvage from our tragic predicament is a sense of "honor" in facing up to the finality of tragedy.[5] There is no place then for sunny religious naturalism and its compromises with the bitter truth of our actual situation.

If I were to become a naturalist I would have to side with the sober rather than the sunny. Sober naturalists are at least less cavalier about what all naturalists take to be the truth. As far as naturalism can tell, after all, science has shown the universe to be devoid of meaning. So wouldn't it be both dishonorable and dishonest to pretend that we could ever find lasting personal fulfillment in a pointless cosmos? If the option were forced, logic would compel me to go along with tragic realism of Camus and Weinberg rather than the groundless optimism of the more sprightly naturalist romantics. Fortunately, as I shall indicate later, there is a reasonable alternative to both sober and sunny naturalism.

That naturalism is spiritually disproportionate to the fact of tragedy, of course, does not make it untrue. Let us concede for the moment that the six tenets of naturalism listed above are indeed true. But if they are true, then as the philosopher John Hick states, naturalism 'is very bad news for humanity as a whole'.[6] The physical pain, poverty and unbearable suffering of most people throughout history keeps them from ever fulfilling their hopes within the limits of nature alone. 'Even those who have lived the longest can seldom be said to have arrived, before they die, at a fulfillment of their potential.' Naturalists, therefore, are hiding from the truth unless 'they acknowledge the fact that naturalism is not good news for much of humanity'.[7]

The classic religious traditions, on the other hand, at least according to Hick, do respond to the deepest aspirations of *all* people:

> We human beings are for so much of the time selfish, narrow-minded, emotionally impoverished, unconcerned about others, often vicious and cruel, but according to the great religions there are wonderfully better possibilities concealed within us. . . . We see around us the different levels that the human spirit has reached, and we know . . . that the generality of us have a very long way to go before we can be said to have become fully human. But if the naturalistic picture is correct, this can never happen. For according to naturalism, the evil that has afflicted so much of human life is final and irrevocable as the victims have ceased to exist.[8]

Again, this does not by itself prove that naturalism is unreasonable or untrue. But, says Hick, naturalists at least

> . . . ought frankly to acknowledge that if they are right the human situation is irredeemably bleak and painful for vast numbers of people. For—if they are right—in the case of that innumerable multitude whose quality of life

has been rendered predominantly negative by pain, anxiety, extreme deprivation, oppression, or whose lives have been cut off in childhood or youth, there is no chance of ever participating in an eventual fulfillment of the human potential. There is no possibility of this vast century-upon-century tragedy being part of a much larger process which leads ultimately to limitless good.[9]

Is naturalist explanation enough?

Hick makes an interesting point. But even though naturalism may be spiritually inadequate, this alone does not make it unreasonable, as Hick would agree. That it is unreasonable, I shall argue below. But before doing so, there is a second question that I would like to ask: can naturalism, even in principle, ever fulfill its promise of explaining completely every natural event or actuality by way of other natural events? Do we not have to appeal, at some point in our attempt to make *complete* sense of things, to something beyond the natural world and beyond the competency of science?

Are naturalistic explanations enough to explain adequately and ultimately the existence of the universe, or why the universe would give rise to life, mind, ethics and religion? Granted, science can say a lot about all of these, but can it say everything? Is science enough? Is it certain that all causes are natural causes? Can science, for example, explain why there is anything at all rather than nothing? (Even the astronomer Martin Rees places this question outside the scope of science.) If there is nothing that lies beyond or deeper than the scientifically accessible world, then of course natural causes would be the ultimate and exhaustive explanation for everything. Scientific or naturalistic explanation would then amount to final or ultimate explanation. Then there would be no logical space left for theological interpretations of reality. And religion would stand in a competitive, conflictive relationship to science.

Contemporary naturalists, fortified by the success of science, are confident that through science alone we can discover the adequate and final explanation of everything. Life can be fully explained in chemical terms.[10] Mind is the outcome of natural selection alone.[11] Language (Pinker), ethics (Ruse), and even religion (Boyer) can be explained in full naturalistically. Given the fact that naturalists deny the existence of anything other than nature, they are compelled logically to maintain that natural causes provide the final explanation of all phenomena, including intellectual, ethical and religious expression. But can naturalism even give us an ultimate and exhaustive explanation of anything whatsoever, let alone everything?

Many evolutionists think it can. Today naturalistic confidence flourishes especially among Darwinians. Evolutionary naturalists are certain that the neo-Darwinian recipe—random (contingent) genetic events, natural selection, and deep cosmic time—can account fully for all the features of living beings. Is this confidence justifiable? As a theologian I am willing to push evolutionary understanding as far as it can legitimately take us. I agree completely that evolutionary science has to be an aspect of every serious attempt to understand life, including ethics and religion. But there is no certainty that the *deepest* explanations of living phenomena do not elude evolutionary naturalism (for a fuller discussion see my book *Deeper Than Darwin* 2003).

For example, beneath life's evolutionary story, the universe is an exquisite blend of contingent unpredictability, lawful necessity and eons of time. Life's evolution jumps astride this foundational cosmic mix. The three essential ingredients for evolution have been laid out on the cosmic table long before life begins to stew. Darwinism presupposes a specific cosmic setting; it does not account for it. The physical sciences may have something to say about it, of course, but even after they are finished the question will still remain: Why is the universe such an exciting, adventurous blend of contingency, predictability and temporality that it can give rise to an evolutionary story at all? Perhaps at this foundational point theology may have at least something to say.

In any case, by definition, there can be only one primary or *ultimate* explanation of life—and of the universe for that matter—whereas there can be many intermediate or secondary explanations. Darwinian explanations are intermediate, not ultimate. We put too heavy a burden on science whenever we make its provisional accounts into ultimate ones, as naturalism does. What I propose instead, as a way of giving a place to both science and religion, is 'layered explanation'. By this I mean that everything in the universe, and indeed the universe itself, is open to a plurality of levels of explanation. The alternative to layered explanation or explanatory pluralism is 'explanatory monism', an approach generally favored by naturalists.

Here is an example of what I mean by layered explanation. Suppose you have a wood fire burning in your back yard. Your neighbor comes over and asks you to explain why the fire is burning. A very good response would be: it is burning because the carbon in the wood is combining with oxygen to make carbon dioxide. This is an acceptable explanation, and for a certain kind of mentality it is enough. Still, there can be other levels of explanation. For example, you might just as easily have answered your friend by saying: the fire is burning because I lit a match to it. And an even more illuminating answer would be: 'The fire is burning because I want to roast marshmallows.'

Different levels of explanation, as we see here, can coexist without conflict. 'I want to roast marshmallows' does not compete with physical explanations of the burning wood. The deeper the explanation lies, in fact, the harder it is to grasp in physical terms. 'I want to roast marshmallows', for example, cannot be squeezed into the explanatory slot that focuses on the chemistry of combustion. And yet, there is no inherent contradiction between the chemistry of combustion and my overarching purpose of having something to eat.

Analogously, let us suppose that there is an ultimate reality which for some mysterious reason wants to create a life-bearing universe. We should not expect this divine intentionality to show up within a physical analysis of nature—including scientific speculations on the big bang and the origin of life—any more than we should expect to find 'I want marshmallows' to be inscribed on the burning wood or molecules of carbon dioxide.

And yet, it is just such direct 'evidence' that scientific naturalism demands from those who adopt a theological understanding of the universe. Almost inevitably the reason naturalists give for their opposition to theology is that if there were a deeper than natural explanation, it should show up as scientifically graspable evidence. Since it does not show up at that layer of explanation, it must not exist. Underlying this judgment, of course, is the more fundamental assumption that there is really only one explanatory slot available. And if science now fills this slot, there is no room for theology.

Good theology, however, allows for many layers of explanation. It argues that divine action or divine creativity stands in relation to nature—to such occurrences as the emergence of the cosmos, life, mind, ethics and religion—analogously to the way in which 'I want marshmallows' stands in relation to the chemistry of burning logs. The ultimate explanation will necessarily be hidden from view while we are preoccupied with physical explanations. Even the most painstaking analysis of the molecular movement in the fire will not reveal, at this physical level of examination, the "ultimate" reason why the fire is burning. Likewise, even the most detailed scientific examination of natural processes can neither discover nor rule out a deeper reason why the universe, life, mind, language, ethics or religion exist. There is plenty of logical room for ultimate, theological understanding of the universe to exist alongside of scientific accounts without in any way contradicting or competing with them.

Layered explanation is in fact much more open to the unknown than is the doctrinaire explanatory monism of scientific naturalism. Take, for example, the question of why life came about in this universe. Layered explanation allows that this question can be answered quite nicely by several natural sciences. Even scientific explanation, after all, comes in layers. Physics, for example, can explain the emergence of life in terms of thermodynamics or the self-organizing properties of matter.[12] Chemistry can explain life and its origin in terms of the bonding properties of atoms. And molecular biology may do so in terms of RNA cycles and protein replication (De Duve). Even astrophysics now has a place in the explanation of life, taking us all the way back to the initial cosmic conditions and fundamental constants that made ours a life-bearing universe (Rees).

We justifiably push each science as far as it can possibly go at its own level without fear that it is invading the turf of others. So we may not be wrong to allow also for a theological level at the very foundation of our stack of explanatory levels. Theology can be the foundational layer in an extended hierarchy of explanations without in any way treading on the methodologically specified pathways of the various fields of scientific inquiry. Thus we may rationally suppose that the *ultimate* explanation of life's origin consists of the creative and attractive power of an infinite generosity—of what some people call God—without implying that this explanation is 'better than' or in competition with physical, chemical or biological explanations of life.

Perhaps, after all, adequate explanation runs endlessly deep. No one science, or even the whole set of sciences, can ever comprehend the rich *totality* of causal ingredients that underlie each cosmic event. Every branch of science works on the tacit premise that it does not have to account fully for everything. Every science, for the sake of clarity, leaves something out. In fact the sciences reach clarity about the world only by *abstracting from* most of the world's actual causal depth. Consequently, Cartesian clarity and distinctness in our scientific thinking is not a sign that we have arrived at deep understanding.[13] And conversely, the deepest explanations—precisely because they leave less out—will inevitably be the least clear and distinct. This is why religious and theological explanations will always have a fuzziness and vagueness that will frustrate the scientific naturalist.

Naturalism, on the other hand, typically demands that ultimate explanation be clear and distinct. In doing so, its devotees often appeal to the idea of Ockham's razor, which asserts that 'things [explanations] should not be multiplied without necessity (*sine necessitate*)'. Accordingly, since Darwin's recipe can explain life, mind, behavior, language, ethics, religion and so on very simply in terms of natural selection, the naturalist claims that there is no need to appeal to the obscure notion of an unseen deity in order to make ultimate sense of these fascinating developments. The promise of explaining all the great 'mysteries' of life in terms of the economical notion of reproductive success is hard to resist. It has led to the cult of 'universal

Darwinism' and the creed that natural selection is the bottommost explanation of all the manifestations of life (for a good illustration see Cziko).

This exclusionary singleness of mind, however, is comparable to explaining the fire in my back yard by leaving out as completely irrelevant the fact that 'I want to roast marshmallows'. If we can reach a *simpler* explanation at the level of the fire's chemistry, why bring in the fuzzy idea that someone just may want something to eat?

Methodologically speaking, of course, science rightly leaves out any considerations of purpose and intentionality in nature. There is no argument here. The issue is whether science takes us to the ultimate level of explanation. Those who say it does are not making scientific but instead theological assertions.

Ockham's razor, moreover, was never intended to suppress layered explanation as such, even though this is exactly how explanatory monists typically tend to use it. If life were as simple as evolutionary naturalists think, then, of course, Darwinian explanation would be adequate. Theological explanation of life and evolution would be superfluous. Remember, though, that William of Ockham said that explanations should not be multiplied unless they are necessary. Sometimes they are necessary. There is no justification either in Ockham's maxim or in science itself for closing off the road to explanatory depth.

Is naturalism a reasonable worldview?

Finally, my third and focal question is whether naturalism is rationally sound. Given the fact that naturalism falls in the same camp as theology, namely, that it is a set of beliefs or a worldview, is it consistent with the innate dictates of reason and logic? My way of addressing this question will be to ask you the reader to suppose, for the sake of discussion, that you subscribe to the six tenets of naturalism listed above. Then I want to ask you whether the actual performance of your own mind is logically compatible with these teachings. If not, then you will be compelled to judge naturalism unreasonable.

Suppose you are an evolutionary naturalist. If so, you are obliged to explain all living phenomena including *your own mind,* as much as possible in purely natural (physical, chemical, and biological) terms. If you are an evolutionary naturalist, then the *ultimate* explanation of your various organs, your eyes, your ears—everything that is functionally adaptive about you—is Darwinian.[14] To be consistent, you are compelled to admit that your own mind (which is a function of your physical brain) can be explained ultimately as an adaptive organ also. If you follow paleontologist Stephen Jay Gould you will appeal also to the role of accidents in natural history, and not just to selective adaptation, in explaining why you have a mind.

In any case, if Darwinian adaptation or sheer accident (or a combination of the two) is the *ultimate* explanation of your capacity to think, then how can you trust your thought processes to lead you to the truth? And why should I believe you when you tell me that evolutionary naturalism is the rock-bottom truth about life? How do I know—if I follow your own premises—that your mind is not just taking part in one more adaptive (and possibly fictitious) exercise?

You are telling me that evolution is the deepest explanation of your mind and its properties. Darwinism, you say, is true. But what I want to know is how your mind's capacity for truth-telling slipped into your naturalist Darwinian universe. If you tell me it is a consequence of cultural conditioning this will not help, since according to the first tenet of naturalism human culture is also just another part of nature, a product of natural (blind and mindless) causes only.

I am not denying that Darwinian biology is one very good level of explanation. But I am questioning whether you can be certain that your own evolutionary naturalism logically accounts, at least *ultimately*, for the trust you have in your own mind to lead you (and me) to the truth? In fact, Darwinians claim that it is often due to a capacity to deceive that the more complex forms of life and mind evolved at all.[15] But if adaptive evolution, or any other blindly material process underlying life, is the *ultimate* explanation of your own brain and its mental functioning, then why aren't you suspicious now that you may be deceiving me rather than telling me the truth? Again, how do you know that in responding to me your avowedly rational mind, which you take to be the outcome of a perfectly mindless process, is not involved in just one more deceptive exercise? If you still believe that a blind and mindless natural process provides the *ultimate* explanation of your mind, then, why should I take seriously anything you tell me?

My point is a simple one. Nature, at least as understood by evolutionary naturalism, is not big enough for your own intelligent functioning. And if it is not big enough for your own mind, then naturalism must be incoherent. As a naturalist you believe that your mind is fully part of nature. But if your mind and your view of nature don't fit each other, then something has to give. My suggestion is not to abandon evolutionary explanations, but to accept them as intermediate rather than ultimate. Then dig down into the murky cosmic depth that lies beneath Darwinian accounts and the restrictive tenets of scientific naturalism. There you may find an endless realm of discovery open to layer upon layer of even deeper explanation.

Evolutionary naturalism by itself cannot justify the spontaneous trust you have placed in your own mind as you seek to arrive at truth. To justify your implicit trust in the possibility of arriving at truth, you need to look for a wider and deeper understanding of the universe than naturalism alone can provide. Perhaps your own mind's spontaneous and persistent trust in the possibility of reaching truth is itself a hint that the physical universe, at least as naturalism conceives it, is only a small fragment of all there is, all there ever was and all there ever will be.

End Notes

1. Holmes Rolston III, *Science and Religion: A Critical Survey* (Philadelphia: Temple University Press, 1987), 247–58.
2. Ursula Goodenough, *The Sacred Depths of Nature* (New York: Oxford University Press, 1998).
3. Albert Camus, *The Myth of Sisyphus, and Other Essays*. Translated by Justin O'Brien (New York: Knopf, 1955), 88–91.
4. Steven Weinberg, *Dreams of a Final Theory* (New York: Pantheon Books,1992), 256.
5. Weinberg, *Dreams,* 255, 260.
6. John Hick, *The Fifth Dimension: An Exploration of the Spiritual Realm* (Oxford: Oneworld Press, 1999), 22.
7. *Ibid,* 24
8. *Ibid*.
9. *Ibid,* 24–25
10. Francis HC Crick, *Of Molecules and Men*.(Seattle: University of Washington Press, 1966), 10; JD Watson, *The Molecular Biology of the Gene* (New York: WA Benjamin, Inc, 1965), 67.
11. Gary Cziko, *Without Miracles: Universal Selection Theory and the Second Darwinian Revolution* (Cambridge, Mass: MIT Press, 1995), 121.
12. Stuart A Kauffman, *The Origins of Order: Self Organisation and Selection in Evolution* (New York:Oxford University Press, 1993); Harold Morowitz, *The Emergence of Everything: How the World Became Complex* (New York: Oxford University Press, 2002).
13. Alfred North Whitehead, *Science and the Modern World* (New York: The Free Press, 1967), 173.
14. Cziko, *Without Miracles,* 121.
15. See Rue for a convenient summary. Loyal Rue, *By the Grace of Guile: The Role of Deception in Natural History and Human Affairs* (New York: Oxford University Press, 1994), 82–127.

Science, Religion And The Quest For Cosmic Purpose

John F Haught

Abstract

Vaclav Havel, president of the Czech Republic, recently stated that 'the crisis of the much-needed global responsibility is in principle due to the fact that we have lost the certainty that the Universe ... has a definite meaning and follows a definite purpose.'[1] I would hasten to agree that if we fail to trust that the cosmos is, at heart, the unfolding of a transcending purpose, our ethical aspirations and our zest for life will eventually wither on the vine. Today, I believe we need to recapture in a fresh way the religious sense of a purposeful universe. The future of religion is, in a very deep sense, tied to the plausibility of the idea that the universe is here for a reason. The question, however, is whether we can we embrace such a sweeping idea without contradicting the discoveries of science. Yet, I shall argue here, with the help of such scientifically enlightened religious thinkers as Michael Polanyi, Teilhard de Chardin and Alfred North Whitehead, that we may plausibly view the discoveries of natural science as a springboard toward a wider and more vibrant sense of an ultimately meaningful universe than has ever been available to us before.

Traditionally most religions led us to believe that the universe is inherently meaningful. This belief gave human lives a sense of belonging to something of great importance. Most of our ancestors considered the universe and our lives to be *timelessly* grounded in a transcendent principle of 'rightness' (*Dharma, Rta, Tao*) or ultimate meaning (*Brahman, Yahweh, Allah,* amongst others). They felt that the cosmos pulsed with meaning, and this intuition gave them a sound reason for ethical aspiration. The ideals that shape the ethical sensitivity of most humans today, including that of skeptics, still draw their authority from the moral heroism of our religious predecessors, most of whom believed they lived in a meaningful world. Today, whenever people surrender to the demands of virtue, regardless of how much this propensity may have been fashioned by evolutionary factors, we can assume it has been amplified and molded by religious cultures of the past that attributed meaning to the whole universe. Contemporary efforts to live a life of justice or compassion—even where consciousness has become fully secularised—are connected, at least remotely, to ancient religious traditions that assumed the universe is here for a reason.

Traditional faiths, originating as they did prior to the scientific discovery of deep cosmic time (a fifteen billion year old universe), usually arranged their pictures of the world in a hierarchical way. At the lowest level were inanimate things such as minerals. Above this stratum lay the more elusive levels of plants, then animals and finally humans with their capacity for reflective self-awareness, free choice, ethical aspiration and religious longing. Presiding over all of the levels of being was the ultimate source of being and meaning, identified in theistic faiths as 'God'.[2]

As we journey up this 'great chain of being', the levels become increasingly harder to grasp in a controlling way.

When we move up to the level of mind, we encounter something that is literally incomprehensible. For if we try to grasp our own subjective consciousness objectively, the subjective or 'inner' side of this consciousness will not show up in our objectifying vision. The subjective aspect of our consciousness cannot completely become an object of consciousness without losing its essential character of being subjective. And if even the human mind is so incomprehensible, it is not surprising that the highest level of all in the classic hierarchy, that of ultimate reality, would be utterly beyond our comprehension. If there is an ultimate level of reality that gives meaning or purpose to the universe, therefore, it would comprehend us, but we could not comprehend it.[3]

According to most religious traditions, a 'purposeful' universe must possess at least some kind and degree of hierarchical arrangement. In order to be the carrier of meaning the book of nature, in other words, has to consist of various levels or dimensions, the lower able to be informed 'from above' by higher levels of meaning. For this reason, traditional religions and philosophies have almost unanimously resisted modernist attempts to collapse their hierarchical visions down to a single, desacralised flatland.

One appealing feature of any hierarchical scheme has been that it embeds our own brief lives—and, indeed, the entire cosmos—within the larger context of an eternal reality immune to transience and death. Participation in the imperishable permanence of God rescues the flux of transitory cosmic and human events from the oblivion of nothingness. I suspect that the most serious challenge the new scientific picture of the universe poses to religion and its future, therefore, consists in great measure of its 'horizontalising' and 'atomising' the sacred, vertical hierarchy of traditional religions. By compressing, and decomposing into lifeless atoms, the richly layered symbolic, mythic and metaphysical constructs in which the sense of a purposeful universe has for ages typically been conceptualised, the new science and cosmology seem to have destroyed the spinal column on which the various impressions of cosmic meaning had been entwined for thousands of years.

We cannot exaggerate the sense of anxiety that the evolutionary scientific world-view has thus brought about. For many thoughtful people today, not only Darwinian biology, but also astrophysics and cosmology, have rendered the classical hierarchical religious schemes unbelievable, and along with them any plausible intuition that the entirety of nature participates in the eternal. In modern evolutionary materialism, for example, the inanimate level, formerly thought of as the lowest of all, is now identified as the most real or 'fundamental'. Lifeless and mindless 'matter' is now the ground or source of all beings, including those beings endowed with what we call 'life' and 'mind'. In modern times the universe of 'matter' has been thought of as *essentially* lifeless and mindless. Accordingly, whatever has evolved out of matter must also be essentially lifeless and mindless—even if it seems, to our naive 'folk psychology', to be alive and intelligent.[4]

An essentially mindless cosmos, moreover, is not the sort of reality that could be permeated by meaning or purpose. Instead of being a book or a 'teaching' whose meaningful content would gradually become transparent to the religiously awakened, the universe that evolves from dumb matter must always be intrinsically pointless. The formerly lowest level, that of inanimate matter, is now the 'ultimate' explanation of the 'higher', and the 'higher' levels of life and mind are 'epiphenomenal' derivatives of an inherently meaningless material underpinning. In the absence of any sacred hierarchical information flowing downward from higher to lower levels, the physical universe no longer symbolically represents any kind of eternal significance. And so, apparently, no grounds remain for our attributing lasting value or importance to it.

Evolutionary science, moreover, has blurred the former sense of ontological discontinuity between non-life, life, humanity and culture to the point where we can no longer clearly decide where one leaves off and the other begins. Evolutionary thinking sees only a physical and historical continuity running across all the levels of nature formerly thought to be discontinuous and hierarchically distinct. In all of science, in fact, nothing seems to have melted down the classic hierarchical vision more thoroughly than has the evolutionary picture of nature. In combination with physics, chemistry, molecular biology, geology and other sciences, neo-Darwinism has now made the traditional sense that nature leads us gradually upward to God, by way of a series of hierarchically distinct levels, seem quite unbelievable. For this reason, the future of any plausible religion will depend, at least to a great extent, on how well it deals with the fact of cosmic evolution.

At the very same time that the ancient hierarchy has been flattened, historicised, and horizontalised, it has also been 'atomised'. Atomism is the method of breaking organisms or complex entities down into more elemental units (such as atoms, molecules, genes, or cells). Atomistic reduction is an essential duty of science, but when atomistic analysis becomes a world-view it inevitably demolishes hierarchies and the meanings embedded in them. Once the complexity of nature has undergone granulation ontologically into irreducible particulate units—units that are themselves dumb and dead—it becomes difficult for us to discern the crisp hierarchical boundaries that formerly allowed us to make distinctions among the levels of material, living and thinking beings. As the analytic method of science becomes fixated on the atomic constituents of things, our intuitive sense that some hidden integrating principle of coherence fashions these elements into ontologically discontinuous grades of being begins gradually to dissolve. All we have left, then, are atomic, molecular or (today) genetic monads. The comprehensive wholeness that used to make organisms seem qualitatively different and hierarchically more elevated than their inanimate constituents, melts away. The future survival of any intellectually coherent religion requires also, therefore, a competent critique of metaphysical reductionism.

As if atomistic reductionism were not enough of a wound to the ancient religious visions of reality, the specifically Darwinian cast of contemporary biology has lately made it more and more difficult for many scientifically educated people to feel the deep connection their ancestors experienced between human ethical life and the universe itself. A universe that allows for so much randomness, struggle, suffering, elimination of the weak, and impersonal 'natural selection', seems to be utterly indifferent to us, and opaque to our ethical sensitivities. Consequently, any suggestion that the universe is an intrinsically meaningful process appears more gratuitous than ever after Darwin. Nature, at least as it is now understood by neo-Darwinism, is blind, aimless, and apparently pointless. Religious thought in the future will have to address this cosmic pessimism more directly than ever before.[5]

Purpose after Darwin

Even in the wake of Darwin and the new cosmology, I would propose, however, that it has not been decisively demonstrated that a trust in cosmic purpose is silly or stupid. Here I shall offer four considerations that may offer something of a challenge to the horizontalsing and atomising reductionism that has reigned so confidently in modern and current intellectual culture.

1). Let me begin by suggesting that the 'historicising' and 'atomising' of nature by our new sense of deep evolutionary time and molecular biology does not *logically* eliminate a hierarchical universe. Since a purposeful universe requires some kind of hierarchical ordering, it is not without interest that the new scientific rediscovery of the idea of *information* now allows in principle for the logical and ontological discontinuity in nature that saves the idea of hierarchy—albeit not in the static sense of pre-evolutionary thought. The scientist and philosopher Michael Polanyi, for example, has logically demonstrated that the quiet entry of informational novelty into the course of evolution allows us to hold onto the venerable conviction that there abides in nature, after all, a real discontinuity of levels (or dimensions)—and therefore an ontological hierarchy—and that we can affirm its reality without our having to deny the chemical and historical continuity in evolution.[6]

The most obvious evidence of the presence of information in nature is found in DNA. DNA is a chain of chemicals, but it is not 'just chemistry'. The DNA in living beings is also a *specific informational sequence* of four acid bases (A, T, C, and G). And it is this informational aspect of DNA that figuratively outlines the distinctive shapes and identities of all living beings. Although, at a certain level of analysis, DNA appears to be 'just chemistry', the informational aspect is logically distinguishable from the strictly deterministic chemical processes operative in all living beings. The specific sequence of the 'letters' in the DNA of any particular organism consists of an informational arrangement that cannot be reduced without remainder to chemistry.

A simple analogy may help clarify this point.⁷ Suppose I scribble aimlessly with my pen on a piece of paper, but then suddenly begin writing a coherent sentence. From the point of view of the chemistry that bonds ink to paper there is a physical continuity between the scrawl on the one side and the sentence on the other—at least when we look at it from a 'lower' level of analysis. But from a 'higher', informational, point of view, the specific arrangement of letters in a code that forms a sentence introduces discontinuity. Physico-chemical continuity remains, but it does not rule out an overriding logical and informational discontinuity.

Analogously, the informational arrangement of nucleotides in DNA does not violate, but instead relies on, the laws of chemistry and their uniform operation. And so, if we look at DNA from a purely materialist perspective we will see 'just chemistry'. But even though physical and chemical determinism is essential to DNA, the nucleotides can be arranged in an indefinite number of sequences. Their *specific sequence* is not chemically determined. A quiet, and even physically invisible, introduction of informational patterning, therefore, can bring about sharp ontological discontinuity even though strict continuity of nature's inviolable physical laws still prevails at the lower, chemical level. An informational discontinuity at one level can exist simultaneously with unbroken physical and historical continuity at another.

2). A second consideration is that the universe, as viewed by astrophysics, may not be *essentially* lifeless and mindless, after all, even though a great deal of modern thought since Descartes has assumed this to be the case. The whole edifice of modern cosmic pessimism (the denial of purpose in the universe) has been built on the assumption of an inherently mindless universe. Yet, we now know how exquisitely sensitive the existence of mind is to initial conditions and fundamental constants established at the time of the big bang. Therefore we have good *scientific* reasons for questioning the metaphysical foundations of modern materialism. The reasoning goes as follows:

In order to have 'mind' (in the sense of human consciousness) science now realises that there must be brains with sufficient physiological complexity to entertain what we call 'thought'. But for nature to bring about complex brains, a process of Darwinian evolution was necessary. To have evolution, in turn, there must first be life. And to get to life there have to be planets in the universe with the right chemical composition, including especially carbon. But where does the carbon come from? The existence of massive stars was required to 'cook' the lighter elements (hydrogen and helium) into carbon and other heavy elements. But the existence of the massive stars, some of which have exploded as supernovae, cannot be taken for granted either. For them to exist at all the rate of cosmic expansion (Hubble constant) and the gravitational coupling constant had to have precisely the values they in fact possess—values that have been fixed from the very first moment of the universe's existence. An infinitesimally slower or faster expansion of the universe, or a weaker or stronger gravitational force, would have forbidden the evolution of supernovae, carbon, life and mind. 'Mind', therefore, is much more intricately tied up with the basic structure of the early universe than most scientists imagined half a century ago.

I do not intend here to utilise the current physics of the early universe as the basis for a new natural theology or a post-Darwinian design argument for God's existence (although some scientists do precisely this). Rather, I wish only to emphasise that when we locate the story of life and mind within the larger cosmic narrative, they look a lot less improbable or accidental than they did prior to recent developments in astrophysics. Without denying that there is still plenty of room for contingency in evolution, we cannot be as certain as was biologist Jacques Monod only thirty years ago, for example, that matter is inherently hostile to life, or that the universe is *essentially* mindless.[8] And since most modern scientific materialism and cosmic pessimism have rejected the idea of cosmic purpose because they assumed that the universe is essentially mindless, contemporary cosmology makes us suspect that in some way mind has been woven into the fabric of the universe from its earliest beginnings.

3). In pondering the question of science and cosmic purpose, as my third consideration I propose that it would be most worthwhile for us to take a careful look once again at the evolutionary ideas of Teilhard de Chardin (1881–1955). Perhaps more than any other important thinker in the late modern world, this famous Jesuit geologist was convinced that the universe is not indifferent to mind (or spirit). Rather, he insisted, the emergence and intensification of consciousness is central to the very essence and meaning of cosmic reality. As matter has become increasingly complex, it has become ever more fully endowed with consciousness. It has also become more social and more free. Moreover, from the beginning of the universe, matter has exhibited a tendency to cluster around a center. (Teilhard called this 'centration'.) Already at the level of the atom we see the tendency of matter to organise itself around a center. Centration is manifested later in the eukaryotic cell that is arranged around a nucleus, and—much later in evolution—in anthills and beehives where the queen is central. Further intensification of 'centredness' occurs in vertebrates, primates and eventually in the self-awareness of human persons. And centration continues now at the social and planetary phase of evolution in the phenomenon of religion. Religions carry forward at the human level (that is, at the level of what Teilhard called the 'noosphere') the very same cosmic search for the center that began long ago with the atom.

So there is clear evidence of directionality in the cosmic process. But is there purpose in our evolving universe? For a process to have meaning or purpose it must give evidence of being oriented toward achieving some value. Purpose means the 'realising of a value'. Inasmuch as the cosmic process, at least according to Teilhard, is bent on giving birth to more and more *consciousness*, it exhibits the character of being purposeful. Consciousness, after all, is self-evidently a value. Even to deny this, one would be implicitly valuing his or her consciousness.[9]

4.) Fourth, and above all, I would like now to consider at more length the contributions of the philosopher Alfred North Whitehead to the question of purpose in an evolving universe. Whitehead (1861–1946), the renowned British and American philosopher and mathematician, was quite familiar with evolutionary science. This great philosopher's wide vision weaves our human existence tightly into the fabric of an organic cosmic development, and it does so in a way that can embrace, on the one hand, contemporary scientific (including Darwinian) understandings of how the universe works, and, on the other, a religious conviction that the cosmos is the repository of a timeless meaning. Without suppressing the ideas of Darwin or any other segments of natural science, Whitehead's understanding of nature rescues the universe and human existence from what modern thought had prematurely claimed to be an inherent pointlessness.

Like Teilhard, Whitehead was impressed by the relatively recent scientific discovery that the cosmos is not a state but an unfinished process. The universe has always been discontent with the status quo. According to Whitehead an appropriate way of thinking about cosmic purpose in an evolutionary world is to view the universe as a restless aim toward ever more intense configurations of beauty.[10] Beauty, of course, is a difficult notion to define clearly. However, many philosophers have agreed that 'beauty' implies, at the very least, a delicate balance of form and content, a blend of unity with multiplicity.[11] Similarly for Whitehead beauty is the 'harmony of contrasts' or the 'ordering of novelty'.[12] Without the novelty of contrast there will remain only the monotony of bland order. But without some degree of order the elements of novelty and contrast will dissolve into the ugliness of chaos. At times order may suppress the element of contrast, leveling it down to flat uniformity. At other times variety may threaten to overwhelm unity, fragmenting it into incoherent particulars. Every instance of genuine beauty stands somewhere between chaos on the one side and monotony or triviality on the other. Beauty arouses our appreciation because it turns what would otherwise be contradictions or clashes into aesthetic patterns that preserve both nuance and coherence. Beauty embraces local conflict, placing it in a 'wider vision' wherein difference enhances the whole instead of being mere chaos that destroys it.

It is toward bringing about such instances of beauty that our universe seems always to have tended overall, though not always successfully. And beauty has emerged with increasingly more intensity. In view of the discoveries of sciences ranging from astrophysics to biology, today there can be little doubt, at least when we view it over the long run, that the universe has wended its way directionally from simplicity to complexity, from triviality to more intense versions of ordered novelty, that is, toward emergent beauty.

For a process to be called purposeful, to repeat what I said earlier, it must be oriented toward the realising of what we take to be self-evidently valuable. Thus, in its aiming toward beauty, which is a 'transcendental' value (along with being, unity, truth and goodness), the universe, in spite or all the randomness we see in the life story, shows itself to be something more than a mere hit-or-miss affair. Even though its 'aim toward beauty' may not always have been effectively realised in every cosmic episode or domain, it is not rash to suspect that from its beginning the cosmos has had at least a 'loose' kind of teleology or purposiveness. It has been aiming toward and achieving beauty in the sense defined above.

Of course, from our own finite perspective the universe will often seem at least locally to bear features that are more discordant than harmonious. But this does not warrant the modern extrapolating from local disorder to the pessimistic claim that the universe is pointless overall. The judgment that the universe is ultimately pointless is often made on the basis of a purely materialist reading of the Darwinian picture of life. With Whitehead and our ancient religious traditions, however, I suggest that we look for a 'wider vision', without having to overlook what Darwin has said.

The 'aesthetic' understanding of the cosmos that I am proposing here admonishes us that our human vantage point is inevitably limited, even if it seems to enjoy the apparent support of science. The great religious and metaphysical traditions almost universally instruct us that there is always a more expansive perspective on the cosmos than any individual human being, or any particular culture, or historical epoch, can legitimately claim to have, and that our own impressions are only fleeting glimpses of an immeasurable and still unfolding panorama. If we follow the intuitions of our great wisdom traditions, even the scientifically educated can allow for a perspective—beyond our own vision—that can in the long run resolve local contradictions, monotonies and absurdities into a harmonious and beautiful whole. Even though our finite vistas cannot, at least for now, encompass such a whole, we can allow it gradually to encompass us.

The general features of the universe, I would propose, may be shaped, therefore, by an 'aesthetic cosmological principle'. Unlike the so-called 'anthropic cosmological principle', which views the physical constants and initial conditions of the universe primarily as pointing toward the eventual emergence of human consciousness, the aesthetic cosmological principle suggests, more generously, that the universe has apparently been 'set up' from the very beginning in such a manner as to allow for the ongoing creation of manifold forms of beauty.[13] The physicist Freeman Dyson has recently speculated that the universe is fashioned according to a 'principle of maximum diversity', according to which 'the laws of nature and initial conditions are such as to make the universe as interesting as possible'.[14] The aesthetic principle that I am proposing here, on the basis of Whitehead's metaphysics and contemporary astrophysics, expresses a deeper intuition: the 'point' of the universe it to maximise beauty and, along with it, modes of experience capable of appreciating and enjoying beauty in ever greater depth of intensity. Such a vision, it goes without saying, dramatises all the more, by way of contrast, the ugliness and evil of our current destruction of earth's life-systems, the precious and irreplaceable products of an immensely long evolutionary creation of diversity and beauty. In their ecological recklessness our current cultures and economies are clearly moving against the grain of the universe.

Conclusion

In a post-Darwinian world our moral lives can be securely grounded, and religion can have an effective future, if we think of them in connection with the universe's own purposeful impetus toward intensifying beauty. The universe, as it turns out, is not fundamentally indifferent or hostile to the realisation of value, for it has always had an adventurous inclination to expand the domain of beauty, a beauty *intrinsic* to things and not simply 'in the eyes of the beholder'. It is true that Darwinian process leads toward the intensification of beauty in ways that may not conform neatly to our human standards of good design. But this need not obscure from us the more generic cosmic propensity to amplify the scope of beauty.

The purpose of human life, when situated in a cosmos that aims toward aesthetic intensity must have something to do with preserving and enlarging the dominion of beauty in the universe. An awareness that our own conduct can contribute to the ongoing creation and expansion of *cosmic* beauty may give our moral lives a sense of being meaningfully and creatively tied into what is going on in the *universe* at large. I would like to suggest that we link our own sense of meaning and morality, as well as our vocations, to the deep and ageless cosmic striving to intensify beauty.

This way of understanding ethical life and cosmic purpose still begs the irrepressible question of why the world is apparently shaped by an 'aesthetic cosmological principle' in the first place. Did things have to be this way? Why does the universe have an urge to move beyond the status quo? Why the impetus for so much novelty, contrast and diversity? And why is the cosmic creation of beauty spread out over so many billions of years and over such an immensity of spatial magnitude? Why has there been so much evolutionary drama, including not only the invention of unpredictable beauty, but also an enormous amount of struggle and loss? And why did life have to take so long to become complex enough to be endowed with consciousness and the capacity for ethical aspiration?

These are humanly unanswerable questions, of course, but the 'long view' proposed by the great religions, and mediated by an aesthetically understood evolutionary cosmology, would consider all of the puzzling features of the cosmos revealed by modern science to be consistent with the notion of an *ultimate reality* whose intention for the cosmos is the maximising of beauty. Moreover, if this ultimate reality is conceived of as essentially infinite love, then it would apparently act most effectively not by forcing its will onto the cosmos in some instantaneous display of divine magicianship, but by inviting the universe to unfold freely and spontaneously from within itself, at its own pace. 'God', as we name this ultimate reality in the context of Western theistic religions, longs for the freedom, self-coherence and the risk-filled aesthetic intensification of the cosmos.

End Notes

1. Vaclav Havel, *Civilization*, (April/May), 1998, 53.
2. One rendition of this so-called 'perennial philosophy' may be found in EF Schumacher, *A Guide for the Perplexed (New* York: Harper Colophon Books, 1978), 18ff.
3. Again, see Schumacher's book *A Guide for the Perplexed*.
4. See Hans Jonas, *The Phenomenon of Life* (New York: Harper & Row, 1966), 9.
5. I have attempted to do this in *God After Darwin: A Theology of Evolution* (Boulder, Colo, 2000); and *Deeper Than Darwin: The Prospect for Religion in the Age of Evolution* (Boulder, Colo: 2003).
6. See Michael Polanyi, *Knowing and Being,* edited by Majorie Grene (Chicago: University of Chicago Press, 1969), 225–39.
7. This analogy is suggested by Polanyi in *The Tacit Dimension,* 31–34.
8. Jacques Monod, *Chance and Necessity,* translated by. Austryn Wainhouse (New York: Vintage Books, 1972); See also Daniel C Dennett, *Consciousness Explained* (New York: Little, Brown, 1991).
9. The most accessible introduction to these ideas is Teilhard de Chardin, *The Future of Man*, translated by Norman Denny (New York: Harper & Row, 1964).
10. Alfred North Whitehead, *Adventures of Ideas* (New York: The Free Press, 1967), 265.
11. See Louis Dupré, *Passage to Modernity* (Cambridge: Harvard University Press, 1993), 17–19.
12. For the following see Whitehead, *Adventures of Ideas,* 252–96; *Process and Reality,* 62, 183–85, 255 and *passim; Modes of Thought,* 57–63. Cf also Charles Hartshorne, *Man's Vision of God* (Chicago and New York: Willett, Clark & Company, 1941), 212–29.
13. I develop these points more fully in my books *God After Darwin* and *Deeper Than Darwin*. See note # 5 above.
14. Freeman Dyson, *Infinite in All Directions* (New York: HarperCollins, 1988), 298.

Darwin And Divine Providence

John F Haught

Abstract

Darwin challenges religious trust in a providential God who purposefully creates, influences and eternally cares for the world. Our religious ancestors did not have our knowledge of biological evolution, though they were certainly aware of the suffering of humans and other living beings. Darwinian science, however, vastly extends the story of life's suffering (and creativity as well) beyond that of traditional theological awareness. In what sense, then, after Darwin, might we still trust in divine providence, if at all? Is it perhaps possible that evolutionary portraits of life may open up fresh ways of thinking about God and cosmic purpose? After Darwin can we have a plausible understanding of God that is both consistent with traditional belief and adequate to the reality of evolution?

In biology as well as other sciences Charles Darwin has probably never been more important than he is today. Although he published *On the Origin of Species* almost a century and half ago, biologists today still consider his ideas to have enormous explanatory power. Darwin's theory has been updated by the contributions of Gregor Mendel and recent genetics. But in the contemporary 'neo-Darwinian synthesis' of genetics with the idea of natural selection the core of Darwin's original theory stands intact. Today most scientists would probably agree with geneticist Theodosius

Dobzhansky that nothing in biology makes sense except in the light of neo-Darwinian evolution.

Theologically speaking, however, the name of Darwin and the notion of evolution continue to invite impassioned discussion and at times bitter opposition. Christians today are still deeply divided over what to make of evolutionary biology. Specifically, it seems to me, what is most at issue after Darwin is whether we can plausibly reconcile the new evolutionary picture of nature and life with the theological notion of divine providence. Does embracing Darwinism (or neo-Darwinism) mean that one can no longer be a Christian in good faith, as many maintain? Or is it perhaps conceivable that evolutionary biology will prove in the end to be the occasion for deepening our belief in a God who graciously "provides" for the world?

The suspicion that providence and evolution do not go well together seems easily justifiable. Darwin's 'dangerous idea' exposes the story of life on earth as being dramatically different from what most people before the last century had expected. The vast amount of randomness, the extravagantly wasteful and impersonal discarding of innocent organisms by natural selection, and the enormous extent of time required by evolution—about 3.8 billion years of life history in a universe estimated to be around fourteen billion years old—have been so unsettling that many religious people have turned away in horror from the Darwinian abyss.

In order to allow a place for providence the universe of classical theism was structured hierarchically. That is, it consisted of at least several levels, typically thought of—moving from lower to higher—as the inanimate, the living, the sentient and the self-aware. Presiding over all of these levels is a hidden but eminently real dimension of divine Care and source of meaning identified as 'God'.

The persistent attraction of a hierarchical scheme consists of the fact that it embeds the temporal world within the framework of an eternal, absolute and sacred reality immune to transience and death. Only participation in such a permanence could give meaning to the perishable flux of finite existence and a sense that the universe is ultimately cared for. However, modern science has made the classical hierarchical vision untenable for many, and in doing so it has made it more difficult for to think seriously of nature as the expression of an eternal meaning or the universe as superintended by divine providence. Perhaps it isn't too much of an oversimplification to say that the main threat modern science has posed to religion is its apparent collapsing of the sacred hierarchical representation of being without which it is difficult to imagine how the universe could be the object of divine care or the expression of divine meaning. In the absence of a hierarchical vision how can there be any sense of the participation of the temporal in the eternal, and therefore any basis for attributing transcendent value, importance or meaning to the physical universe?

How, also, could the notion of providence ever make sense in terms compatible with biological evolution? Is the idea of divine providence even conceivable in a Darwinian universe, and if it is, how is it manifested? The following possible responses suggest themselves:

1. Providence is absent. The cruelty and indifference of evolution have banished as implausible any notion of providence once and for all.
2. Providence may still be present, even after Darwin, in the form of cosmic design or living complexity.

3. Providence makes sense when seen as Divine pedagogy, even in the harshest features of evolution.
4. Providence is manifested, after Darwin, in the form of loosely directional, and at least faintly discernible, evolutionary trends?
5. Providence is expressed in those fundamental cosmic features that constitute the very recipe of Darwinian evolution itself: chance, law and time. In the contingency, predictability and deep temporality of nature, theology after Darwin can discern the matrix of a richer and more biblical understanding of providence than has ever before been available.

Let us look more closely at each of these five proposals.

Providence as absent
Recently an ex-clergyman sent me a book that he had just written in which he set forth in great detail how Darwin's picture of the cruelty of nature had driven him to atheism. Could an omnipotent, omniscient, and omnibenevolent God have devised such a cold-blooded competition of beast with beast, beast with man, man with man, species with species, in which the clever, the cunning, and the cruel survive? . . . How could a loving God have planned a cruel system in which sensitive living creatures must either eat other sensitive living creatures or be eaten themselves, thereby causing untold suffering among these creatures? Would a benevolent God have created animals to devour others when he could have designed them all as vegetarians. What kind of deity would have designed the beaks which rip sensitive flesh? What God would intend every leaf,

blade of grass, and drop of water to be a battleground in which living organisms pursue, capture, kill, and eat one another? What God would design creatures to prey upon one another and, at the same time, instill into such creatures a capacity for intense pain and suffering?

In a similar vein David Hull, a philosopher of biology, has written:

> [Evolution is] rife with happenstance, contingency, incredible waste, death, pain and horror. Any God who would oversee a Darwinian world must be careless, indifferent, almost diabolical. This is not the sort of God to whom anyone would be inclined to pray.[1]

George Williams and other renowned biologists have expressed similar sentiments. And if 'cruelty' seems to be too moral or anthropomorphic a term to characterize the apparent mindlessness of Darwinian processes, nature's obvious 'indifference' is scarcely more consoling. 'So long as DNA is passed on', Richard Dawkins writes, 'it does not matter who or what gets hurt in the process. It is better for the genes of Darwin's ichneumon wasp that the caterpillar should be alive, and therefore fresh, when it is eaten, no matter what the cost in suffering. Genes don't care about suffering, because they don't care about anything.'

And so: 'The universe we observe has precisely the properties we should expect if there is, at bottom, no design, no purpose, no evil and no good, nothing but blind, pitiless indifference.'[2] Evolution has destroyed the idea of providence for good.

Providence manifested in pockets of intelligent design
Prior to Darwin, as Dawkins observes, a very common reason for belief providence was the adaptive design in

living organisms. This of course is the position William Paley made famous in his watchmaker analogy.[3] The intricate design in living organisms points us toward an intelligent providential divine designer no less certainly than the intricate mechanism of a watch points us to an intelligent watchmaker.

However, Darwin seems to have provided an adequate explanation of the design in living beings without resorting to theology at all. Natural selection of random variations, now called mutations, can explain life's 'design', that is, if you just give it enough time. And scientists today think that life originated as long as 3.8 billion years ago, leaving more than enough opportunity for the seemingly improbable design in living beings to come about gradually in a purely naturalistic way. So the story of life does not require any special *ad hoc* interventions of the supernatural, and we can discard the design argument of natural theology.

We may note in passing that the evolutionary materialists are not alone in celebrating the apparent death of natural theology. Many mainstream theologians, both liberal and conservative, want nothing to do with it either. They view the design argument as an idolatrous attempt on the part of finite humans to grasp the infinite and incomprehensible God in rational or scientific terms. Rational arguments diminish the mystery of God, seeking to bring it under the control of the limited human mind. For religious reasons, therefore, we should be grateful to Darwinians for helping us get rid of the pretentiousness of natural theology.

But natural theology has not gone away. It still lives on after Darwin, and under the stimulus of its encounter with evolutionary ideas, it has taken on new breadth and fresh confidence. Even though much of the revival of natural theology is now the work of scientists rather than professional theologians, it is an important instance of contemporary engagement of religious thought with evolution.

Instead of looking too closely and minutely at living organisms and their delicate adaptivity as the primary evidence of a designing Deity, this revived natural theology today stands back and surveys with wider-angled lenses the larger cosmic story in which Darwinian evolution is only a relatively recent episode. For example, John Polkinghorne, an emeritus Cambridge University physicist and now a practicing Anglican clergyman, argues that contemporary scientific advances in astronomy and physics place the whole story of life on our planet in an entirely new light.[4] We cannot divorce our understanding of the fact of biological evolution from its larger cosmic context or the history of the universe as a whole. In the light of today's astrophysics we not only have to account for life, but also for the physical and cosmic conditions that made life possible in the first place.

Among these conditions is the existence of carbon and the other heavy elements essential to the complex makeup of living beings. These elements were not yet present in the early universe, which featured only an abundance of hydrogen and helium; so if we are to understand the remote origins of biological phenomena we need to review the process that eventually brought the chemical conditions for life into existence in the first place. Recently the physics of the early universe has provided us with a fascinating account of this process, one that seems—at least in Polkinghorne's updated version of natural theology—to point once again toward something like intelligent design at the very foundations of the universe itself. In the overall evolution of the universe the eventual appearance of carbon and other heavy chemical elements depends upon cosmic features that had to have been very precisely fixed during the first micro-seconds of the universe's existence at the time of the big bang. To a good number of scientists today the initial conditions and fundamental cosmic constants seem so precisely bent toward the eventual production of carbon, and then life, that they suggest a new basis for natural theology, not in biology but in physics.

For life to be possible at all, the argument goes, the rate of expansion of the universe, the force of gravity, the ratio of electron to proton mass, and innumerable other cosmic birthmarks had to have been fixed infinitesimally close to their now established values. Otherwise the universe could never have produced hydrogen atoms, supernovae, carbon and other ingredients essential to life. Details of this fine-tuning can be found in many scientific works today, and it is not necessary to discuss them any further here.[5] We need only note that natural theology's encounter with Darwin has not inevitably led to its death but, in some cases at least, to the search for a more expansive cosmic setting in which to look for signs of divine design. As Polkinghorne argues, there must have been an extremely high degree of "'improbable order' even at the very beginning of cosmic time if life was eventually to come about, to evolve into the countless species, and eventually to become conscious in us humans. Human reason needs some intelligible account of this improbable initial ordering. Since such intricate and precise patterning was already present at the very beginning of cosmic history, it would not have had the 'time' (since there was no time 'before' the first cosmic moment) to come about by a process of evolution. Thus, the initial ordering of the cosmos strongly suggests, Polkinghorne claims, the work of a supremely intelligent Creator. Consequently, there is room even after Darwin for a revived and revised natural theology focusing on design in nature.[6]

Of course, if you are truly addicted to the idea that our life-bearing universe is a purely random, undirected and unintelligible occurrence, and that life within it *must* in no sense be the product of divine intelligence and wisdom, you may then imaginatively conjure up an endless series or proliferation of other 'universes', so as to increase the probability that randomness rules. Though most of the alleged 'universes' will be unsuited to life, you may still find it conceivable that purely by chance a life-biased set of initial conditions and fundamental physical constants such as we know to exist in our Big Bang universe, might eventually pop up.

However, to Polkinghorne such unrestrained and purely ungrounded speculation is certainly less elegant, and indeed no less metaphysical, than the theological idea of 'intelligent design'. Polkinghorne admits that his revised natural theology is not a 'knock down' argument for God's existence, but he views it as strongly suggestive of the contemporary relevance and reasonableness of theistic explanation.[7] In any case, we can see here that natural theology has been compelled by its encounter with evolutionary biology to seek a 'wider teleology' than it did prior to Darwin.

Providence as Divine pedagogy

Guy Murchie, in his colorful book *The Seven Mysteries of Life* agrees that Darwinian process is harsh, but precisely as such it is also educational. Earth, in all its Darwinian waywardness may best be thought of as a 'soul school'. Try to imagine that you are the creator, Murchie advises us. What kind of a world would you create? Would it be one in which we could luxuriate in blissful and undisturbed tranquility or hedonistic enjoyment?

> Honestly now, if you were God, could you possibly dream up any more educational, contrasty, thrilling, beautiful, tantalizing

> world than Earth to develop spirit in? If you think you could, do you imagine you would be outdoing Earth if you designed a world free of germs, diseases, poisons, pain, malice, explosives and conflicts so its people could relax and enjoy it? Would you, in other words, try to make the world nice and safe-- or would you let it be provocative, dangerous and exciting? In actual fact, if it ever came to that, I'm sure you would find it impossible to make a better world than God has already created.[8]

Divine care, therefore, may be present in the severity as well as the creativity in evolution.

Today many of us would find Murchie's proposal too anthropocentric and too earth-centered. And we would have to ask about the pain of other living beings? Why do they have to go to 'school' with us? Why does there have to be so much suffering? And why do we need such a big universe for such a small soul school? There is a venerable pedigree for the view that God chastises those whom God loves. Examples can be found in Proverbs, I Corinthians and especially Hebrews 12. The theme of divine pedagogy is present in Irenaeus, and abundantly so in popular spirituality, in the writings of John Hick. It was the poet John Keats who first used the expression 'Valley of soul-making' to make sense of our suffering. Still, it is not hard to see how such a view could build resentment and hatred of God. Moreover, it renders the story of the universe ultimately inconsequential except as providing a stage for the human drama. Surely there must be a better way of thinking about providence in a post-Darwinian context.

Providence manifested in general cosmic trends

Here I believe that the works of Teilhard de Chardin and Alfred North Whitehead can provide a vision of the cosmos that might allow one to think of providence in a fresher and wider way than ever before. I have space to point only in a very sketchy way how each of these great thinkers may contribute to a renewal of a sense of purpose. (A fuller picture is available in my book God After Darwin.)

From Teilhard de Chardin we can learn to 'see' trends in nature that are often overlooked by an atomistically or mechanistically oriented science. We need not accept it as a priori evident that the universe has no general aim or orientation. Whatever one may think of Teilhard's broad understanding of 'science' or his mystical cosmology, his general vision of a universe of emerging complexity-consciousness deserves our continuing study. This is the case especially today as we contemplate a future in which global com-plexification will probably continue to intensify as a result of economic, technological, communication, and informational developments. Teilhard's association of cosmic purpose with the ongoing heightening of consciousness does not seem at all preposterous today. And an increasing number of experts are now acknowledging that the rapid shrinking of our planet by satellite communications and especially the Internet are completely consistent with Teilhard's vision.

What is often forgotten, however, is Teilhard's constant counsel that any genuine planetary or cosmic advance will also require an intensification of faith, hope and love. Without the contributions of these fundamentally religious dispositions we cannot anticipate a meaningful future for the earth. For Teilhard, a 'scientific' reason for this claim is that empirical studies have observed in evolution, along with emerging complexity-consciousness, an increasing 'centration' at the heart of 'socialization'. That is, from the very origins of the universe 'matter' has had a fascinating tendency to gather and complexify in terms of a center. We find this centration in the atom's 'nucleus', in the eukaryotic cell, in anthills and beehives organized around a 'queen', in the emerging of the central nervous system in vertebrates, and most obviously in our own intensely centered 'subjectivity'. But now that humans have become the dominant terrestrial species the 'search for a center' is manifested most representatively in our religions. Religions are fundamentally ways through which the universe continues, at least at the terrestrial and human levels, its ageless search for a Center. Instead of interpreting religion and evolution as incompatibles, as do many religious believers and scientific skeptics today, the Teilhardian vision portrays our religions as the privileged ways by which our unfinished universe orients itself—at this point in its evolution—toward its ultimate destiny.

From Whitehead we may learn to see that at least one way of thinking about general directionality in an evolutionary world, and hence of providing a way to think about divine providence, is to note that the cosmos is a restless aim toward ever more intense configurations of beauty. The general features of the universe are fashioned by what I like to call the 'aesthetic cosmological principle'. Unlike the so-called 'anthropic cosmological principle', which all too easily suggests that the physical constants and initial conditions of the 'big bang' universe are oriented focally toward the emergence of humans, the 'aesthetic cosmological principle' proposes more broadly—and in a manner less controversial in terms of ecology—that the universe is structured so as to strive openendedly and experimentally toward more and more intense versions of beauty. What I mean here by beauty would be inclusive of, but by no means exhausted in, the emergence of human consciousness and culture. In this aesthetic cosmological perspective our own lives could be seen as meaningful, and our moral aspiration connected once again to the cosmos; but our relative position in the cosmos would be rendered more modestly than in some of our inherited theological formulations.

Providence present in contingency, law and deep time underlying evolution (my own approach).
In the interest of maintaining a sense of the unity of truth we must go beyond merely demonstrating that evolution is logically compatible with the notion of providence. Unfortunately, however, most contemporary theology has still not faced up to the fact that a Darwinian universe is a lot different from the hierarchical cosmographies that shaped classical theologies and that continue to inform the rather acosmic, and often anemic, spiritualities of the Christian churches. Evolution, though perhaps the most important idea to have emerged in the last two centuries, still remains outside the central concern of academic theology and seminary education. Even when the topic comes up at all, evolution does not receive a very close examination, and many of its most challenging features are glossed over.

This oversight, it seems to me, is a lost opportunity for theology and religious education. I believe that a close encounter of theology with contemporary versions of evolutionary biology can reinvigorate our sense of divine providence and deepen our appreciation of God's love and eternal care for the cosmos. But how could this be, especially given the randomness or contingency in life's evolution?

Unlike those theological approaches that virtually deny the reality of randomness, my own theology of evolution insists that chance is no illusion. Accidents— such as mutations and meteorite impacts that redirect the pathways of life's evolution in indeterminate ways—are a simple fact of nature and should not be made to seem unreal. The contingency in evolution which to a Dawkins or Gould suggests a pointless universe, is theologically precious because it points to a spontaneity in nature that, paradoxically perhaps, helps illuminate belief that God deeply loves and cares for creation. After all, if it is truly the case that the universe is grounded in divine self-giving love, as Christian faith maintains, at least some degree of indeterminacy in the world is just what we should expect. We can say this on the basis of the analogy of one human being's love for another, an analogy that Christians find so resplendent in the life of Jesus. The essential point is that genuine love never forces or compels. True love, by definition, allows the other the space to be and become truly other.

If we seriously believe that God loves the universe, then, it seems to me that we must make intellectual room for the astounding and liberating idea that the universe possesses at least some degree of autonomy. Evolutionary biology is expressive of such a universe. The autonomy of the world manifests itself in unpredictable eruptions of spontaneity—including what we refer to as the randomness in evolution. Without such scope for indeterminacy the world would be little more than an appendage to God's own being rather than something distinct from God. It is important to keep in mind here the fundamental teaching of the theistic religions that *the world is not God*. And a world devoid of contingency or internal spontaneity could not be truly 'other' than God, for if it were not truly distinct from God it could not be the recipient of divine love. There must be ample scope for contingency in any universe that is both distinct from and loved by God. Moreover, the appearance of human freedom would never have been possible in a universe that had been created by a manipulative magician who did not allow the cosmos to emerge gradually toward an independence that allows it to be increasingly distinct from the One who calls it into being.

At the same time, the remorseless consistency and invariance of the laws of physics, and the unbending rule of natural selection, though these are seemingly impersonal, indifferent and even cruel at times, are easily indicative of a creator who does not wish to intrude into the autonomous coherence of the world as it emerges into ever deeper independence vis-à-vis its creator. Moreover, the predictable routines defined as natural laws are absolutely necessary if an emerging universe is not to collapse back into chaos at any moment in the process of its becoming. As such, the laws of nature are signs not of divine indifference but of divine fidelity and care.

Finally, if nature is truly differentiated from God, as it must be if we are to avoid pantheism, it has to have considerable scope for wandering about experimentally 'on its own' This means that creation will be nonlinear and serendipitous--as evolution shows it to be. And if God's creative and providential presence to the world includes 'letting the world be', rather than manipulatively controlling it, then it would be strange indeed if the world's coming into being occurred in a single magical instant instead of taking a considerable amount of time--perhaps many billions of terrestrially calculated years.

The point is, there could be no self-giving of God to the universe unless the universe is first allowed in some way to become itself, though of course within the wide limits of the creator's vision of the world's future. The evolutionary materialists, as well as the creationists and 'intelligent design' proponents, suspect that a universe whose evolution takes so much time could not conceivably reside in the bosom of any kind of divine care. But listen to these words of theologian Jürgen Moltmann:

> God acts in the history of nature and human beings through his patient and silent presence, by way of which he gives those he has created space to unfold, time to develop, and power for their own movement. We look in vain for God in the history of nature or in human history if what we are looking for are special divine interventions. Is it not much more that God waits and awaits, that—as process theology rightly says—he 'experiences' the history of the world and human beings, that he is 'patient and of great goodness' as Psalm 103:8 puts it? . . . 'Waiting' is never disinterested passivity, but the highest form of interest in the other. Waiting means expecting, expecting means inviting, inviting means attracting, alluring and enticing. By doing this, the waiting and awaiting keeps an open space for the other, gives the other time, and creates possibilities of life for the other.[9]

The theology of evolution I am proposing here locates the epochs of evolutionary experimentation, the spontaneous emergence of life, the indeterminate genetic variations, the implacable consistency of natural selection and the unfathomable depth of time itself within a divine eternity that both embraces the cosmos and invites it to become increasingly more independent.

However, this independence does not entail the separation or mutual aloofness of the world and God. Rather this is an independence without which there can be no true relationship or climactic union of the world with God. Moreover, this hoped for union will in no way abrogate the world's distinctness from God. The reason is that, as Teilhard de Chardin often emphasized, 'true union differentiates.'[10] As the world becomes more and more independent of God, the opportunity for intimate relationship and dialogue of the world with God intensifies. So also, of course, does the risk of an ungrateful human turning away from the freedom-bestowing creator.

Nevertheless, the promissory thrust of biblical faith encourages us to trust that God, the font of all freedom will never forsake the world. And so theology may picture the entirety of cosmic and biological evolution, along with human history, as destined for an ever deeper intimacy with God. A trust that God is infinite self-giving love would imply that divine providence influences the world in a persuasive rather than coercive way. God's humility would allow creation to emerge as something other than God. And since a limitless love cannot force things onto a rigid pathway of growth, the life-story would quite understandably be peppered with a contingency or spontaneity that opens it to an indeterminate future.

If God is love, and not controlling power, the world will be given leeway to experiment with an array of creative possibilities. And if life is allowed such an amplitude of possibilities, it may turn out that some experiments will succeed and others fail. We may at first balk at such an idea, but let us consider the alternative. A more directively dictatorial deity might bring the universe to completion in one magical moment, but what a bland, lifeless, storyless world that would be. If God were to follow our human sense of 'design', the story of life on earth would have been shorter and less ragged. It would probably have gone without the outlandish organisms of the Cambrian explosion, the creepy age of reptiles, and most of the other episodes of creation that seem so alien to us. Our divine designer would have fashioned from primordial chaos a much more respectable, and certainly a less mysterious, world than the one that so troubles us with its strange evolutionary pathways.

In describing the inefficient way that human organs are cobbled together by evolution, science writer Chet Raymo captures nicely the disjunction between the actual pathways of evolution on the one hand and our own narrow sense of 'intelligent design' on the other. Raymo is a severe critic of Intelligent Design Theory, not least because defenders of design overlook the marvelously creative power of evolution. Living phenomena hardly fit our own ideas of good engineering. For example, our digestive tract is so twisted and tangled that it's a wonder that anything can move from one end to the other. 'An engineer might sort it out. Roll that small intestine up into a nice neat coil. Straighten out those kinks in the large intestine. Can you imagine the exhaust system of your car in such a tangle?' Likewise, Raymo notes, the human ear seems unnecessarily complex from an engineer's point of view. 'Hammer, anvil and stirrup: Where did those crazy little mechanisms come from? Five separate membranes. And three fleshy loops that seem, on the face of it, superfluous.' According to Raymo

> ... much of the human body is an engineer's nightmare, showing little in the way of intelligent design: which is just what you'd expect if our bodies evolved by a process of incremental changes acted upon by natural selection. The thing about evolution is this: Inevitably it moves toward ever more finely adapted organisms, but the end is not foreordained and the journey is something of a drunken stagger.

And here is Raymo's message to advocates of 'intelligent design':

> Now, before you accuse me of tossing an Intelligent Designer out of the picture, consider this: For all of the improvements an engineer might suggest for the human body, the body is still a thing that no engineer could hope to equal. Fabulously resilient. Capable of stunning feats of endurance. Exquisitely attuned to the environment. Agile, disease-repelling, self-repairing, purposeful, cunning.
>
> Evolution by natural selection, for all of its jerry-rigged solutions, for all its failed experiments and blind alleys, is a wonderfully efficient way to populate a universe with diverse and interesting creatures. If I were an Intelligent Designer, and I had a hundred billion galaxies (at least) to fill with wonders, I can think of no way more efficient to do it than by genetic variations and natural selection of self-reproducing organisms.
>
> You want intelligent design? Try evolution.[11]

Conclusion

Evolution helps us realise that God is much more interested in arousing adventure in the world than in establishing impeccable design. Evolutionary science allows us to connect our ideas of God to the larger story of life's arduous, ageless liberation from triviality. And when divine providence is thought of in a consistently biblical spirit it must not be separated from the theme of *promise*. Divine care for the world has to do fundamentally with God's opening the world to an always new and unpredictable future. And evolution now invites theology to extend the sweep of the divine promise beyond the narrow sphere of human history so as to embrace the story of the entire universe.

In response to the outpouring of God's boundless love the universe is invited, but never forced, to undergo a process of perpetual self-transformation. As it adapts to an infinitely self-giving love and an always faithful promise of a new future, the finite cosmos undergoes what we now take to be a dramatic evolution toward increasing complexity, life, consciousness and expanding beauty. Viewed in this way, the evolution of life is more than just 'compatible' with a biblically informed notion of providence. Faith in a humble, promising, self-giving God should already have prepared us for the idea of evolution.

End Notes

1. David Hull, 'The God of the Galapagos', in *Nature*, 1992, 486.
2. *River Out of Eden* (New York: Basic Books, 1995), 131.
3. William Paley, *Natural Theology* (New York: Boston, Gould and Lincoln, 1873).
4. John Polkinghorne, 'Creation and the Structure of the Physical World', in *Theology Today,* 44 (April, 1987): 53-68.
5. See especially John D Barrow and Frank J Tipler, *The Anthropic Cosmological Principle* (New York: Oxford University Press, 1986).
6. Polkinghorne, 53–68.
7. *Ibid.*
8. Guy Murchie, *The Seven Mysteries of Life: An Exploration in Science and Philosophy* (Boston: Houghton Mifflin, 1978), 621—22.
9. Jürgen Moltmann, 'God's Kenosis in the Creation and Consummation of the World', in John Polkinghorne, editor, *The Work of Love: Creation as Kenosis* (Grand Rapids: Eerdmans Publishing Company, 2001), 149.
10. Pierre Teilhard de Chardin, *The Human Phenomenon,* trans. Sarah Appleton-Weber (Portland: Sussex Academic Press, 1999), 186.
11. Chet Raymo, 'Intelligent Design Happens Naturally', in *The Boston Globe*, 14 May 14, 2002.

Theology, Ecology And Cosmology

John F Haught

Abstract

A major assumption of any compelling ecological ethic is that humans belong to the universe and the earth. In some versions of Christian spirituality, however, the earth sometimes came to be thought of as a place *to get away from* in order to find salvation. Nature in this understanding became little more than a point of departure for the human religious journey to another world. Secular environmentalists have claimed that this religious otherworldliness has compromised our planet's ecological integrity. This lecture will respond to that accusation and argue that contemporary science and cosmology, unlike earlier views of the universe, provide a refreshing background for a Christian understanding of humanity's relation to nature.

Holmes Rolston III, one of America's most renowned environmental ethicists, has written that because of human factors and failings

> ... nature is more at peril than at any time in the last two and a half billion years. The sun will rise tomorrow, because it rose yesterday and the day before; but nature may no longer be there. Unless in the next millennium, indeed in the next century, we can regulate and control the escalating human devastation of our planet, we may face the end of nature as it

> has hitherto been known. Several billion years worth of creative toil, several million species of teeming life, have now been handed over to the care of this late-coming species in which mind has flowered and morals have emerged. Science has revealed to us this glorious natural history; and religion invites us to be stewards of it. That could be a glorious future story. But the sole moral and allegedly wise species has so far been able to do little more than use this science to convert whatever we can into resources for our own self-interested and escalating consumption, and we have done even that with great inequity between persons.[1]

Our species, Rolston and other environmentalists agree, is ruining the natural world. We humans are destroying rain forests, allowing the soil to erode, poisoning the air, and polluting rivers, lakes and oceans. We have created a dangerous greenhouse atmosphere, and reduced the protective ozone layer. And we are daily destroying many irreplaceable living species. Common sense demands that we change our ways, but apparently we need much more than common sense to fire our ethical responsibility for the earth. What we need is a vision, one that can move us to a firm and permanent commitment to ecological responsibility within the context of natural flux and cosmic evolution.

Can Christian faith provide such a vision? And can theological reflection discover in tradition or scripture a groundwork for dedicated ecological action? It seems to me, speaking here as a Christian theologian, that this is one of theology's most important contemporary challenges, especially in view of well-known accusations that Christianity is itself in some way responsible for our environmental neglect. Such a serious indictment forces us to ask whether theology can demonstrate an essential connection between Christian faith and ecological concern. Can Christian faith provide truly motivating reasons for taking care of the nonhuman natural world?[2]

The Australian philosopher John Passmore, for one, doubts that it can. Belief in God and the 'next world,' he says, softens our sense of obligation to this world. Otherworldly piety even gives rise to an implicit hostility toward nature. The only substantial basis for environmental concern, therefore, is a radical naturalism, a belief system that sees nothing beyond the existence of the physical universe. According to Passmore, only if humans accept the fact that we are situated here on this planet in a universe barren of any transcendent governance, will we begin to take full responsibility for our terrestrial home.[3]

Passmore is right in characterising much traditional Christianity as otherworldly to the point of neglecting the earth's wellbeing. His complaint is justifiable, given his understanding of what Christianity essentially is. Moreover, he compels us to acknowledge that Christian theology must do a much better job of displaying whatever ecological relevance it might have than it has done so far.

So, precisely how can Christian theology respond? It may begin by emphasizing that according to biblical faith the natural world is inherently good and that God has even become incarnate in the cosmos. It can point to exceptional exemplars of love of nature such as St Francis, Hildegard of Bingen, Meister Eckhart, or Gerard Manley Hopkins. It must in all candor acknowledge that most of our saints, poets and theologians have had little formal concern about the well-being of nature. But at the same time it may point to the fact that several distinct kinds of 'ecological theology' are now emerging. For convenience's sake I shall call these respectively the tradition-centered (or 'apologetic') approach, 2) the sacramental approach, and 3) the cosmic promise approach. The latter weaves the biblical theme of promise into the new scientific awareness of a universe still in the making.

Each of these three proposals is insufficient when taken alone, but taken together they constitute a substantial beginning for a Christian ecological theology. Cumulatively they are capable not only of responding to accusations that Christian faith is indifferent to the welfare of nature, but they can provide the underpinning of a new vision of religiously inspired responsibility to the earth. Each of the three approaches relies on points made by the other, but it adds its own emphasis. There is a good deal of overlap, but each has an accent not visible in the others. The three types are complementary in an additive sense: each is a piece of a whole puzzle.

As we shall see, the cosmic promise (or, more technically, the 'cosmological-eschatological') approach becomes especially significant once we situate our reflections in the context of what science has demonstrated to be the unfinished condition of the physical universe and what the editors of this volume refer to as ecological flux. Cosmology has recently undergone a radical transformation, one that allows theology now to link up with ecological understanding in a way that would not have been available to our religious ancestors. Today it is imperative that theologians who address the contemporary ecological predicament attend very closely to what geology, evolutionary biology, genetics and especially scientific cosmology are telling us about the natural world. We shall find, I believe, that theological reflection on what science has shown to be a world still in the making can reconfigure the meaning of stewardship in an entirely fresh manner, one that may bring about a new appreciation of the close connection between biblical faith and our obligations to nature in process. But first let us see what we can say about Christian responsibility to nature even independently of any encounter with the world of contemporary natural science. (In this paper I shall limit myself to the world of Christian thought.)

A tradition-centered (apologetic) approach

The first and probably the most familiar approach to ecological theology is one that finds in scripture and tradition adequate resources for a Christian response to the ecological predicament. We may call this approach 'apologetic' because, as the Latin world *apologia* suggests, it 'defends' biblical faith against the charge that it is ecologically hazardous or inconsequential. Examples of the apologetic approach include recent statements on environmental issues by the Pope, Catholic Bishops, the World Council of Churches and a growing number of theologians.[4] Their common message is that we have ignored the wealth of ecologically relevant material in the Bible and Christian tradition. Accordingly, what theology should be doing now is to retrieve this lost wisdom and allow it to address the present crisis. Theology will find numerous, often previously ignored, biblical passages and many other texts from the great teachers in the Church's history that proclaim the goodness and beauty of creation. It will come upon numerous ecologically relevant texts that it had barely noticed before we began recently to become aware of the fragility of life on this planet. How many of us, for example, had thought very much about the words in the Noah story in *Genesis*, where after the flood God made a covenant not only with human beings but with 'every living creature'? And had we even reflected on the profound significance of the familiar words in Genesis

1:31 may have today: 'And God looked at everything he had made, and he found it very good.'

The backbone of the 'apologetic' approach, of course, is God's giving humans the task of 'caring for' the garden in which they are situated (Gen 2:15). Responsible stewardship, however, entails the practice of ecologically appropriate virtues: compassion, humility, moderation, detachment and gratitude. Since the immediate 'causes' of our ecological crisis are commonly said to be human arrogance, greed, violence and the crude exercise of power, a renewed commitment to a biblically inspired ethic should lead directly to the repair of nature. Indeed, it is tempting to say that the solution to our ecological crisis lies simply in a serious return on the part of human beings to the practice of fundamental biblical values and classic religious virtues. Contrary to what critics of Christianity maintain, therefore, the apologetic approach insists that this tradition by no means lacks the basis for ecological conscientiousness. The fact is, we have not attended to its ethical directives. Environmental abuse is not the fault of Christianity, as Passmore and other secular thinkers have argued. Rather, it is the result of our failure to take seriously the imperatives embedded in Christian faith.

What could be more fundamental in restoring our relationship to the natural world, for example, than earnestly practicing compassion? Would we be stretching Christian faith beyond its boundaries were we to extend its emphasis on sisterly and brotherly love toward all of creation? Is St Francis' compassion toward animals or his discourse about brother sun and sister moon an unnecessarily revisionist straining of the meaning of love? For Christians the paradigm of such widening of compassion for, and deeper relationship to, all of creation is revealed in the picture of Jesus as the Christ. The Gospels picture Jesus as one who constantly sought out deeper connections than those required by the customs of his time. They see him as passionately desirous of relating to those who were by all ordinary standards relationless: the sinners, the religiously despised, the sick, and even the dead. Perhaps the central motif of his life was the embracing of what did not belong. Is it not conceivable then that the contemporary movement to include all of life and all of nature within the circle of our own compassionate care is a justifiable extension of the Spirit of Christ in our own time? An ecological theology may extend the circumference of Jesus' inclusive compassion for the unincluded to embrace the totality of nature.

Finally, there is an even more fundamental way in which theology may ground ecological concern in Christian tradition—while at the same time defending itself (apologetically) against the claim that radical secularism or pure naturalism provides a more favorable climate for ecological solicitude than does theistic belief. Numerous classic texts of Christian tradition echo St Augustine's oft-repeated observation that each of us is restless until we rest in God.[5] According to many religious traditions, in fact, we are each born with an insatiable desire for the infinite. From the Jewish, Christian and Islamic perspectives, only the inexhaustible mystery of God can ultimately satisfy us. But when the modern world formally abandoned the idea of God it did not eliminate the infinity of our native longing. We remain *capax infiniti* (open to the infinite). Our unquenchable thirst for 'more and more' stays with us as an anthropological constant. Having lost sight of its ultimate objective—the infinite God—this longing does not go away, but instead turns itself toward devouring our proximate environment, the planet we live on. The restless human search for satisfaction is now engaged in the hollow project of squeezing the infinite out of what is increasingly exposing itself as utterly finite. Our tiny planet is unable to deliver the boundlessness that renders the human heart forever restless. We have not found in the earth a transcendent plenitude proportionate to the abysmal emptiness of our hearts. Thus, many of the earth's resources are now being used up with disproportionate rapidity, all in the senseless enterprise of milking infinity from a conspicuously bounded resource. Logically speaking, then, the solution to our disastrous exploitation of the planetary environment is not to deny the existence of the infinite mystery of God, but in conformity with our great religious traditions to direct our longing toward it once again.

Evaluation of the tradition-centered approach

Over the past fifteen years or so, I have witnessed at close hand the emergence of ecological theology, and I would say that most theologians, along with many other Christians, have made the tradition-centered or apologetic approach the substantial core of their response to our present ecological situation. There is much to recommend this approach, and its retrieval of the tradition must surely be part of any adequate ecological theology today. However, I fear that it does not adequately address all dimensions of the current situation. On the positive side, it has made us read the Bible and traditional theology with new eyes, and helped us peer more deeply into the ethical significance of the venerable teachings about creation, incarnation, divine wisdom, etc. But, as I shall argue below, it needs to be supplemented by the 'sacramental' and 'cosmic promise' approaches. It is not enough by itself to deal with what this book is calling 'ecological flux.'

Before taking up the alternatives, however, I should first emphasize that the 'apologetic' stance is entirely justified in opposing the simplistic allegations made by Passmore, Lynn White, Jr. and others that Christianity is the main cause of our environmental ills. The fact is that the secularist and scientistic assumptions of modern intellectual culture have led to a radical desacralising of nature that in turn has permitted us to treat the earth as though it were merely instrumentally good rather than a value in itself.[6] In addition, the modern secularist outlook has generated a materialist philosophy of nature according to which life is reducible to lifeless chemicals, and in which insensate 'matter' is elevated to the status of ultimate reality.[7] It is hard to imagine how such a picture of things could ever lead people toward the reverencing of nature that ecological ethics now requires. Barry Commoner points out that if we consistently followed the materialist creed that life is reducible to lifeless matter *in principle*, sooner of later this reduction will take place *in fact* as well.[8] Moreover, as Hermann Daly and John Cobb have shown at length, the causes of nature's present distress include runaway industrialization and naive economic assumptions about the unlimited resourcefulness of the earth, both of which are rooted in the materialist assumptions of modernity.[9] Christians, like others, bear much of the blame, but Christianity's and other religions' antimaterialism is inherently a restraining influence, and their cultivation of virtues of moderation and humility, were we to take them seriously, would lead us to accept our finitude, and temper our will to exploit and destroy the natural world.

However, after acknowledging all of this, there is room to doubt whether it is enough for Christian ecological theology simply to restore the most familiar elements of the tradition. I strongly suspect that the present crisis calls for something more from theology than simply pointing us to relevant and often forgotten texts and teachings. Today we may need a more animating and far-reaching articulation of what it means to be Christian in an ecological age. In view of the unprecedented modern and contemporary devastation of nature, perhaps we should not place too protective a shield around our traditions, but instead allow them also to be creatively transformed, as indeed nature itself is being transformed in its own evolution. Religious faith, after all, springs to life most floridly during those periods of history when it faces radically new challenges. Can we be certain that Christian tradition in its purely classical formulations is fully adequate to the dimensions of the current environmental crisis? Is it perhaps conceivable that faith and theology are now being summoned by radically new circumstances, and especially by developments in scientific cosmology, to undergo a more sweeping metamorphosis than the apologetic approach alone would permit?

There seems to me to be something utterly interruptive about our current ecological situation, and so our religions are now being challenged to a much more thoroughgoing self-renewal than an exclusively apologetic approach would allow. For Christianity, as for all other traditions, innovative responses may be needed. Consequently, I shall now outline two alternative routes—not completely separable from each other or from our first approach—that theology may take in our time as it looks toward the future of humanity's relationship with the natural world.

The sacramental approach

For Christians the theological resources for an ecological renewal of faith can be found not only in Biblical texts and doctrinal tradition, but also, and no less fundamentally, in the 'sacramental' character of nature itself. To say that nature is sacramental simply means that, even apart from biblical revelation, nature in all of its beauty and diversity reveals the divine mystery—not just to Christians, of course, but to people of many traditions. A sacrament is anything through which we are gifted with a sense of the sacred; and it is especially nature's beauty and vitality that have communicated to humans an impression of the divine. In fact, it takes only a moment's reflection to realise that we really could not say very much about God at all apart from the richness and variety present in nature. Nature's sunlight, oceanic depths, fresh air, water, storms, rocks, trees, soil, growth, fertility, life, abundance, power, just to name several obvious examples, are perennially essential to religious metaphor. Even apart from traditional religious texts, therefore, nature's sacramental character gives us a deeply religious reason for taking care of it.

By acknowledging nature's inherent transparency to the divine, sacramentalism keeps us from turning our world into nothing more than raw material for our own human projects. Its sacramental capacity, therefore, should shield nature from diminishment at our hands. Without pantheistically identifying nature with God, as some traditionalists fear, the sacramental approach sees the natural world is at heart a symbolic disclosure of God.[10] This gives nature a 'sacral' quality that should divert our manipulative tendencies. And today, after Darwin and Einstein, we are in a position to envisage all natural sacraments as embedded in an even more encompassing sacrament, that of an entire evolving universe gradually revealing the divine to us in a dramatic way that previous theological age could never have imagined. For ecological theology not to notice and profit from this magnificent revelation would be a most appalling oversight.

Sacramental ecology argues that apologetics, with its emphasis on classic texts, is not enough to ground an ethically motivating ecological theology. If we want a theology capable of responding to the full dimensions of the ecological crisis we must learn once more to revere the natural world itself for showing forth to us the sacred reality that underlies it.[11] And as I shall argue below, we cannot do this without the help of contemporary science and cosmology. Our spirituality has become so acosmic, so obsessed with themes of history and human freedom, so concerned with interpreting written texts, that it has lost touch with the sacramentality of nature. It is now time to resacramentalize theology.

For Christians this means especially that they place fresh emphasis on the biblical theme of creation. Western religious tradition has unnecessarily subordinated creation — and by implication sacramentalism — to the theme of redemption.[12] An exclusive emphasis on redemption has led Christian theology to exaggerate the 'fallenness' not only of ourselves but also of the natural world. The assumption has been that redemption would be a momentous event only in proportion to the abysmal depths of a primordial Fall. By over-emphasizing the fallenness of both humanity and nature 'in the beginning,' nature has been made at times to seem perverse and therefore undeserving of our care. By exaggerating the fallenness of nature we have too easily lost sight of the original goodness of the entire creation that God declared to be 'good'. At the same time, an undue focus on the human need for redemption from evil has distracted us from the travail of the entire creation which, in St Paul's words, also 'groans' for radical renewal (Rom 8:22). The renewal of nature to which Christian faith alludes need not be postponed until the 'last day,' but it can begin to become a reality here and now — no less so than the renewal of our personal lives can begin in the present.

The sacramental approach emphasises the present renewal of nature when it interprets 'sin' to mean more than just our human separation from God or from each other. Sin also signifies the current alienation of nature from humanity, its estrangement from God and from its own creative possibilities envisaged by God from the outset of creation. Accordingly 'redemption' and 'reconciliation' must mean not only the restoring of the divine-human relationship, but also the healing of the entire earth-community and indeed the renewal of the whole creation, beginning right now. The redemption of nature no more has to be delayed to the 'end of time' than does the new creation of our own personal lives.

Likewise, for a sacramental-ecological theology, the redeeming 'Christ' is no longer exclusively a personal, historical savior but, even more fundamentally, a cosmic presence--indeed the rejuvenating heart of an entire universe--as represented in the writings of Paul, John, Irenaeus and Teilhard de Chardin. We may even say that the whole cosmos is in some sense the 'body of Christ.' Concentrated and epitomized in the flesh and blood of Christ, the entire evolution of the universe becomes the corporeal expression of the very being of God.

A sacramentally shaped ecological vision also gives a cosmic dimensionality to eucharistic celebration. Eucharist symbolizes the healing not only of damaged human relationships but of our broken connection with the natural world as well. At the same time, a sacramental ecology gives fresh relevance to the doctrine of the Holy Spirit, the creative power that the Psalmist implores God to 'pour out' so as to 'renew the face of the earth.'

This sacramental face-lift of theology calls in turn for new directions in Christian spirituality. It encourages, for example, a wholesome new sense of our intricate relationship to the natural world. In the past, the spiritual sensitivities of Christians have often been shaped by an anti-incarnational dualism that separates spirit from matter and thus distances us humans from nature. This dualism suppresses our natural intuition of being connected to an incalculably rich cosmic diversity and to a bodily existence completely continuous with the rest of the story of life on earth. The same dualism, incidentally, has also undergirded patriarchal exclusivism with its sinful oppression of women.[13] Sacramentalism, in alliance with prophetic themes of biblical faith, links respect for the earth very closely to the social and religious liberation of women; and it argues that our religious institutions will not seriously accept ecological responsibility until they have begun to treat women with justice, both socially and ecclesially.

The sacramental approach is typically allied with a sense of the interrelationship of all forms of life. For this reason a renewed sacramental realization of the intricate way in which human life is woven into the natural world should lead us to see how inseparable ecological concern is from the demands of economic justice. Much of our mistreatment of this planet's life-systems, after all, stems from the inequitable way in which the world's goods are distributed from region to region, or from nation to nation. Impoverished places on earth are often the most ecologically spoiled simply because their inhabitants must strip them bare for the sake of mere subsistence. Hence we cannot hope to restore the ecological integrity of such locales without also addressing the extreme poverty that exists there. At the same time, those of us who live in areas of material bounty and wealth must realize that our own extravagant use of the world's resources contributes disproportionately to the global perpetuation of ecological disarray. The Christian tradition is powerfully relevant and often effective on issues of social justice, but social justice must now become allied closely—and everywhere—with a more sacramentally oriented focus on *eco-justice*.

Evaluation

Along with the tradition-centered approach, a sacramental vision adds indispensable ingredients to the larger project of formulating an ecological theology. Today Christian theology in particular needs to retrieve a sacramental sense of the cosmos. Our ancient intuition of the revelatory character of the universe, now brought up to date by scientific cosmology, is perhaps the most significant theological and ecological contribution our second approach has to make. More explicitly than the traditional apologetics, a sacramental theology allows us to recognize the *intrinsic* relation between religious faith and contemporary ecological concern. It helps us to realise, for example, that without the freshness of air, the purity of water, and the fertility of soil, the power of our most enduring symbols of God is diminished or lost. The integrity of nature is inseparable from the flourishing of religion. If we lose nature, as Thomas Berry puts it, we will also lose God.

Nevertheless, the sacramental approach is unable to give us a fully biblical or a distinctively Christian ecological theology. It can easily allow us to overlook the pivotal motif of biblical religion, namely, the theme of promise for the future.[14] In its justifiable longing to recapture the sense of our connectedness to the natural world the sacramental approach does not always pay enough attention to the Bible's fundamental orientation toward *future* fulfillment. That is, it is often inclined to ignore what theology refers to as 'eschatology', the biblical concern for future fulfilment. A biblically informed sense of what we may call 'the *promise* of nature' must become central, I believe, to any explicitly Christian reflections on ecology. Moreover, when eschatology is conjoined with contemporary scientific cosmology the theme of 'nature as promise' can preserve the best of both the classical and sacramental contributions to ecological theology while extending them into fresh territory.

The 'cosmic promise' approach

Biblical scholars over the last century or so have gradually rediscovered eschatology as the core of biblical religion. Promise of future fulfillment is the central message of the Hebraic scriptures, of the teachings of Jesus, and it is the driving force of the Christian vision of the world.[15] But theology has also come to realize that eschatology—concern for future fulfillment—means not simply a hope for human survival in the 'next world', but a conviction that *everything that happens* in the present world (or the present age) occurs within the context of a divine promise of future fulfillment.[16] Although 'what happens in the world' has usually meant primarily the affairs of human history, neither the doctrine of creation nor contemporary scientific cosmology permits us to leave the natural world out of the compass of Christian hope. An integral theology, one attuned to the biblical spirit of promise as well as to astrophysics, geology, evolutionary biology and ecology, demands that we now view the entire universe, from its earliest beginnings to whatever end awaits it, as sharing in the same promise that the evangelist Luke, for example, beheld in the events associated with the birth of the Messiah.

An expansive and inclusive eschatological faith is convinced that the same divine promise that brought Israel and the church into being has in fact always encompassed the totality of the cosmos. Eschatology, in its deepest and widest meaning, therefore, implies that a resplendent fulfillment awaits the *entire universe*. The divine promise first announced to Abraham pertains not only to the 'people of God' but also, if we listen attentively to St Paul in *Romans* 8:22, to the 'whole of creation.'

However, the question immediately arises as to whether Christianity's eschatological orientation is ecologically helpful. Doesn't future expectation actually uproot us from nature instead of reconciling us to it? Some ecologists fear that religious concern for a future fulfillment will allow us to tolerate ecological indifference in the present. Hope for a future new creation, the argument goes, causes us to dream so extravagantly of the age to come that we will lose interest in this one, and even let it slip toward catastrophe. We cannot ignore this concern. After all, some kinds of biblical expectation, if taken in isolation, are ecologically dangerous. For example, apocalyptic visions, when interpreted too literally and independently of other biblical forms of anticipation, may even take consolation in the prospect of this world's imminent dissolution. Additionally, those individualistic earth-despising brands of supernaturalist optimism--more a heritage of the Greek than the biblical world--which seek an acosmic 'spiritual' world as our final destiny, seem to consign our present natural abode to final insignificance. Certain versions of eschatological fervor, in other words, do indeed appear to be ecologically problematic whenever they make 'this world' only instrumental to the human religious journey.

Secular environmental ethicists characteristically charge that Christianity's futurist preoccupations make it inescapably indifferent to the present well-being of the nonhuman natural world. Western religious doctrine and spirituality appear so otherworldly that the conservation of this world cannot easily become a priority for believers. Christianity, after all, has often taught that 'we have here no lasting home' and that our true abode lies elsewhere. But ecological responsibility demands that we think of the earth, and the entire cosmos for that matter, as our *home*.[17] If we are going to have any lasting incentive to save the beauties of creation we need to feel deeply that we belong to nature here and now. Much of the enthusiasm that ecological ethicists now have for native peoples and non-Christian religions can be explained by the impression that alternative faith systems seem to nest us more comfortably within nature than do the dominant Western religious traditions. In the religions of many indigenous groups, for example, nature and humanity together formed a much more organic unity than they do in the classic Christian view of the world. Primary religions, generally speaking, do not seek to separate humans from nature. Perhaps, then, the emergence of eschatology in religious history is more of problem than a solution to the ecological question.

Biblical eschatology, in fact, seems to partake of a general religious restlessness that emerged in several places around the world in the first millennium BC. During a historical period that philosopher Karl Jaspers has called the Axial Age, Indian mystics and Greek philosophers at times began to portray human destiny in terms of a withdrawal from 'this world'. Plato, for example, interpreted the natural world 'here below' as a pale reflection of an ideal world that exists beyond time. The goal of our lives, from this perspective, is to find our way out of temporal existence into an eternity beyond time. Thus a sense of 'cosmic homelessness' drifted into Western religion, and it became easier for us ever since to think of ourselves as strangers to nature. Christian spirituality has inherited much of this sense of cosmic homelessness; and so for that reason its eschatology often gives the impression of contradicting the ecological requirement that we experience ourselves as belonging to the wider world of nature.

How, then, is an ecological theology to address this troubling impression? It is undeniable, after all, that many influential religious teachings instruct us that excessive attachment to things, or to 'this present age,' or to natural objects, does tie us down, enchaining and enslaving the human spirit. Moreover, Jews, Christians and Muslims view the restless, wandering figure of Abraham as a model of the deeply religious calling to leave the narrowness of 'home' in pursuit of deeper fulfillment. In heeding the call to religious life it seems that we are encouraged to pursue a life of detachment. Christianity, following ancient biblical patterns of thought, sees our life here on earth as an exodus journey, a pilgrimage, a desert wandering. In the New Testament, Jesus, the 'Son of Man' is portrayed as having 'no place to lay his head,' and in Luke's Gospel he calls his followers to set their eyes on Jerusalem and not to look back toward what they have left behind. The Kingdom is more important than home and family.

If we turn to the East we notice that the Buddha also has to leave home, to cease clinging to things and even to family, so as to find 'enlightenment'. And in Hinduism the *sannyasin* finally forsakes home and family also, wandering to the edge of a forest or some other remote spot, so as to get closer to God. A great deal of the world's religious instruction, especially since the Axial Age, persuades us to accept the fundamentally homeless character of our existence as a condition of redemptive liberation. Accepting this homelessness is apparently essential to the religious adventure. But how do we reconcile religious pilgrimage with the ecological imperative to implant ourselves more deeply than ever in the earth? Can we practice 'religious homelessness,' in other words, without turning it into an ecologically ominous 'cosmic homelessness'?

After some reflection on this question, I have come to the tentative conclusion that it is not the ideal of religious homelessness *per se* that is problematic. Rather it is our careless and unnecessary translation of religious into *cosmic* homelessness. The former, I propose, does not inevitably entail the latter. The endorsement of cosmic homelessness twists the ideal of religious homelessness into an escapism that makes nature a victim of our religious restlessness. Earth, for example, comes to be seen as a place to get *away from* in order to find salvation. The natural world becomes little more than a 'vale of soul-making' in which to prove ourselves worthy of eternal life in some extra-cosmic domain. But if we love nature how can we keep this affection from slipping toward a pure naturalism that enchains our spirits and frustrates our search for the ultimate liberation that faith promises? Can we ever truly learn to love God without turning our backs on earth? Can we come to cherish the natural world without surrendering our longing for the beyond? These are questions, perhaps the main questions, to which a Christian theology of nature must now attend.

I believe that we must admit in all candor that the religious formation that many if not most Christians have received has led them to harbor a deep suspicion that the human species does not essentially belong to nature or to the earth; and so in the name of religious aspiration they sometimes still hold themselves at a distance from nature. Many fear that it would be a capitulation to paganism, pantheism or romantic naturalism if they allowed the roots of their being to penetrate very far into the terrestrial soil. Unhappily, modern theology has done little to prevent the divorce from nature. Especially in the modern period it has handed over the natural world to science and left to itself the task of interpreting classic religious texts, personal life and human history. It has left questions about nature and its future out of the field of theological interest. The majority of theologians still have little formal interest in the welfare of the nonhuman natural world.

However, I should hasten to add that it is not only religion and theology that have made us feel that we do not really belong to the cosmos. The so-called modern 'scientific world-view' has also left us with the strong impression that we humans are essentially exiles from nature. In recent centuries much scientific thought has come to see nature as lifeless and mindless 'stuff'. As a result modern intellectual life has often assumed a materialist and pessimistic philosophy that gives the status of reality primarily to dead matter and views life and human consciousness as ephemeral accidents. Thus, in an essentially lifeless and spiritless world it is not surprising that the human spirit can hardly feel at home.

Together, scientific materialism and religious dualism have perpetuated the ancient Gnostic idea that we are 'lost in the cosmos'. Can we, therefore find a way to reconcile the religious requirement of living homelessly, on the one hand, with the ecological imperative to make nature our home on the other. We are torn—or so it would seem—between two appealing but apparently conflicting persuasions. We are drawn spiritually to the religious ideal of living without clinging to things that will diminish us and ultimately disappoint us. A spiritual homelessness is essential to the religious adventure even if physically we are tied to nature; and spiritual detachment can make us reluctant to see nature itself as an ethical concern. But, at the same time, many of us are now attracted to the ecological sentiment that the natural world has values worth preserving, that it is indeed our home.

How do we hold these two propensities together? Fortunately, and perhaps ironically, recent developments in natural science can come to our aid here. Careful reflection on the implications of contemporary scientific cosmology may allow us to belong to nature while at the same time letting us also pursue the life of religious detachment. Only a little knowledge of what science now teaches us about the universe can help us spiritually and intellectually to link our religious journey of homelessness to the ecological requirement of remaining friendly with and even firmly fixed to nature. We can now reasonably claim, in other words, that religious homelessness may exist harmoniously with a sense of our being quite at home in the cosmos. The following is an attempt to say why this solution is plausible.

Over the last century and a half science has demonstrated that the natural world itself is a restless adventure. No previous age had ever known—at least with the assuredness that we now possess—that the natural world is on a pilgrimage of its own. Our religions, including Christianity emerged long before science had discovered that nature is itself a historical process and not something fixed or static. Today scientists realize that the physical universe is not changeless, eternal or necessary, as they formerly may have thought it to be. Although many people still do not believe it, the cosmos is most certainly a process, an evolution, an ongoing story. Humans live, in other words, in a universe that is still being created. The cosmos is not a stationary set of things frozen in essentially the same plodding status from all eternity, but an unfinished adventure open to what is perpetually new.

The famous Jesuit geologist and paleontologist Teilhard de Chardin (1881–1955), has probably done more than any other Christian thinker to demonstrate how we can remain fully a part of the earth and the cosmos, while also embarking on a momentous religious journey—along with the universe, not apart from it. Although, like others in his day, Teilhard was not fully aware of the scale of ecological degradation that modernity had unleashed, he developed a deeply incarnational and hopeful spirituality that can now frame our own efforts to construct an ecological theology. He did this by reinterpreting Christian faith in the context of cosmic and biological evolution.[18]

What evolution implies first and foremost is that creation is not yet finished. It is *in via*, on the way. The cosmos itself is essentially a pilgrimage. Hence, for us to embrace *this* universe we must align our own human existence with its inherent restlessness. Biology, geology and astrophysics now converge in challenging the ancient assumption that the universe is eternal and essentially unchanging. Taking seriously the new scientific picture of the world allows—even requires—that we embed our own unsettled lives within the much larger context of a *cosmic* restlessness. Only by accepting the universe's own homelessness, in other words, can we be at home in nature. Billions of years before we humans came along in evolution the universe had already been on the move. During the past century and a half science has filled out in remarkable detail the various episodes of this immense journey. I believe that there are implications for an ecological theology in these new accounts of the cosmic adventure.

At first glance, of course, one may wonder just what ecological-theological significance could possibly be squeezed out of the initially disturbing news that the cosmos itself is not at rest. According to the Big Bang theory, which almost all scientists accept today, the universe has a finite evolutionary past and an irreversible temporal trajectory. For all we know, therefore, our big-bang cosmos may presently be only in the early stages of a creative process that will last for many more billions of years. The point is, it is now clear that the universe is a still unfolding story. But what does this mean for our own question about the relationship of ecology to theology? It means, most fundamentally, that it is not only the human spirit that has undertaken an immense journey (especially through its religious wanderings) but that the entire cosmos is partner and prologue to our own homeless religious passage. Therefore, we do not need to abandon the natural world in order to follow the spiritual counsel to live homelessly. Indeed, we may even be permitted to say that our religious restlessness is a blossoming forth of the universe's own ageless adventuring. Our human hunger for transcendence is a conscious development of a general leaning toward the open future that has always been a hidden feature of the physical universe. Our religious striving toward the infinite is to be satisfied only by our attuning ourselves to the larger and longer cosmic odyssey into the future, not by extricating ourselves from it. The new scientific cosmology allows us to belong to the universe without our having to sacrifice the ideal of religious sojourning. Eschatology can embrace cosmology—'Your promise O Lord is as wide as the heavens'.[19]

So our religious homelessness does not have to be turned into cosmic homelessness after all. Theologically viewed, we may now say that the universe—at its very core—is inseparable from promise. And so, we may learn to revere the natural world not simply because faith sees it as sacramentally transparent to God, but even more because it carries in its present perishable nature the seeds of a final, glorious future flowering. This means, in turn, that our current abuse of nature is not only a violation of nature's sacramentality; it is also a turning away from the promise that lies embedded in God's creation. In a properly biblical framework, then, our ecological recklessness is not just disobedience to our mission of stewardship, nor simply a sacrilege in violation of nature's sacramentality. It is fundamentally an expression of despair, of the distrust that the Bible considers to lie at the base of human sinfulness.

This promissory way of looking at nature requires that we give a fresh understanding to the notion of stewardship. Stewardship, in the framework of a cosmology framed by the theme of promise, must amount to much more than conservation. Conservation is essential of course. We need to appreciate the many millions of years of evolutionary striving and achievement that produced the ecological richness that preceded human emergence. It goes without saying that there is an intrinsic worth in earth's biosphere that deserves our best efforts at preservation. But perhaps the most fundamentally Christian reason to participate in the saving of living diversity is that nature is always pregnant with the promise of humanly incalculable future outcomes. We do not have access to the creator's vision of the cosmic future, but we may confidently believe that every present contains the promise of future fulfillment.[20] A Christian vision will lead us to strive not to get out of the world but to do what we can to shepherd this still unfinished universe toward the fulfillment of the promise that underlies and impels it toward the future.[21]

End Notes

1. Holmes Rolston, III, 'Science, Religion, and the Future,' in Mark Richardson and Wesley Wildman, Editors, *Religion and Science: History, Method, Dialogue* (New York and London: Routledge, 1996), 79.
2. For a fuller development of the present essay see my book *The Promise of Nature (Mahwah: Paulist Press, 1993)*.
3. John Passmore, *Man's Responsibility for Nature* (New York: Scribner, 1974), 184.
4. Pope John Paul II, 'Peace with God the Creator, Peace with All of Creation' (World Day of Peace Message, Jan 1, 1990); Pope John Paul II, *The Ecological Crisis: A Common Responsibility*, nos 1, 15, December 8, 1989. The American Conference of Catholic Bishops, Renewing the Earth (1991). Drew Christiansen, SJ and Walter Grazer, editor *And God Saw That It Was Good* (Washington, DC: United States Catholic Conference, 1996); Bishops' Pastoral letter, 'The Columbia River Watershed: Caring for Creation and the Common Good', (February, 2001). Documents and discussion of some of the earliest work on ecological issues by the World Council of Churches may be found in Charles Birch, William Eakin, and Jay B McDaniel, editors, *Liberating Life: Contemporary Approaches to Ecological Theology* (Maryknoll, NY: Orbis Books, 1990).
5. Augustine of Hippo, *The Confessions of St Augustine* (Garden City, NY: Image Books, 1960), 44.
6. This point is persuasively argued by Rupert Sheldrake in *The Rebirth of Nature: The Greening of Science and God* (New York: Bantam Books, 1991), 9–96.
7. For a thorough discussion of the implications of materialist philosophical assumptions (based on the 'fallacy of misplaced concreteness') for both economics and our treatment of the natural world see Herman E Daly and John B Cobb, Jr, *For the Common Good* (Boston: Beacon Press, 1989), 25–110. See also my book *The Promise of Nature*, 11–38.
8. Barry Commoner, 'In Defense of Biology', in Ronald Munson, editor, *Man and Nature* (New York: Dell Publishing Co, 1971), 44.
9. For support of this claim, once again, I recommend a close reading of Daly's and Cobb's book *For the Common Good*.

10. See Michael J Himes and Kenneth R Himes, 'The Sacrament of Creation,' *Commonweal*, volume CXVII (12 January 1990): 45.
11. See Thomas Berry, *The Dream of the Earth* (San Francisco: Sierra Club Books, 1988).
12. *Ibid.* See also Matthew Fox, *Original Blessing* (Santa Fe, NM: Bear, 1983).
13. Both Rupert Sheldrake and Thomas Berry have made this point respectively in their books referred to above. See Sheldrake, 43, 56, 74f, and Berry, 138–62. They are both indebted to Carolyn Merchant, *The Death of Nature* (San Francisco: Harper & Row, 1980).
14. To readers unfamiliar with theological method, let me explain briefly why Christian theology cannot ignore the theme of promise, even when it is dealing with nature. Theology, as David Tracy has written, is systematic, critical reflection on the classics of a religious tradition. (*Blessed Rage for Order: The New Pluralism in Theology*, New York: Seabury Press, 1975). Among the classics of Christian tradition of foremost importance is the Bible. In this vast and variegated body of sacred texts, the most fundamental and recurrent theme is that God is a maker and keeper of promises. Hence, for Christian theology to make the theme of promise optional, as both the apologetic and the sacramental approach tend at times to do, would be to abandon what is central to the tradition. By emphasizing the theme of the 'promise of nature' I am attempting to take the biblical substance of Christian tradition much more seriously than other ecological theologies, especially that of Thomas Berry, have done.
15. For support see the writings of Jürgen Moltmann, for example, *Theology of Hope*, translated by James Leitch (New York: Harper & Row, 1967; and *The Experiment Hope*, edited and translated by M Douglas Meeks (Philadelphia: Fortress Press, 1975).
16. For an earlier development of points made in this section see my book *God After Darwin*, 159-64.
17. As I will show later on, being fully at home in nature does not require that one adopt an exclusively sacramentalist approach.
18. See especially Pierre Teilhard de Chardin, *Christianity and Evolution*, translated by by Rene Hague (New York: Harcourt Brace & Co, 1969)
19. Psalm 138: 2 (New English Bible translation).
20. For us to throw away our natural heritage would be equivalent to throwing away a promise. For this reason we may be glad that

the American Catholic Bishops' pastoral *Renewing the Earth* has identified the virtue of hope as the fundamental posture of Christianity toward the ecological situation of our time.

21. I do not have space here to consider the anticipated questions that arise from recent astrophysical scenarios of a universe that will sometime in the distant future no longer be able to sustain life. The eventual demise of the cosmos, however, does not vitiate the theme of nature's promise that I have been highlighting. To the Christian there should in principle be no more difficulty trusting that the whole universe-story will be taken redemptively into God's life than there is in trusting that we ourselves will be saved by God's compassionate care. For now I must be content to affirm that it is no longer theologically or cosmologically conceivable that human destiny could ever be separated from cosmic destiny and vice-versa. If we dwell within the compass of God's promise, so also does the entire universe.

Part Two

Myths Of Origination In Early Chinese Thought

Cheng, Chih-Ming

Abstract

Origin myth, or creation myth, is the kind of myth that concers the origin of the whole creation, including the creation of the universe, the origin of human beings, the birth of peoples, the beginning of all the things on earth and so on. To bring up and ponder the question of the origin of the heavens and earth and all the things on earth demands broad-minded views and a certain ability to think abstractly. Origin myth is rustic practical thinking; or it can even be said to be the earliest form of philosophy. It reveals that the longing, the pursuit and the investigation of the life of human beings in the early stages were made possible through people's efforts to make use of their own practical living to grasp life.

    Among all these efforts, witchcraft is one outstanding example. It is not a philosophical meditation or a religious prayer in silence. Nor is it an aesthetic gaze. Rather, it is an operation. It is a way of thinking and a spiritual product in virtue of the process of its actual operation. Origin myth is a linguistic interpretation system accompanying witchcraft, to explain the life relationship of mutual inspiration between human beings and the heavens, earth, ghosts and gods. It projects the movements of human beings as subject to, and as the object of, all the things in nature. It is also conscious of the practical function of the mutual communication between human beings and spirituality in nature. Witchcraft is a behavior of concrete operation generated by the realization of animism. Origin myth, in this case, is a collective linguistic system to propagate the kind of life experience evidenced by witchcraft.

This essay, making use of origin myth, traces the cosmological conceptions systematized by early human beings and the operational function of religious praxis resulting from these conceptions. Origin myth displays the fact that human beings, as their realization was under the influence of collective consciousness, do not rely solely on biological instincts to investigate the thoughts and views of all the things in the heavens and earth. In fact, for their investigation, they also resort to their cultural realization such as social praxis and life experiences to imagine and analogize the formation and development of all kinds of life in the cosmos. In origin myth the life of human beings is entangled with that of the cosmos. The gods are possessed of emotion, volition and life similar to that of the human beings. The realm of gods is actually an extension and sublimation of the human one. The numerous kinds of great creation gods in origin myth correspond to the order of existence in human society. On the one hand, the principles of existence of human beings are brought into the natural structure of the cosmos; on the other hand, the latter has to satisfy the former in return. Human beings and the cosmos thus constitute cooperatively a mutually dependent relationship of symbiosis and reciprocal inspiration between each other. Origin myth is not just a mere description of how the great creation gods brought into being the human beings and all the things in the cosmos. It is also a reconsideration of the meaning and value of life and being—a reconsideration conducted not for the materialistic purpose of scientific research but, as culture gradually develops, for spiritual enrichment which has intuited the metaphysical function of life and being.

Introduction

Human beings possessed the ability to think with language prior to the invention of writing. This type of thinking is usually called 'primitive thinking'. Around 10,000 years ago human beings began to move from intuitive action thinking and concrete imagery thinking into analogous abstract thinking so as to understand and process information.[1] This 'primitive thinking' is the birth of the ability to express human experiences and consciousness, enabling the human beings to invest their lives with purpose, hopes, emotions and volition. Culture begins in the ability of individuals to express themselves. This eventually leads to the formation of a collective worldview.[2]

'Primitive thinking' can be regarded as the 'childhood' of mankind. It is the long-term sedimentation of wisdom after hundreds of thousand years. Unavoidably tainted with naïve and immature conceptions, it is however not to be seen as simple ignorance. It has its own rationality and logic. It displays the ability of human beings to create cultures, seeing themselves as social subjects able to constitute the object.[3] 'Mythical thinking' can be seen as the product of highly developed primitive thinking. It shows that, before the invention of writing, human beings were able to cope with the challenges of cosmic time and space, with the birth and death of the world's creatures.

They used language to formulate a knowledge tradition and an origin of culture, from generation to generation, to develop principles of living, of technique and of order.[4]

'Mythical thinking' is used to signify the knowledge tradition of the period mentioned above. It is a mode of thinking that is conscious of the existence of the living principle of mutual inspiration, temporally and spatially, between human beings and all the things in the heavens and earth. With the help of this kind of consciousness, human beings can experience the spiritual existence of ghosts and gods in a metaphysical way. By utilising language as a means of expression, human beings develop thoughts about the real or apparent relationship between themselves and spiritual beings. Concepts and activities pertaining to belief—spirits and gods, witchcraft and sacrifice—were thus effected.[5] 'Mythical thinking' is a mode of thinking relevant to the spiritual praxis of human beings.

On the one hand myth can enrich the design and diffusion of religious rituals; on the other hand more and more fascinating mythic stories are created because of the religious relationship of mutual inspiration between human beings and gods. The creation of myths was anything but free associations without aims. Rather, it was utilised as a mode of thinking—representation, undertaken actively and purposively in accordance with the various kinds of needs and directions of human beings. It was displayed as a unique combination of fantasy and reality so as to enable human beings, by relying on their own experiences, to find out the way to survive, to secure their own safety in the heavens and earth.

The purpose of the creation of myths is threefold: to understand nature, to conquer nature and to pray to nature.[6] Human beings as subject are unified in the myths with the object of nature, through the real and apparent relationship between the two. This characteristic in the myths gives birth to a peculiar culture of belief that lays emphasis on the unity of things and oneself as well as the mutual inspiration between human beings and the heavens.[7]

Chang Kuang-chih proposes the notion of 'Chinese culture as an entity of continuity'. The humanist aspects of Chinese society should not be severed from its primitive predecessors. The two kinds of society are not opposed to each other. In fact the humanist society has succeeded the conceptions imbedded in those pre-historical myths— cosmology, witchcraft, the communication between the heavens, earth, human beings and gods, and the monopolised political privileges enjoyed by those who could appeal to different kinds of communication and so on.[8] The humanist society and the primitive one were developed out of the same cosmology. Both of them contain the worldview of shamanism.[9]

Around 5,000 years ago, due to the flow between different peoples, Chinese culture underwent a convergence and consolidation. Between 3,000 and 5,000 years ago, with the introduction of the written word, culture further flourished.[10] While the accumulation of knowledge has become more diversified and complicated, nevertheless, the basic cultural characteristics and principles of thoughts of today have been influenced by the racial knowledge acquired 3,000 years ago.[11]

While the development of writing allowed the expression of more and more complicated thoughts, mythical thinking did not disappear as a result. The imagination still remained as an artistic means for human beings to convey and express their thoughts and wishes. The creation of quasi-myth enabled them to reflect their lives and emotions, to preserve their realisation of nature and society and even to record and reflect on their own thoughts and history. Mythical thinking does not fade away even after a period of 3,000 years. It still exists in folk belief and worship of ghosts and gods. Through those activities, the primitive thinking and myth are not only preserved but also augmented and modified to become new mythical thinking.¹² More than that, the mass of mythical thinking, found in the documents with annotations, can result in a cohesion of the Chinese spirit passed down from the primordial era. *Shan Hai Jing* (The Book of Mountain and Sea) is an excellent example of this. It can be regarded as a classic which has continued the mythic age. In it is preserved a lot of prehistoric mythical material that enables us to investigate the forms of ancient Chinese society and characteristics of the racial spirit.¹³

Origin myths, or creation myths, are the kind of myths which are concerned with the origin of all things on earth, including the creation of the universe, the origin of human beings, the birth of peoples, the beginning of all the things on earth. Questions of origins demand broad-minded views and a certain ability to think abstractly. In view of the issues raised in it, origin myth is apt to be a product of the later stages of primitive thinking, that is, the period of maturity of mythical thinking.¹⁴ It is an early practical thinking which may be seen as the earliest form of philosophy. It reveals that the early longings, the pursuits and the investigations of life were made possible through their practical efforts to grasp life. Amongst these practices, witchcraft is of great importance. It is not a philosophical meditation or a religious prayer in silence. Nor is it an aesthetic gaze. Rather, it is an operation. It combines practical and spiritual thinking with an actual practice.¹⁵ Origin myth is a system of linguistic interpretation accompanying witchcraft, explaining the mutually inspiring relationship between human beings and the heavens, earth, ghosts and gods. It projects the movements of human beings as subject to, as object, all the things in nature. It is also conscious of the practical function of the mutual communication between human beings and spirituality in nature. Witchcraft is a behaviour of concrete operation generated by the realisation of animism. Origin myth, in this case, is a collective linguistic system to diffuse life experiences. This essay, making use of origin myths, traces the cosmological conceptions systematised by early human beings and the operational function of religious praxis resulting from these conceptions.

The properties of ancient origin myths

Origin myth is the attempt of human beings to investigate life being with their self-consciousness. In primitive thinking, there was the tendency to see that all the things were endowed with life. The notions of human life were expanded and applied to all the things in nature, personifying it. EB Tylor, an anthropologist, in his *Primitive Culture* (originally published in 1871), remarks that the origin of both witchcraft and myth is closely related to this animism. He further asserts that animism serves as the philosophical foundation of these early societies as well as the civilised peoples.[16] Tylor's conception of animism has been questioned and criticised by some scholars; however, it is hard to deny the assertion that the thinking of early human beings was really governed by the view of soul.[17]

The operation of witchcraft can be considered as the practical performance of human beings under the influence of animism. Human beings attempted to have a mutual relationship with the spiritual beings in nature. Myth was the attempt through language to investigate the divine world relevant to all being. Mythical thinking can be considered as a mode of inspirational thinking, stemming from the practices of witchcraft combined with language, to inquire into the spirituality common to the human beings on the one hand and the heavens, earth, ghosts and gods (with whom they could commune), on the other hand.

Some of the characteristics of this worldview include: being unconscious of the boundary between one's self and the external world; no differentiation between subject and object; and the unity of the heavens and man.[18] Some scholars also call the mode of mythical inspiration thinking as 'chaos thinking' in view of the lack of differentiation between the thinking subject and its object in the structure of thinking. This causes myth to be pervaded unconsciously with the characteristic of the sameness of oneself and the external world and that of the mutual inspiration between the heavens and man. To put it in another way, the thinking subject and its object infiltrate each other and merge to become a unity.[19]

Origin myth can be said to be the product of inspiration thinking or chaos thinking. Origin myth displays the fact that human beings, under the influence of the collective consciousness, did not rely solely on biological instincts to investigate. In fact, they also resorted to their social praxis and life experiences to imagine and analogise the formation and development of all kinds of life in the cosmos. In origin myth the life of human beings is entangled with that of the cosmos. The gods are possessed of emotion, volition and life similar to those of the human beings. The realm of the gods is actually an extension and sublimation of the human one. The numerous kinds of great creation gods in origin myth correspond to the order of existence in human society. On the one hand, the principles of existence of human beings are brought into the natural structure of the cosmos; on the other hand, the latter has to satisfy the former in return. The human beings and the cosmos thus constitute cooperatively a mutually dependent relationship of symbiosis and reciprocal inspiration between each other.

Origin myth is not just a mere description of how the great creation gods brought into being the human beings and all the things in the cosmos. It is also a reconsideration of the meaning and value of life—a reconsideration conducted not for the materialistic purpose of scientific research but, as culture develops gradually, for the spiritual requirement which has intuited the metaphysical function of being.

After the collation and systematisation by scholars, origin myth can be generally classified into five kinds, according to their motifs.

Myths concerning the origin of the heavens and earth
In this kind of myth, Pan Gu is generally found as the major god. He performed the miracle of having chiselled out the universe and separated the earth from the heavens. Written accounts of the myths about Pan Gu can only be found in a relatively later period.

Scholars are unsure whether Pan Gu is an ancient myth about the origin of universe. He Xin contends that Pan Gu is a metamorphosis of an Indian myth that was spread to south-western China. Rather than an archetypal myth originating in China, the myth of Pan Gu is seen as a transformation of the myth of Brahma of ancient Brahminism.[20] Chen Jun refutes the viewpoint that the myth of Pan Gu was spread to China from the West, insisting that it is a transformation of the myth of Fu Xi and focuses on the managing, in chaos, of the divinity and functions of the heavens and earth.[21] In the Period of the Six Dynasties the myth of Pan Gu was tainted with the atmosphere of Daoism. Pan Fu was then transformed into a deity, Yuanshi Tianzun.[22] It is also subject to controversy as to whether the myth recorded in the documents is really the exact original myth. Hu Zhongshi claims that Xu Zheng must have modified the myth of Pan Gu, infusing into it conceptions popular in the Qin and Han dynasties such as *yuan qi* (primordial vital energy), and *ying-yang*, 'man as a copy of heaven'.

Xu Zheng's modification of the myth caused it to become a story told by human beings. Thus the original appearance of the myth vanished.[23] To restore the myth of Pan Gu, we need to pay special attention to two motifs: the universe emerges from the cosmic egg and the body of Pan Gu, after his death, turns into different things in the cosmos.

In myths about the universe emerging from cosmic egg, all things—including the heavens, earth, sun, moon, and human beings—are products generated from the gyration of the round substance called chaos. As to Pan Gu, he can be taken as a deity who transcends the heavens, earth and material world and symbolises the primordial life that existed at the commencement of the cosmos.

Pan Gu is not the supreme arbitrator to create the cosmos, but the common spring of all the things in it. His life has to be succeeded and passed down forever by all the things in the world as well as human beings. This kind of myth can be viewed as a creation of synthetic generalisation. All the things—from the heavens and earth, to insects and animals as well as from the sun, the moon and stars to rivers, valleys, lakes and seas—are involved in the account of the origin of the cosmos. Such a myth demonstrates an outstanding capability to generalise and is therefore apt to be the product at the later stage of a primitive society.[24] We can also sense in it an earlier form of the cosmology of the unity of man and the heaven. It reveals that human beings and nature share a common regularity; life and death can be reciprocally transformed and interacted; and life is characterised by the possibility of continuous generation and immortality.

Myths concerning the origin of human beings
This kind of creation myth mainly takes Nu Wa as the major goddess and gives an account of her moulding human beings out of yellow clay. A more detailed account of this myth can be seen in *Taiping Yulan* (*Taiping Anthologies*

for the Emperor) of Song dynasty. The book cites in scroll seventy-eight the myth of Nu Wa as recorded in *Fengsu Tongyi* (*Comprehensive Meanings of Customs and Habits*) by Ying Shao of Eastern Han dynasty: 'It is said that there were no human beings when the sky and the earth were separated. It was Nu Wa who made human beings by moulding yellow clay. The work was so taxing that her strength was not equal to it. So she dipped a rope into the mud and then lifted it. The mud that dripped from the rope also became human beings.'

In mythological thinking the origin of the cosmos is by no means the only concern. We can also find in it the questioning and investigation of the source of the birth of human beings, requiring an interactive relationship between human beings and nature. If all the things in the heavens and earth were created by god, then the life of human beings was also inevitably endowed by god. Nu Wa, the great goddess in the cosmos, symbolises the mother of human beings. However, where does this great goddess in the cosmos come from? In the chapter 'Tian Wen' of *Chu Ci* (*Poetry of the South*), the question of the origin of Nu Wa had already been asked, 'Nu Wa has a body. Who made it?' This is a comparatively more rational thinking of later periods. It brings forth the query: If Nu Wa created the bodies of human beings, then who created her body? In scroll twelve of *Shuo Wen Jie Zi* (*A Character Dictionary*) by Xu Shen of Eastern Han dynasty, the explanation of the word 'Wa' can be found: 'Wa, goddess of antiquity, is the one who generates all the things.'

In regard to their divinity, Pan Gu and Nu Wa are of no difference. Both of them are the source of the creation of the cosmos, even though Pan Gu is more inclined to be related to the creation of the heavens and earth while Nu Wa to the origin of all the things, including human beings.[25] Nu Wa is the original mother-goddess who breeds all the things. Therefore, the creation of human beings is a necessary duty that she needs to fulfil. The way she created human beings with mud is also a motif of myths, which is seen to spread in many races and regions all over the world. The appearance of this myth is probably related to the invention of the technique of pottery.[26]

The myths of Nu Wa express not only an attempt to trace the origin of the birth of human lives but also the concern of the order of existence for human beings in responding to the cosmos. Moreover, they could enable early human beings to understand the way of existence and assure their belief in Nu Wa. Under her blessing, the cosmos would last forever. In such a case, the myths also bear with them the function to pacify early human beings who had to strive in a tough and disastrous ecological environment.

Human harmony included both the natural and social environments. The myth of Nu Wa being a matchmaker lays the foundation for the everlasting and continual being of human offspring. This myth is closely related to reproduction worship in antique society. As early human beings gradually realised that sexual intercourse could produce offspring, totem worship declined and was replaced by the worship of sexual behaviour and the reproductive organ. Some scholars regard that the original appearance of Nu Wa herself was as the female reproductive organ. She was worshipped as the prominent god of matriarchal society, symbolising the root of all the things in the cosmos.[27] This reveals that early human beings attached much importance to the propagation of their ethnic group. This is in fact a sublimation of the consciousness of human propagation.[28]

Besides the worship of the female reproductive organ, there also existed the worship of fish in matriarchal society for the purpose of praying for the flourishing of population. Fish worship was developed later to become *gao mei* or *jiao mei*, a sacrifice to pray for male offspring by worshipping the female reproductive organ.[29] The deity worshipped in this ritual is none other than Nu Wa. As a result of the later development of society, the system of marriage was devised. That Nu Wa became the goddess of marriage could more or less be regarded as a continuity of the myth of her creation of human beings.

Myths concerning the rebirth of human beings
In this kind of myth, Fu Xi or 'a brother called Fu Xi and his younger sister' are taken as the main gods. It describes the rebirth of human beings after a deluge. In some myths Nu Wa is taken as the younger sister of Fu Xi. This is why the main gods in them are named 'a brother and a sister called Nu Wa'. According to Volume Three of *Duyi Zhi* by Li Rong of the Tang Dynasty, 'At the opening of the universe, there were a brother and a sister called Nu Wa, living in the Kunlun Mountain, and there were no ordinary people at that time. They discussed to become husband and wife.' Although it was recorded in a comparatively later period, this myth about victims who survive the deluge and bring forth a rebirth of human beings is still preserved in the oral tradition of the races spreading across north-eastern, north-western, southern, and south-western China.[30]

Perhaps we can say that Nu Wa is the major goddess of matriarchal society while Fu Xi the major god of patriarchy. The image of Fu Xi is one of semi-god and semi-mankind; or he can be said to be a human being possessed of divine traits. He represents an age in which people had the precise idea that the propagation of human beings could be made possible only through sexual intercourse between male and female. The saying that 'only one man and one woman were left after the deluge' can be considered as a symbolic use of the language of myths to manifest the divine function of marriage system in culture. The myth of the deluge and of the rebirth of human beings reflects that, in confronting the natural catastrophes, early human beings had constituted the cyclic view of the repeatedly happening of devastation done to the world and the re-establishment after that. They maintained that there must have been an order of operation in the cosmos—first, the stage of chaos; next, that of orderliness; then, that of devastation caused by disorderliness and lastly, that of maintenance and re-creation after the devastation.

Nu Wa is the great god that represents the former two stages, while Fu Xi the latter two stages. By the time of the appearance of Fu Xi, gods were portrayed with the image of mankind. This portrayal reflects the mode of thinking that human beings can win over heavens. Human beings can propagate their offspring by means of forming families through marriage. Similarly, they are possessed of the ability to participate in the creation of the heavens and earth. Furthermore, they can also make use of their wisdom to constitute the order of existence.

Myths concerning the origin of culture

This kind of myth usually takes Huang Di as its major god. The story about how Fu Xi's created *Bagua* can actually be categorised under this kind of myth. In the myth of Huang Di we find that all the acts concerning the creation of culture are ascribed to him only. This is a kind of social myth to account for how human beings, in the process of their surviving in nature, constituted the cultural forms necessary to their living. These cultural forms include the invention of tools and methods for production, the discovery and use of fire, the development from fishing and hunting society to agricultural society, the creation and application of various handiwork tools and the development of laws and institutions from daily living. The invention and creation of these cultures could hardly be attained by any single person, in a certain place and at one time. These cultures were products accumulated, improved and completed in a long process of time. Then, why do we find in the myth of Huang Di that all the acts about the creation and invention of cultures are ascribed only to him and his liegemen? To answer this question requires an understanding of the divine nature of Huang Di. In the myths about him, Huang Di is simultaneously a god and an emperor of human beings. He should be the ancestor god of a clan society, with an appearance of a half god and half man. In the myths he is regarded as the ancestor of the development of a race. His image is changed from *Tian Di* (emperor of heaven) for worship to an emperor, as a historical ancestor of a race and as a cultural hero unifying the Central Plains.[31]

In 'Lu Yu', a chapter in *Guo Yu* (*Discourses of the States*), a portrait of Huang Di is given. 'Huang Di is able to give names to all the things so as to enable people to understand reasons and supply the state with wealth and expense.' In the myths Huang Di becomes the symbol of the ancestral emperor of a race. He initiates the decrees and institutions of subsequent eras. Only after all the things are given names by Huang Di can they obtain appropriate official names and, consequently, can the human society be operated.[32] Although he is not the great god who creates the universe and human beings, he can still accomplish, as a human being, the order of being in real life. He becomes a symbolic figure who signifies that the human beings have come out of the chaos. That is why the long-term cultural creation of primitive society has been focused on him. Huang Di can actually be regarded as an ancestor god who integrates the lineage of gods and that of a clan. On the one hand, such integration preserves god worship, the inner substance of ancient belief; on the other hand, it conveys ancestor worship found in tribes established due to consanguinity and societies formed according to geographical factors. The integration therefore can be considered as a way to extend and expand the cohesion of a clan, just as an ancestor god can be taken as a symbol of the incessant succession of a clan. Huang Di is a human being and an ancestor. At the same time, he is also a god. Human beings cherish the memory of, and pay homage to, their ancestors. In myths they are proud of praising the brave deeds of their ancestors. To utilise such act of praising as a foundation, they proceed to lay emphasis on the conception and the sensation of not betraying their ancestors' teachings.[33]

In Chinese myths Huang Di is assigned the role of a wise and able emperor, an ancestor and a cultural hero. He is even regarded as the first great man of the race in that he serves as the first cornerstone in establishing Chinese civilisation. According to the legend, both political and military achievements, under his reign, were at the height of power and splendours. Thus the foundation of the development of the country was stabilised. Huang Di therefore became the leader accepted by all the races then. More than that, he became the manufacturer and the inventor of all things. Under the spread of such a kind of myth, the deification of human beings and the humanisation of deities entangled with each other to the extent that it was hard to differentiate one from the other.[34]

In its essence, hero worship itself is also a kind of religious consciousness. Amid the historical cycle of turmoil and reconstruction, people in the past were inclined to desire the appearance of sage and virtuous heroes. This kind of thinking—to transform super-natural deities to become folk heroes in flesh and blood—has a twofold function. It gives expression to both deism and humanism—to be more specific, a kind of deism blended with humanism and vice versa. Both deism and humanism, however, turn out to bear the same function to indicate the awakening of self-consciousness of human beings and the affirmation of their independent status in the process of social and historical progress.[35] The deeds of heroes are described under the influence of both mythical and historical heritage. Thus the heroes become 'supermen' of semi-supernatural and semi-human. Such a kind of description reflects that there exists in human beings the force of regeneration in facing various kinds of disasters. Those uncommon deeds symbolise the ability of human beings in conquering the external dreadful environment. They include not only combating and military deeds but also the invention of technology that can civilise the society and benefit the descendants.[36]

Myths concerning the origin of races
In ancient China many races coexisted. Each race has its own origin myth. The myth about Huang Di is actually an origin myth of a race, even though he became the first leader of a federation later. Master Yin Shun contends that there are four major clans in ancient China: the Divine Goat Clan, the Divine Bird Clan, the Divine Fish Clan and the Divine Dragon Clan.

The first ancestor myth is not used to trace the historical process of the origin of ancient races and their division. The pedigree of the ancient emperors in the myths may only be one of the integration of divine gods and ancestor gods. Different branches of first ancestor myths may come out from the same race. It is hard to investigate in these branches of myths the succession of emperors only by means of blood relationship. Moreover, it is by no means necessary to find out the pedigrees of the clans for those first ancestors.[37] The first ancestor myth is no different from the origin myth. Its major function lies in accounting how a race, under the leadership of the first ancestor, transformed from a primitive tribe to a clan society. It is not strange that first female ancestor myths are widespread in matriarchal society and first male ancestor myths in patriarchal society. The first ancestor myths of ancient China are mainly focused on the male. From these myths we can observe the historical change of the replacement of matriarchy by patriarchy. As the male had played a more and more important role in the process of reproduction, it is unavoidable for them to replace the female in dominating the society. To be sure, the transition from a matriarchal society to a patriarchal one could only be the result of a series of violent clashes.[38] Most of the first ancestor myths present an account of how the male ancestors lead their tribesmen to survive the serious challenges found in the external arduous environment.

These first ancestors are also cultural heroes. The descendants of different races accumulate various kinds of cultural creation for their competition to survive. They praise in myths their first ancestors' heroic deeds, including the slaying of demons and monsters, and the invention and creation of weapons and systems. Xiao Bing classifies these first ancestor heroes into five types: heroes who are great archers, heroes who are abandoned in their infancy, heroes who eliminate heinous forces, heroes who regulate floods and heroes who are sapient. Especially in myths about heroes who are abandoned in their infancy, we can witness the process of the transition from matriarchy to patriarchy. Why are these heroes abandoned in their infancy? In the past not a few books attempted to explain it from the ethical viewpoint. As a consequence, numerous ridiculous explanations are offered. Nevertheless, the phenomena can simply be explained as a way of dealing with redundant male babies in matriarchal societies. Some of these heroes obtain special care from gods. An outstanding example is the first ancestor of Zhou, Qi. Qi was abandoned three times and adopted three times as well. However, he could become the chosen hero to found a race.³⁹ In the myths the first ancestors often appear in human images, but most of them bear a blood relationship with gods. They, as human beings, come to this world to fulfil the orders of gods. Their various kinds of creation and invention are ways to realise the gods' will. It shows that there exists a relationship of interaction between human beings and gods.⁴⁰

The first ancestors are the ones who are in between human beings and gods. They are also the ones who can accomplish the gods' orders. They are creators who initiate the heavens and earth. The modelling of the first ancestors expresses the collective subconscious of early human beings in viewing the cosmos. These semi-human and semi-god first ancestors reflect the desire of human beings in investigating the origin of themselves and their races. They regard men can be the embodiment of gods and constitute a culture of living in corresponding to the heavens and earth. This kind of men is not ordinary men but the few chosen heroes who obtain special care from gods. They can make use of their power of interacting with gods to initiate human societies for their posterior. Under such a kind of conception, all ethnic societies of human beings can be said to be inspired by gods. All kinds of origin are hardly detached from religious relationship that lays emphasis on the interaction with gods. The cosmology found in the myths is consistent; no matter they are concerned with the origin of the cosmos or that of a race. This cosmology is formed on the basis of the chaos thinking which stresses that man and god can be found in the same body. It reflects the cultural psychology common to all the members of a race. Myth is interactive with the spirit of a race. Myth can be utilised to express the development and transformation of the essence of human beings and to understand how they strive to improve and perfect themselves in social praxis.⁴¹

Cosmology in ancient origin myths

Problems that arise from the decoding of prehistoric myths preserved in Chinese documents result largely from the entanglement of myth and history, where myth is treated as history. Some scholars attempt to study myth by doing research on history, while some endeavour to analyse history by relying on the interpretation of myths. The motivation of these two factions of scholars causes them to overlook the uniqueness of myth. Undoubtedly, myth is closely related to history. However, myth is not equal to history. Myth is at most a projection of history to reflect the cultural consciousness developed from the real living of early human beings, the kind of origin myth especially. In this kind of myth, we can find a projection of the process of the long-term transformation and development of ancient social systems. In spite of that, myth can never be viewed as true and reliable history and counted as part of prehistoric history. When myth is treated as history, it will be explained as, or reduced to, history. In order to suit the causal relationship valued by history and some unchallengeable principles, the myths will be deprived of their imaginative and romantic characteristics to become merely a record of past events. For the same reason, those supernatural deities and heroes will be turned into idealised virtuous emperors and sage ministers.[42] As a consequence, gods in myths and emperors as human beings will be mixed up. Thus myths can hardly be differentiated from stories of human beings.

Myth can be taken as a linguistically open, dynamic system. It is a totality in which the inner cultural and psychological structure of human beings can exchange messages with the outer natural and social environment. It is a psychological schema and cognitive structure transformed from the repetitious practice of human beings. As the society becomes more and more rationalised, there is the tendency for myths to pass into man's stories. This tendency causes the mythical sense to shed gradually. At the same time, it also strengthens the dominant position of human beings themselves in conquering and reining nature.[43] There is an obvious tendency for those prehistoric ancient myths to turn into the stories of human beings. The focus shifts from religious divinity to the humanity of the ancient emperors.

The power and function of gods are replaced by the creation and invention of human beings. The protagonists of myths are not the gods any more but those people who can communicate, and maintain a mutual inspiration relationship, with gods. The gods recede from the dominant role to a subordinate one. People who appear in the role of heroes become the subject of cultural creation. No more do human beings rely on and worship gods unconditionally. Although the gods can still preserve the lofty image of creating and dominating all the things in the heavens and earth, human beings are elevated to the divine status of participating in the growth of things and the initiation of systems in the heavens and earth.[44] They can even communicate with the spirituality of gods to accomplish the way of life being—god and man can be in the same body.

In discussing the environment in which human beings dwell, Martin Heidegger (1889–1976), a German philosopher, proposes the cosmology of the unity of the heavens, earth, man, and god. He asserts that they form a whole and cannot be cut apart. The environment in which human beings dwell is an expression of the unity of the four elements. As an inner substance, the unified entity of the heavens, earth, man and god enters the site to protect and arrange man's living. What Heidegger asserts is actually a way of putting into practice a cosmological conception in a living space. It is the nature and the expression of the demand for the settlement of human beings.[45] According to the inner substance of ancient Chinese mythological thinking, we may change Heidegger's conception to the unity of the heavens, earth, man, ghost and god. It is the re-fusion of the unity of the heavens, earth and man with that of man, ghost and god. Human beings become the subject of this re-fusion. He needs to maintain the relationship of mutual inspiration with the heavens and earth and, at the same time, with ghosts and gods as well. They are conscious that they, for their existence, ought to maintain a natural harmony with the heavens and earth and, more than that, consolidate a supernatural harmony with ghosts and gods. 'The heavens and earth' and 'ghost and god' are abstract meta-physical being of human beings' intuition. They admit that their existence has to depend on such kinds of transcendental force. Thus they place 'the heavens and earth' and 'ghost and god' in the core position of their living space.[46]

These origin myths express the subjective intentionality of the mass and the dialectical structure of cultural history. As they can spread by means of language, they can accumulate the values and the systems of praxis admitted by collective consensus.[47]

The application of the cosmological model of 'round heaven and square earth' is very popular in China. What is mentioned in the ancient books as the principles of square and circle can actually be taken as the norms for the heavens and earth. The cultural creation of ancient people in 'manufacturing instruments according to celestial phenomena' is itself a guiding principle for them to manufacture instruments by learning from the principle of 'round heaven and square earth'. As a consequence, the instruments are possessed of the mysterious force of drawing and summoning the heavens and earth. The invention of vehicle can be taken as an example. The body of a vehicle is square like earth. The top of it is round like heaven. The four flags stuck onto it represent the four directions. The two wheels operate like the periodic operation of the sun and the moon.[48] We can see a more popular use of the concept of 'round heaven and square house' in architecture. An outstanding example can be observed from the kind of building called *ming-tang* (bright hall). The round top of *ming-tang* and its body symbolise the heavens and earth respectively. The four doors in it symbolise four seasons and the eight windows in it the 'eight wind'. Such a kind of structure is the representation of the cosmology in fortune telling, which is itself an extension of myth.[49] People who espouse this kind of cosmology will believe that the space and direction of their dwelling correspond to the operation order of the cosmos and bring about corresponding effects of fortune and misfortune to them. In order to enjoy peace and stability both physically and spiritually, human beings have to pay much attention to the management of a divine space in their environment and, moreover, the divine time that exists correspondingly. By doing so, they can get hold of the best situation to survive.

Time and space in myth are possessed of special symbolic meaning. They are the divine time and the divine space that correspond to the heavens and earth. What is divine space? It is not an ordinary geographical position. In fact, it is a world manifested by the sacred on the basis of the thought of the creation of the cosmos. It is a world where man can get along with gods. It is a divine world where man can communicate with the heavens, earth, ghosts and gods.[50] What is divine time? It is the starting of the origin of time again. It is also the return of the creation of cosmos. It displays the periodicity of the creation of world, which symbolises the eternal comeback of time.[51] Origin myth is not only to be resounded repetitiously but also accompanied by the rites of witchcraft. It is the way for human beings to face the being of their own lives. They continuously repeat the quest for the creation of the cosmos and world and, by means of the operation of rituals, the demand for activities that enable them to have a rhythmic harmony with the cosmos.

During the process of the rituals, human beings and creation gods, or heroes, are satisfied with hierophanies. The arrangement of space from the core to the four directions or eight directions is a way to construct a divine space with a square and a circle, or just a circular divine space corresponding to the centre.

A circular divine space is not a concrete space in this world but symbolises the divine *jing* (invisible space). It is the space that points back to the centre. The square or circle, drawn with the divine space as the centre, is also only a symbolic form of being. The space of it can be extended infinitely and takes the circle as its symbol. The account of origin myths corresponds to the act of putting *jing* into ritual practice. Through the ritual practice, human beings are projected to the centre where they can be unified with the heavens, earth, ghost and god. As a result, they can understand the divine value of life being and, furthermore, yearn for implementing this value in the outer layer of the circle of divine space, that is, the activity space for life. The centre is divine. The circle of the outer layer is divine, too. Both of them are worlds manifested by the sacred. The circular cosmic world accounted in myths has been handed down from generation to generation. It becomes, in Chinese culture, the most fundamental mode to realise the cosmos. In the chapter of Ze Yang in *Zhuang Zi*, Ran Xiang is described as one who can 'understand the essence of the Way and let all external things grow naturally. He does not know when he begins, or ends, to get along with those things. He even does not know how long he has been with them.' Zhuang Zi's thinking does not come from nothing. It should be regarded as an extension of the cosmological view about centre found in the myths. He intends to fuse with the centre of the cosmos actively. He wants to be at the same pace with and correspond to the time and space of the cosmos.[52]

The religious function of ancient origin myths

The mode of realisation of the cosmos found in origin myth can be actualised only by means of the operation of rituals. The operation of rituals differs not greatly from the religious form of ancient witchcraft. In Chinese myths witchcraft is not opposed to religion. Rather, they come down in one continuous line. The intuitive experiences of a wizard, or a witch, are long lasting. Behind their craft to communicate with gods, there lie the rich metaphysical ideas about the relationship between human beings and god as well as the emotion of belief. Witchcraft is actually a kind of religious activity in worshipping deities. At the same time, it is also a constitution of thinking under the influence of life experiences. In other words, it is a display of the values hidden in their spiritual world.[53] Both myth and witchcraft are products of inspiration thinking of human beings. They get united tightly. They reflect the world of the early human beings' belief in supernatural deities.

Early human beings attempted to evoke inspiration from supernatural, mysterious forces to settle life being. They were not limited to making use of language to investigate the origin and destiny of the world and life. They also attempted, through some certain activities, to communicate with all the things in the heavens and earth.

Ancient origin myth expresses the conceptions of early human beings toward divinity and divine world. In the process of tracing the origin, human beings can understand the meaning of self existence in life. They tend to pay much attention to the communication and mutual inspiration not only between humanity and divinity but also that between this world and the supernatural world. As a result, the origin myths are far more than accounts of the origin of the cosmos and the existence of all things in the heavens and earth. More important, they can enable human beings to understand their spiritual transcendence and the practice of life.[54] Origin myth can be regarded as a system of symbolic discourse unique to primitive religion. It is a kind of spiritual and religious activity resulted from the development of society in the process of human beings' striving to survive. It is also a kind of collective memory about the assimilation of their living situation with the cosmos, which signifies the desire of human beings in yearning that life is not to be destructed by death but to continue immortally and everlastingly. To the ancient people origin myths are not literary works for their amusement. What is embedded in it is a specific world view. It can help people achieve the self-awareness of their own existence. Moreover, it can also contribute to the social praxis of human beings by providing directions for their thoughts and norms for their behaviour. Myth is assigned the function to promote the self-consciousness of human beings. In it they can undertake an eternal pursuit of life through the realisation of cosmological ideas; they can also arrive at a transcendental spiritual world by means of the ritual operation of witchcraft.

Origin myth carries with it a conspicuous religious purpose. It makes use of the thinking mode of language to convey conceptions about the cosmos and ways of behaviour under the influence of collective consciousness. It is a proof of the awakening of the self-consciousness of human beings and of their pursuit of an ethical order of higher meaning. We can find in it divine religious ideas and rationalised practices of belief.[55] There is a world for deities in both myth and religion. Human beings have already been aware that there is a transcendental divinity that, as the origin of all other divine lives, can exert absolute power in controlling and dominating all the things in the heavens and earth. As they live under the influence of ungraspable natural and social forces, human beings are naturally inclined to depend on and revere deities. More than that, human beings even bear with them the inspirational wish to communicate with deities in order to re-constitute their living position in the cosmos. They are aware that they need not worship the deities unconditionally. Instead, they are capable to enter the world of the deities to transcend themselves and even predominate over their own destinies. Ancient origin myth is the life process for human beings to experience the existence of divinity. They endeavour to make use of the language of myth and the rituals of worshipping to come close to the divine world.

What origin myth symbolises are the principles to exist in the cosmos—not only the origin of things in the heavens and earth but also the demand for harmony coloured with religious divinity. By means of origin myth, human beings apprehend that there exist certain principles of operation behind the cosmos so as to re-establish a new living order out of confusion. Originally, it is gods who are responsible for maintaining natural living and social order. Later, human beings realise that they are also possessed of the capability to take part in that responsibility. Through the symbolic unity of human beings and divinities, the latent confusion can become harmonic order in religious living. Hence human beings can live in the kind of harmony similar to that found in the operation of the cosmos.[56] The cosmology in origin myth is established on the ultimate pursuit of the existence of life. Out of the apprehension of divinity human beings initiate the experiences of their inner self. They are conscious that they can utilise some concrete symbols and rituals, in corresponding to the organic rhythm of nature, to find out their own peculiar nature of life and functions to survive. Human beings should not overlook the balance of nature and the interaction between all the things. This is why they are bound to project the life of a self to the orderly cosmos. Through the interpretation of and discourse on the origin in myth, they can enter into religion to hold fast to and to act on the principles of the cosmos.

Through the divine symbols and measures, religion can initiate the good and kind life innate in human beings. Deities are only the personified embodiment of this kind of metaphysical force or, in other words, the final embodiment of the personified divinity. Such embodiment can direct human beings to pursue the divine world that manifests again and to perfect the praxis of life being. Origin myth is utilised in religious belief, the kind of belief that causes people to believe in the existence of divinity. Because of this belief, human beings can overcome the confused living situation to re-establish the harmonic rhythm of life. Furthermore, by learning and practicing the principles of the cosmos, they can set up some norms for human behaviour. In this way, the direction is established for the development of religion in later ages.

According to the cosmology expounded in origin myths, there are three principles for the development of Chinese religion:

a. belief in the centre

The world of ghosts and gods found in myth and witchcraft is not an external predominant authority. Just like human beings, that world has to correspond to the living order of the cosmos. The worship of ghosts and gods by human beings is to initiate the value of self in life and to actualise the purpose of self-existence and self-development.

The forms and types of ghosts and gods are various and complicated.

Origin myth is an evidence of the wish of human beings, bound in their living situation, to obtain consolation from cosmic forces. Pan Gu and Nu Wa, found in the myths about the creation of the heavens and earth and human beings respectively, symbolise the energy of creation that comes from the cosmos. This energy creates a site for human beings to enjoy peace and stability both physically and spiritually. In this site human beings are conscious of the divinity of the heavens and earth as well as that of ghosts and gods. Being affected by the chaos thinking, they unify themselves with the heavens, earth, ghost and god.

'Severing earth from heaven' myth divides ancient religion into two stages. Deities are the focus of the belief activity in the first stage. There are no clear and definite religious acts. Human beings are not separated from nature. At the same time, they are internalised in gods. In the second stage, human beings become the focus of belief activity. Clear and definite religious acts can be witnessed. Belief activity becomes a ceremony in which wizards are relied on to open various kinds of communication between human beings and gods. Due to this kind of ceremony, abundant techniques and culture for living are accumulated. Most of the myths, which are about the rebirth of human beings, the origin of culture and the origin of races, are product of this stage. The rise of wizard is closely related to the creation of human culture. Wizard can be said to be the one who starts the primitive religion; the one who accumulates and spreads knowledge in early ancient ages; and also the one who creates and narrates myths. He develops various ritual activities that are involved with gods. He hopes to summon the help of divine force to fulfil the needs and wishes of human beings. This kind of witchcraft culture is actually the spring of the 'sage culture' in later ages in China. The two kinds of culture share the same cultural gene that enables the 'sage culture' to succeed the witchcraft culture.[57] The most obvious characteristic is that both cultures stress the constitution of a centre inside the living space.

Centre is the most outstanding divine zone. It is the place where human beings can achieve harmonic creation with deities.[58] It is established on the core concept of the unity of the heavens, earth, man, ghost and god to become oneness. In primitive religion wizard is the one who is possessed of the most sophisticated occult power. In his words and actions, he can express gods' will. He can even unify with gods directly. Emperors in myths can be said to the embodiment of the unity of the heavens, earth, man, ghost and god. They appear in human figures to display the divinity that is in compatible with the cosmos and to disclose the mystery of the affinity between self and the cosmos. In this case, these emperors play exactly the same role as the wizards do. Chinese humanistic thoughts of later ages affirm that even an individual can reach the life realm advocated by the wizards. By means of the conservation and manipulation of *qi* (vital matter), the small cosmos of self can reach the big cosmos, the centre where the unity of the heavens, earth, man, ghost and god can be accomplished. Religion, through practice, can help an individual develop his own symbolic cosmos so that he, like a wizard, can experience the whole world anew.

b. Hierophanies in the world of the circle

Emperors in myths symbolise the centre for the unity of human beings and gods. However, these emperors deploy the energy of cosmos creation in the role of human heroes. The role of these emperors can be seen in those myths which are about the rebirth of human beings, the origin of culture and the origin of races. These myths lay much emphasis on the point that human beings should keep on proceeding sacred self-manifestation in the world of circle where they actually live. They should also enrich, with various kinds of cultural invention similar to cosmos creation, the living landscape of the world of circle. Witchcraft values the progress of actualising in the outer layer what can be found in the centre. It also affirms that the world of circle itself is the site in which the spiritual life of human beings can undertake long-term self-practice. Without doubt, the divine centre is important. However, we cannot neglect the kinds of cultural invention actualised in substantial space. Cultural invention can enrich the space which carries the weight of living and custom. Amid those intensely centripetal regressive movements, cultural invention, by resorting to deep cultural experiences, can display the kind of endless, fervent life energy to perfect the living environment. The circle, the outer layer is no less important than centre. 'Centre' is the fundamental thought, while 'circle' is application at the level of praxis. What we emphasise is the divinisation and the purification of self subject when it appears substantially on earth. It is this divinisation and purification that eliminates the anxiety and uneasiness incurred by people who are on the verge of being.[59]

Myth is helpful to the divine initiation of rituals. It symbolises a new undertaking of the deeds of creation pertaining to the origin of the cosmos. Through the repetitious operation of the rituals, the divine force in the cosmos can keep on recurring continuously. The traditional cosmology of circle shows that space and time are recurring and regressive. In facing the recurring process of the destruction and the re-establishment of order, myths about the rebirth of human beings place emphasis on the destruction and the reconstruction of this world. Life is viewed as a cycle, just like the periodically waxing and waning of the moon. The cosmos also falls into the recurring and regression archetype of death and rebirth. First there is the orderly primitive cosmos. Then the panic of disorder caused by different kinds of disasters threatens the cosmos. Finally, the original cosmic order is restored after the effort of re-establishment.[60] Human beings have the rigorous desire to return to the realm of divinity, especially after earth was severed from the heavens. The rise of wizards brings forth the expectation of the restoration of the communication between human beings and gods. Through the operation of rituals, wizards become the ones who can communicate with gods and gods in human figures. Although they cannot take over the status of gods, they can make use of their words and deeds as the medium to express gods' will. Thus the realm of divinity can be actualised in this world.

Originally, god is the arbitrator of the cosmos which governs the motion of heavenly bodies and the change of seasons. In the rebirth activities performed by wizards, the status of human beings is elevated. Like the gods, human beings can have the chance to face their own life cycle— birth, agedness, sickness, and death. Inevitably, a sense of living experience that transcends time and space will be generated. Human beings tend more and more towards the eternal pursuit of a perfect realm. They believe that their life progress is a segment of the evolution of the cosmos. Their life cycle is like the way of evolution of the heavens and earth. Both of them are incessant, with numerous uprisings and downfalls; and, most important of all, head towards perfection.[61] The operation of the rituals can help people overcome adversity and turn back luck into good fortune.

Myth is not only the application of language. It works together with witchcraft to make it possible the sacred reappearance of self. It makes use of the experience of hierophanies to eliminate the nervousness and anxiety of being in this world. Rituals can be repeated. They are endowed with the symbolic significance of cosmos creation. The realm of divinity is brought to the living world of human beings; and the paradigm of cosmos creation is utilised to perfect human living. Each performance of ritual represents a re-combination of the religious divine realm with the mundane human one.[62] As the religious divine realm is placed in the mundane human realm, the real situation can be blessed and protected by divinity. By returning to the divine realm, the people in the mundane world can be freshened up. As a consequence, human beings can enter the spiritual life space from the ecological materialistic space in which they exist. In the divine realm they can succeed the culture of symbiosis that has been handed down by heroes and ancestors. By creating and inventing instruments and systems, they can purify the living wisdom of the world of circle. They are also aware that there exists the rhythm of natural operation in the cosmos. After they are baptised by ritual of the divine realm, human beings can re-establish the principle for living—human beings are unified with nature into a harmonic whole, and perfect the form of the motion to shuttle between the divine realm and the mundane one.

c. Belief in both the centre and its outer layer

Both myth and religion are made use to accomplish the life world of human beings. Both of them originate from the cosmological schema of circle, consisting of a centre and its outer layer. Spiritually, centre and its outer layer are of the same importance. It is revealed in origin myth that life, like the cosmos, is not transient. Life is not a materialistic existing form but a conceptual metaphysical constitution. In origin myth the life of human beings is associated with cosmic phenomena. For example, in addition to his chiselling out the universe and separating the earth from the heavens, Pan Gu also turned his body into different things in the cosmos. This myth about Pan Gu reveals that the mystery of being lies in the coordination of gathering gods in nature and understanding the operational principle of the heavens and earth.[63] Human beings can learn from the formation principle of the cosmos to understand the ultimate concern of life—to transcend birth and death in order to pursue self-perfection and self-fulfilment. The nature of human beings can only be accomplished only when one can face the requirement of harmony from both centre and its outer layer. It is a process which has to undergo troubles and unity. The myths about Nu Wa and Fu Xi symbolise how human beings, in facing calamities, bring into full play their ability to transcend and integrate.[64]

The conception of emphasising both the centre and its outer layer represents that system and application are not different from each other. Essence and function are equal in importance. Life of human beings has to regress to its primitive nature and lays great stress on humanistic function at the same time. Primitiveness and humanism are not opposed to each other. They originate and develop from the same source. Even though it is hard for human culture to avoid dichotomous opposition, there is still the strong demand for regressing to holism. It does not mean that human beings had to cut off their relationship with language once they invented characters. Both language and characters can hand down the ability to create originally to later generations. Primitiveness itself is a kind of creation. It bears with it the mental activity of transiting from living individually to living in groups. It is the awakening of real being of life. It is the self-accomplishment of human beings, awarded only to people who care both inner self and external living situation.[65] To regress to primitiveness does not mean to deny humanism. It is possible that a crisis of ignorance is latent in primitiveness. However, we should not forget that a similar crisis of alienation is latent in humanism as well. It is essential that primitiveness and humanism ought not to focus only on the blind spot of its counterpart and make use of it to deny each other. We should return to the rationality of being of human beings as subject and probe into the origin of life that is unified with the cosmos.

Myth, religion and philosophy are the crystal of wisdom of human beings. All of them are achievements after long-term pursuit and retrospection of the life of self. Prior to the invention of characters, human beings have already been able to investigate the birth and development of the cosmos with the mentality of encompassing all the things in the heavens and earth. At that time, human beings are possessed of the realisation that they are unified with nature to become a whole. They are able to differentiate things in the heavens and earth later, yet their life subject is still associated with those things. This kind of relationship is emphasised to so a great extent that we are warned not to lose it. It is affirmed that the life of nature is interlinked with that of human beings. Human beings, therefore, lay more emphasis on the originally existing spiritual communication between man and nature.[66] Human beings are conscious of the metaphysical being of the heavens and earth and sense the transcendental existence of ghosts and gods. Bearing with them such realisation, human beings proceed to stress on the deploying of divine energy of self. By means of the operation of witchcraft, human beings can be unified to repeat the primitive rhythm of the cosmos and to remember the contribution of their first ancestors and heroes in beginning the culture for them. The primitive rhythm of the cosmos and the culture are subsequently turned into spiritual force to settle real living. This process demonstrates the actualisation of the cosmology which emphasises on both centre and its outer layer. The living order and the ethical principles in the outer layer are affirmed by the conservation of and acting up to the beliefs of the centre.

The inner conceptual system of myth, through witchcraft, can be rendered as an external cultural system. Myth and witchcraft are interactive with each other and they maintain a two-way communication between them. They are characterised with the life concern that emphasises both the centre and its outer layer. Both of them value the experiences of the self subject as well as their succession and transmittal. They utilise the cosmological schema of circle to establish cultural order that serves as a paradigm. What is embedded in myth and witchcraft is the history of metaphysics and of praxis. By opening the soul of his self, one can observe the metaphysical knowledge and moral praxis displayed in myth and witchcraft. By no means do they remain at the linguistic and written forms of cognition. Rather, they are the real intuition and action of life. Origin myth is actually the immediate action of people's quest for origin.[67] It is an act of making use of the experiences of inner soul to investigate the possibility of infinity through finite forms. To be sure, such a mode of cognition is not the one espoused by science of later ages. Quite to the contrary, it is the religious activity that enables early human beings to display their mental wisdom. It is an act of belief that comes directly from cosmic consciousness. If modern religion lacks the dynamic to investigate the origin of the cosmos, it will become ossified at the external forms and remain far away from the spiritual call which reminds us to stress both the centre and its layer.

Conclusion

Origin myth is a comprehensive scrutiny of life existence by early human beings. It is not only a constitution of conceptual system. It can also promote the pursuit of meaning and the emotional experiencing of social and religious living. Early human beings deeply believe that there exists a close, interactive relationship between man and cosmos. Through the interpretation of the origin, they can establish firmly the value of their existence among the heavens, earth, ghost and god. Life is thereby promoted from a finite ecological environment to the infinite spiritual world. It transcends the level of materialistic body to enter that of spiritual, metaphysical identification. The latter level is beyond the scope that can be explained with science. The conception of cosmos embedded in origin myth is not a concrete object. Instead, it is the extension and expansion of life subject. It is a kind of eternal pursuit that interlocks with birth and death. The origin of the heavens, earth and all the things is utilised to prove that human beings are possessed of ceaseless and unquenchable belief nature.

Although myth and witchcraft do not conform to the methodology of scientific positivism, they are the metaphysical praxis of the soul of human subject. Myth and witchcraft are not blind and ignorant superstitious activities. The self-sufficient system of the formation of the cosmos provides human living with definite spiritual support and directions for actions. In the history of civilisation, myth and witchcraft set up the criteria for values and norms for behaviour. Origin myth is by no means nonsense. It is an indication of the direction for life being. It enables self to achieve autonomous spiritual fulfilment in the cosmos. If affirms that human beings are not materialistic animals. On the contrary, human beings are creators, in the sense that they can open a vivid humanistic world of variety with their own sophisticated thinking and action. This kind of spiritual culture, constituted by life subject, should be the most precious civilisation inheritance of human beings. The value of its existence should not be denied even though it cannot be examined by science.

Origin myth expresses the desire of human beings to realise the cosmos. To emphasise on the centre and its outer layer simultaneously can satisfy the wish of human beings to seek dependence and safety and their pursuit of the actualisation of the value of a holistic harmony of life. Through origin myth, human beings can be plunged into the world of the heavens, earth, ghost and god to realise that the nature of life, like the cosmos, exists eternally. Origin myth can bring human beings back to the origin to sense its creativity. By corresponding to those orderly cosmic principles, human beings can confirm their status in the cosmos and the meaning of their existence. The conceptions and actions formulated under human beings' long-term living are possessed of the ultimate purpose and the highest value of the actualisation of self. These conceptions and actions can enable human beings in the state of external natural existence to be possessed with the inner perfection of pursuing *jing* and the destination of life. No matter how dreadful the external environment is, human nature cannot help aiming towards those principles of existence that correspond to the harmony of the cosmos.

End Notes

1. Hau Zhang, *Siwei FashengXue: Cong Dongwu De Siwei Dao Ren De Siwei* (Beijing: China Social Sciences Press, 1994), 133.
2. Qiming Miao, *Yuanshi Siwei* (Shanghai: Shanghai People's Publishing House, 1993), 12.
3. Xiaoling Zhang, *Zhongguo Yuanshi Yishu Jingshen* (Chongqing: Chongqing Publishing House, 1992), 18.
4. Chung-ching Ou, *The Tradition of Knowledge in the Origin of Culture* (Taipei: Traditional Thought Association, 1993), 18.
5. Qiming Miao and Yiqun Wen, *Yuanshi Shehui De Qingshen Lishi Jiagou* (Kunming: Yunnan People's Publishing House, 1993), 61.
6. Yude Qu, 'Shenhua Chuangzuo De Siwei Huodong', in *Shenhua Xinlun* (Shanghai: Shanghai Arts Press, 1987), 23.
7. Qiyao Deng, 'Shenhua Siwei Xinli Jiegou Zhong Siwei Zhuti Yu Siwei Duixiang De Guanxi', in *Shenhua Xinlun* (Shanghai: Shanghai Arts Press, 1987), 42.
8. Kuang-chih Chang, *Six Essays on Archaeology* (Taipei Hsien: Tao Hsiang Publishing House, 1988), 23.
9. Kuang-chih Chang, *Art, Myth and Sacrifice* (Taipei Hsien, Tao Hsiang: Publishing House, 1993), 152.
10. Chung-ching Ou, *Prehistoric Science and Racial Knowledge Tradition: Reflection on the View of History from Prehistoric Time to Shang Dynasty and Chou Dynasty* (Taipei: Traditional Thought Society, 1993), 28.
11. Chung-ching Ou, *The Inheritance of Perceptions in Ancient Chinese Society: The View of Civilization History from Shang Dynasty and Chou Dynasty to Ching Dynasty* (Taipci: Traditional Thought Society 1993), 29.
12. Zhiyong Yang, 'Cong Minjian Xinyang De Shenling Tedian Kan Shenhua De Fazhan', in *Shenhua Xinlun* (Shanghai: Shanghai Arts Press, 1987), 145.
13. Xuanjun Xie, *Shenhua Yu Minzu Jingshen* (Jinan: Shan Dong Arts Press, 1986), 188.
14. Yang and Chung-hsiu Mou, *Creation Myth of China* (Taipei: Tung Hua Book Co, 1990), 19.
15. Chongtian Yi, *Yishu Renleixue* (Shanghai: Shanghai Arts Press, 1992), 157.
16. EB Tylor, *Yuanshi Senhua*, translated by Shusheng lian (Shanghai: Shanghai Arts Press, 1992), 414.

17. Daji Lu, *Zongjiaoxue Tonglun Xinbian* (Beijing: China Social Science Press), 454.
18. Cunming Zhu, *Linggan Siwei Yu Yuanshi Wenhua* (Shanghai: Xue Lin Publishing House, 1995), 71.
19. Qiyao Deng, *Zhongguo Shenhua De Siwei Jiegou* (Chongqing: Chongqing Publishing House), 1992, 120.
20. Xin He, *ZhongguoYuangu Shenhua Yu Lishi Xintan* (Haerbin: Heilongjiang Education Press, 1988), 235–50.
21. Jun Chen, 'Pangu Kao' and 'Pangu Xinkao', in *Zhongguo Shenhua Xinlun* (Guilin: Lijiang Publishing House, 1993), 23–48.
22. Yueli Zhu, *Daojiao Dawen* (Beijing: Huawen Publishing House, 1989), 20.
23. Zhongshi Hu, 'Shilun Pangu Shenhua Zhi Laiyuan Ji Xuzheng Dui Shenhua De Jiagong zhengli', in *Zhongguo Shenhua*, in volume I of *Zhongguo Shenhua* (Beijing: Zhongguo Minjian Wenyi Chubanshe, 1987), 249.
24. Huaicheng Liu, *Zhongguo Shanggu Shenhua Tonglun* (Kunming: Yunnan People's Publishing House, 1992), 318.
25. Ke Yuan, 17.
26. Lihui Yang, *Nu Wa De Shenhua Yu Xinyang* (Beijing: China Social Sciences Press, 1997), 32.
27. Weiying Gong, *Yuanshi Chongbai Gangyao: Zhonghua Tuteng Wenhua Yu Shengzhi Wenhua* (Beijing: Zhongguo Minjian Wenyi Chubanshe, 1989), 198.
28. Zenghua Wang, 'Nu Wa Shenhua Kao', in *Shenhua Yu Minsu* (Xian: Shanxi People's Publishing House, 1993), 15.
29. Guohua Zhao, *Shengzhi Chongbai Wenhua Lun* (Beijing: China Social Sciences Press, 1990), 225.
30. Bingxiang Zhu, *Fu Xi Yu Zhongguo Wenhua* (Hankou: Hubei Education Press, 1997), 86.
31. Zhenli Zhang, *Zhongyuan Gudian Shenhua Liubian Lunkao* (Shanghai: Shanghai Arts Press, 1991), 90.
32. Taro Moriyasu, translated by Hsiao-lien Wang, *The Legend of Huang Di: A Study of Chinese Ancient Mythology* (Taipei: China Times Press, 1988), 176.
33. Zhiyong Yang, 'Shenxi, Zuxi De Yizhixing Yu Zuxian Shenhua De Xingcheng', in *Zongjiao, Shenhua and Minzu* (Kunming: Yunnan Education Publishing Hosuse, 1992), 125.
34. Mu Chien, *Huang Ti* (Taipei: Tung Ta Publishing Company, 1978), 18.

35. Ze Jin, *Hero Worship and Cultural Forms* (Hong Kong: The Commercial Press Ltd, 1991), 145.
36. Xuanjun Xie, *Zhongguo Shenhua* (Hangzhou: Zhe Jiang Education Press, 1995), 127.
37. Masaru Mitarai, 'Zhuan Xu and Qian Huang, Chang Yi, Qing Yang, Yi Gu, Huang Di: about the Pedigree of the Ancestor Gods of the Ying People', in *Myths and Legends of China*, translated by Hsiao-lien Wang (Taipei: Linking Publishing Company, 1977), 239–72.
38. Zhaoyuan Tian, *Shenhua Yu Zhongguo Shehui* (Shanghai: Shanghai People's Publishing House, 1998), 87.
39. Bing Xiao, *Zhongguo Wenhua De Jingying: Taiyang Yingxiong Shenhua Bijiao Yanjiu* (Shanghai: Shanghai Arts Press, 1989), 217.
40. Keisuke Kurihara and Nobuharu Takahashi, translators, 'Primitive Han People and its Mythic-like World View: A Discussion of the Kinship Relationship between Divine Gods and Ancient Han People', in *Gods and Myth* (Taipei: Linking Publishing Company, 1988), 260.
41. Mingzi Qian, *Zhongguo Shenhuaxue* (Yinchuan: Ningxia People's Publishing House, 1994), 18.
42. Peilin Chao, *A Discussion of the History of the Mythical Thought in Early Chin Age* (Wunan Book Co Ltd, 1998), 57.
43. Shizhen Wu, *Shenhuaxue Lungang* (Lanzhou: Dunhuang Arts Press, 1993), 134.
44. Maosong Cai, *Bijiao Shenhuaxue* (Urumqi: Xinjiang University Press, 1993), 29.
45. Martin Heiddeger, 'Building, Dwelling, Thinking', translated by Po-chung Chen', in *An Introduction to Phenomenology of Architecture* (Taipei: Laureate Book Company, 1992), 59.
46. Chi-ming Cheng, *Cultural Consciousness of Chinese Religion, Book II* (Taipei: Chinese Taoist Press, 2003), 70.
47. Chi-ming Cheng, *Cultural Consciousness of Chinese Religion, Book II* (Taipei: Chinese Taoist Press, 2003), 70.
48. Po-shun Chiu, 'A Survey of the Structure of Operation of *Ba Zhai* from the Perspective of "Round Heaven and Square Earth"', in *Space, Force and Society* (Taipei: Institute of Ethnology, Academia Sinica, 1995), 280.
49. Cheng-sheng Tu, 'Inside, Outside and Eight Directions: The Ethical and Cosmological View of Traditional Chinese Dwelling',

in *Space, Force and Society* (Taipei: Institute of Ethnology, Academia Sinica, 1995), 259.
50. Mircea Eliadie, *The Sacred and the Profane: The Nature of Religion*, translated by Su-o Yang (Taipei: Laureate Book Company, 2001), 84.
51. Mircea Eliade, *Cosmos and History: The Myth of the Eternal Return* (Taipei: Linking Publishing Company, 2000), 75.
52. Bing Xiao, 'The View of World Center in Chinese Myths: A Study of the Shift of World Centre in Zhou People', in *Essays Presented in Conference on Chinese Myth and Legend Research* (Taipei: Centre for Chinese Studies, 1996), 88.
53. Chi-ming Cheng, 'Philosophical Reflection on Witchcraft Culture', in *Legein Society Monthly Magazine*, volume 335 (Taipei: Legein Society, 2003), 23.
54. Xinping Zhuo, *Zongjiao Lijie* (Beijing: Social Sciences Documents Press, 1999), 160.
55. Zhufeng Luo, editor, *Ren, Shehui Yu Zongjiao* (Shanghai: Shanghai Social Sciences Academy Press, 1995), 318.
56. Frederick J Streng, *Man and God: Understanding Religious Life*, translated by Ze Jin and Qimin He (Shanghai: Shanghai People's Press, 1991), 111.
57. He Lin, *Zhongguo Wunuo Shi* (Guangzhou: Hua Cheng Publishing House, 2001), 43.
58. Sarah Allan, *The Shape of the Turtle: Myth, Art and the Cosmos in Early China*, translated by Tao Wang (Chengdu: Sichuan People's Press, 1992) 108.
59. Chao-yang Pan, *Outgoing and Incoming: A Study of the Space of Pure Land* (Taipei: Geography Department, National Taiwan Normal University, 2001), 51.
60. Hsiao-lien Wang, 'Death and Rebirth: Regression and Belief of Time', in *The Mythical World of China: Creation Myth and Belief of Different Races* (Taipei: China Times Press, 1987), 573.
61. Yung-chung Kuan, *Myth and Time* (Taipei: Taiwan Book Company. 1997), 297.
62. Louis Dupre, *The Other Dimension: A Search for the Meaning of Religious Attitudes*, translated by Pei-jung Fu (Taipei: Youth Cultural Company Ltd, 1986), 157.
63. Jiakun Zhang, *Zhongguo Zhexue: Renlei Jingshen De Qiyuan Yu Guisu* (Beijing: China Social Sciences Press, 1991), 54.
64. Guangyu Fu, *Sanyuan: Zhongguo Shenhua Jiegou* (Kunming: Yunnan People's Publishing House, 1993), 68.

65. Tso-cheng Shih, *An Introduction to Socioanthropology,* volume 1 (Taipei: Ton San Publications, 1989), 43.
66. Tso-cheng Shih, *The Origin of the Spirit of Chinese Philosophy* (Taipei: Book Land Co Ltd, 2000), 115.
67. Tso-cheng Shih, *The Opening of the Soul and the History of Metaphysics* (Taipei: Ton San Publications, 1988), 131.

One Universe, Two Perspectives: Cosmology, Epistemology and Science-Religion Dialogue[1]

Kang Phee Seng

Abstract

This paper will discuss the Christian understanding of creation in the light of the search for the origin of the universe in science since the early twentieth century. To provide a contemporary focus for the discussion, the epistemological relevance of Stephen Hawking's quantum gravitational cosmology will be explored.

Some of the epistemological issues explored in this paper include:

1. Epistemological dualism: Are science and religion mutually irrelevant?
2. Does science disprove or contradict theology?
3. Epistemological hegemony: Is Science always right?
4. Epistemological suspension: The Return of the God-of-the-gaps?
5. Science or metaphysics?
6. The absence of God?

The epistemological issues serve to illustrate the significance of the dialogue between science and religion in recent decades.

This paper explores some fundamental epistemological issues arising from the dialogue between natural science and Christian theology. To provide a contemporary focus in the discussion, the epistemological relevance of Stephen

Hawking's quantum gravitational cosmology will be drawn upon.[2]

Hawking's quantum gravitational cosmology

The general consensus of cosmologists today is that the universe began at a big bang. For centuries however, scientists believed otherwise. They believed that the universe as a whole was static, that although there were some passing objects like comets, the distances between the galaxies remained constant. With a new understanding of space and time as dynamic quantities, a dynamic, expanding universe based on the general relativity theory was proposed (1922) and later confirmed by empirical observations of redshift (1929) and microwave background radiation (1965). In 1970, Penrose and Hawking showed that general relativity theory implied that the universe like ours must have a beginning, that is, a big bang singularity.[3]

In order to avoid the singularity at which all laws of physics break down, Hawking and Hartle in 1983 proposed a different cosmological model which takes into consideration the strong quantum gravitational effects at the very early stage of the universe.[4] The result is a universe with no singularity and time is without beginning. For Hawking, the religious implication for such a universe is obvious:

> The idea that space and time may form a closed surface without boundary . . . has profound implications for the role of God in the affairs of the universe . . . So long as the universe had a beginning, we could suppose it had a creator. But if the universe is really completely self-contained, having no boundary or edge, it would have neither

beginning nor end: it would simply be. What place, then, for a creator?[5]

Epistemology dualism:
Are science and religion mutually irrelevant?

Many believe that science and religion belong to two different categories. Science is the quest for facts in the physical world and religion is the search for values in the spiritual world. Truth in science is universal and absolute, and in religion individual and relative. The approach in one is cognitive and rational, in the other is emotive and speculative. The ultimate reality for science is nature and for religion is moral. Such epistemological dualism between science and religion is very much Tertullian's — what concourse can there be between Cavendish Laboratories and the Westminster Abbey, between laws of physics and spiritual principles?

It is true that religious symbols cannot be found in an equation of chemical reaction, that the Book of Psalms is not a science treatise, that the law of gravitation may have nothing to do with the doctrine of justification by faith. But it is doubtful whether science and religion can be compartmentalised and separated from each other like an elephant from a whale. Science has never consisted merely of 'facts, nothing but facts'. The so-called 'facts' are never 'pure facts' nor 'raw data'. If natural events are the texts of science, scientific theories are the hermeneutics of these texts. Just as no texts can be abstracted from a language system and its grammatical rules, facts cannot be isolated from their interpretive framework which is metaphysical in nature. Epistemologically, in any scientific endeavour, facts and the theories that are based upon them, together with the values and meanings and philosophies derived are never reduced to physical entities without remainders. Like religion, science has its own metaphysical assumptions that cannot be proved scientifically. Facts, knowledge and theories in science have to be grounded upon some specific conceptual framework or metaphysical categories. Hence, religion and science cannot ignore the implications of the metaphysical assumptions made by the other.

In a similar vein, Christian theology is not confined only within the existential or spiritual. It reaches beyond the realm of individual, inner, and spiritual. If the God of the Christian faith is truly known as 'the Father Almighty, Maker of Heaven and Earth, and all things visible and invisible' and 'the only Son . . . through him all things are made', then all things, cosmological, physical and organic included, are within the knowing and understanding range of Christian theology. Moreover, the core elements of the Christian faith such as the doctrines of creation, revelation, redemption, and above all, the incarnation, are events that had taken place within this our real and physical world. The rejection of Gnosticism by the early fathers affirms the material and the historical dimensions as essential in the Christian faith. That is to say, 'theology has to do not simply with God/man relations but with God/man/world or God/world/man relations, and understanding of the world inevitably enters into the coefficients of theological concepts an statements'.[6] If all truths and realities are ultimately grounded in God, there should be no radical dichotomy between scientific truth and theological truth, between scientific reality and theological reality. Epistemologically, theological values, beliefs and discourses can never be abstracted from this physical world of laws and history, or be deprived of the material and spatio-temporal ingredients. Hence, science and theology cannot ignore the truth claims that are made with respect to the same one world and history by the other, and the conflicts that might arise from the different worldview held by the other.

The quote from Stephen Hawking at the beginning of this paper is a good example to dispel the myth of this mutual irrelevance. Hawking's *A Brief History of Time* is certainly a book on cosmology: 'Where did the universe come from? How and why did it begin? Will it come to an end, and if so, how?'[7] But it is, in the words of Carl Sagan, an atheist, 'also a book about God . . . or perhaps about the absence of God. The word God fills these pages . . . Hawking is attempting, as he explicitly states, to understand the mind of God.'[8] That Hawking's concept of time has religious significance is evident and could well be one of the main reasons for the book's phenomenal sale.

Hawking is not alone in speaking of religious implications of scientific theory. Indeed, the religious relevance of new cosmological discoveries is too striking to be ignored, and are readily acknowledged by even non-theistic or agnostic scientists. Thus, the talk about 'from entropy to God' (Peter Landsberg),[9] 'the waiting of theologians for scientists' (Robert Jastrow),[10] 'a surer path in science to God' (Paul Davies),[11] 'knowing the mind of God' (Stephen Hawking),[12] or simply, 'Science finds God' (*Newsweek*).[13] The dialogue between science and religion in the last three decades has been one of the most successful interdisciplinary studies ever—the rapid growth in publications, the establishment of many new research centres[14] and academic lectureships.[15] Furthermore, more than forty per cent of the winners for the Templeton Prize for Progress in Religion have been actively engaged in science-religion dialogue and, except for Thomas Torrance (1978) and James McCord (1986), are trained scientists.[16] All these speak powerfully of the profound impact of science on religion as well as the immense attraction of religion for scientists.

Perhaps the best argument against the view that science and religion are mutually irrelevant is the fact that the two are in fact engaged in active dialogue. It is now no longer unusual for scientists and theologians to be in the same academic conference exploring the significance of each for the other.[17] The relationship between the two may not always be valued, but is not non-existent. There is no scientific justification for their incommensurability or *incommunicatio*. An epistemological dualism which assumes *a priori* that science and religion are mutually irrelevant to each other is ungrounded.

Does science disprove or contradict theology?

Many believe that if the two are not kept in two different compartments, they will necessarily be in conflict with each other. This 'conflict model' is best illustrated in a strongly-worded editorial response by *Nature*, the renowned science journal, to the announcement of the establishment of a new Starbridge Lectureship in Theology and Natural Science by the University of Cambridge. The editorial pointed to an 'inevitable intellectual conflict' between the two and dismissed the project as an 'empty' venture 'polluting British Universities'. Dialogue or interaction can be 'only in the most superficial sense'. Apart from some kind of 'research on the psychology of religious belief', presumably studies into the psychology of why people would accept religion, 'what other academic purpose can there be?'[18] To this, Richard Dawkins added, 'What has 'theology' ever said that is of the smallest use to anybody? When has 'theology' ever said anything that is demonstrably true and is not obvious?... What makes you think that 'theology' is a subject at all?'[19] However, this myth of intrinsic conflict and perpetual historical battle has been challenged by many. 'Not that Christian and scientific doctrines have never been at odds', observes British historian of science Colin Russell, 'but that to portray them as persistently in conflict is not only historically inaccurate, but actually a caricature so grotesque that what needs to be explained is how it could possibly have achieved any degree of respectability.'[20] A recent study by Larson and Witham showed too that the relationship between science and religion is not zero-sum. Furthermore, even to a very stringent definition of religious faith as believing in 'a personal God to whom one may pray in expectation of receiving an answer' and in 'immortality', nearly forty per cent of scientists answered positively.[21]

It is true that science and religion in an active dialogue do not always see eye-to-eye. They do sometimes contradict each other, as in the case of Galileo versus the church, the conflict was real and they could not be both right.

Hawking's is another case in point. For Hawking, time has no beginning, and thus the universe was not created. The Christian tradition on the other hand believes that the universe is created by God *ex nihilo* and thus time has a beginning. Either time has a beginning or it doesn't. Hence the conflict. If Hawking is right, Christian theology must forgo *creatio ex nihilo*, or at least its traditional interpretation which implies a beginning for the universe and for time. But if the Christian tradition is correct, then Hawking's notion of time can never be justified empirically. It must be emphasised that all parties in a dialogue may be genuine truth seekers, but not all may be in truth. Dialogue if genuine, must be a humble learning process which involves true *metanoia*—turning oneself away from falsehood in which one is found.

Epistemology hegemony: Science is always right!

While dialogue between science and religion is welcomed by many, for some, the two are not true equal partners. For them, if ever there is any disagreement, the truth must always be with science.

The case of Galileo shows that the Church did err in supporting the geocentric view, but those on the side of heliocentrism were not entirely correct either—for we now know that there is no absolute centre or absolute point of reference for the whole universe. All positions and motions in the universe are relative to some frame chosen for convenience of observation. One must not forget that in the camp of geocentrism reside not only clergymen but also scientists. To reduce the whole controversy into science versus religion is historically naïve. The fun-damental question is the conflict between traditional (Aristotelian) science/philosophy and new (Copernican) science, old (Ptolemaic) cosmology and new (math-ematical) cosmology. On both sides of the controversies are scientists, caught in between the old and the new paradigms. Indeed scientists would be the first to know that some of their eminent colleagues can be most resistant to new paradigms. In his recent book *The Genius of Science*, the distinguished physicist Abraham Pais collected astonishingly many stories of physicists who hesitated to announce a great discovery or theory for fear of being ridiculed by colleagues, only to see a Nobel prize stolen from under their noses![22] Moreover, one should also be reminded that many of the conflicts between science and religion in the past happened at a time when modern science was in the infant stage and has yet to establish her credibility as objective and efficient.[23]

Scientific theories are of course always subject to revision and even falsification. They have their own limits and are not infallible. For example, some of the strongest supporters for the 'steady state theory' of the universe had to reluctantly abandon it later when the rival 'big bang theory' was supported by substantial evidence.[24] Hawking himself made two contradictory truth claims about singularity—first in 1970 with Roger Penrose affirming that 'there must have been a big bang singularity provided only that general relativity is correct and the universe contains as much matter as we observe';[25] and then in 1983 with Jim Hartle suggesting that:

> there would be no singularities at which the laws of science broke down and no edge of space-time at which one would have to appeal to God or some new law to set the boundary conditions for space-time . . . The universe would be completely self-contained and not affected by anything outside itself. It would neither be created nor destroyed. It would just BE.[26]

It is interesting to see that while *creatio ex nihilo* was supported by Hawking's former theory of singularity,[27] it was contradicted by his latter notion of time without boundary.

If indeed science is always right, the grand ultimate question would be, 'Whose science? Which cosmology?'

Epistemological suspension: God-of-the-gaps

It was reported that when the first astronaut Gagarin returned from his space travel, he quipped, 'There is no God for I have not seen him up there.' Either God does not exist, or He is not there—driven away by Gagarin's spaceship to look for another shelter place.

The god of scientism is a god-of-the-gaps. He is there only where science has not been. He may be found in gaps of scientific theories and mental blocks. With the exponential advancement in science, God, if he is still with us in the year 3000, will surely be reduced to a cosmological amoeba.

When asked by Napoleon where God came into his theory of the cosmos, the great French mathematician and astronomer Laplace replied arrogantly, 'I have no need of that hypothesis.' Yet Hawking found Laplace's determinism incomplete, for there remained the question of how the laws should be chosen and the specification of the initial configuration of the universe. God was still there—only he was 'confined to the areas that nineteenth-century science did not understand.'[28] In eliminating singularity from the universe, there would simply be no boundary conditions for God to set, neither beginning nor end for him to intervene. In short, there is no place for a creator at all.

Laplace's god remains Hawking's—a god-of-the-gaps, or rather a god-of-the-singularities. He is there only where the laws of science break down, where epistemological probe of science is suspended or prohibited. He is known only where He is not known. Hawking's is a god who is deistically related to the universe at the point of singularity, the only one place where divine action may be required and where prayers and offerings may be made. Deficient in his understanding of the full doctrine of creation as both *creatio continuans* as well as *creatio ex nihilo*, Hawking is unable to engage with the living God of *creatio continuans*. Hawking's dialogue with religion appears to be only a monologue.

Science or metaphysics?

In the quantum theory of gravity, Hawking saw a possibility 'for space-time to be finite in extent and yet to have no singularities that formed a boundary or edge'.[29] It must be emphasised that Hawking's cosmology is essentially a mathematical model which is 'just a proposal' that 'cannot be deduced from some other principle'.[30] Moreover, the immense mathematical complications in solving the wave function of the whole universe will deprive it of exact predictions and verifications, without which it will only remain as a metaphysical system.

More importantly, it is difficult if not impossible to make sense of Hawking's notion of time in our real world. In order to avoid technical difficulties in quantum theory in performing Feynman's sum over histories, Hawking proposed to take the curved space-time of gravitational field as Euclidean, that is, to measure time by imaginary numbers. This has the effect of spatialising time: 'the distinction between time and space disappears completely'[31] When asked what happens to an unfortunate astronaut who falls into a black hole, Hawking replies with a paradox comparable to Schrödinger's cat—there would be no singularities if s/he lived in imaginary time. In real time, s/he is doomed. But Hawking could provide no further answer to the ultimate question of what *actually* happens to the astronaut.

'Only if we could picture the universe in terms of imaginary time, would there be no singularities.'[32] There is indeed no more difficulty in imaging the universe with imaginary time than in picturing a particle that follows every possible path in space-time. Like the sum over histories in quantum theory, imaginary number too is a powerful conceptual tool. The real problem is to make sense of it in our actual experience. Despite its usefulness and beauty in solving the wave function of the universe, what Penrose speaks of quantum theory is also true of Hawking's imaginary number: 'The one thing that can be said against it is that it makes absolutely no sense!'[33] In other words, it is only a useful mathematical model for describing our observations. It has no ontological implications: 'it exists only in our minds',[34] concurs Hawking.

That is why no classical quantum theorists would grant quantum theory a realist status. Hawking's quantum gravitational cosmology would be a real challenge to the Christian concept of *creatio ex nihilo* only if it could make sense in the real world. However, apart from a realist interpretation which Hawking himself rejects, it has no implications in reality. The fundamental issue in the perceived conflicts is ultimately not scientific but metaphysical.[35]

The absence of God?

Much as Carl Sagan would like to believe that Hawking's book is about the absence of God, it is doubtful whether it is what Hawking intends it to be. Indeed, Hawking seems to be fully aware of the fact that science, in spite of its immense contributions, does not provide the ultimate answer.

To be sure, Hawking did boldly declare that time without beginning would signify that the uncaused universe simply is. The universe simply would not need a creator for its existence. But then towards the end of the book, Hawking readily admits that the mathematical model which eliminates the singularity does not answer the questions of why the laws that the universe obeys are such, nor 'why there should be a universe for the model to describe'.[36] Religious questions remain with us even after the discovery of the grand unified theory. In fact, it provides us with a proper context to raise theological questions. In short, religion cannot be reduced to science without remainder as scientism claims.

It has often been said, as did Sagan, that Hawking's cosmological quest is an attempt to understand the mind of God. The last paragraph of his book is revealing. It is only when we have found the answer to the teleological question of human and cosmic existence, then would we know the mind of God. Knowing the wave equation of the universe or even the Grand Unified Theory would not.

> However, if we do discover a complete theory, it should in time be understandable in broad principle by everyone, not just a few scientists. Then we shall all, philosophers, scientists, and just ordinary people, be able to take part in the discussion of the question of why it is that we and the universe exist. If we find the answer to that, it would be the ultimate triumph of human reason—for then we would know the mind of God.[37]

Perhaps we need not wait till the grand discovery of the complete theory, if there is one, to begin the teleological quest for the meaning of human and cosmic existence. Theologians and scientists do not need to work in shifts. They have already begun to work together in their shared endeavour in understanding the origin and the end of humankind and the universe. This is the meaning and significance of the dialogue.

End Notes

1. For the purpose of our discussion, 'science' in this article refers to natural science and 'religion' to the Christian faith. This however should not be taken as neglecting the dialogues between science and other religions such as Islam or Judaism.
2. Stephen Hawking's *A Brief History of Time: From the Big Bang to Black Holes* (New York: Bantam Books, 1988).
3. *Ibid*, 50. SW Hawking and R Penrose, 'The Singularities of Gravitational Collapse and Cosmology', *Proceedings of the Royal Society of London*, A314 (1970): 529–48.
4. *Ibid*, 136. JB Hartle and SW Hawking, 'Wave Function of the Universe', *Physical Review*, D28 (1983): 2960–75.
5. *Ibid*, 140f.
6. Thomas F Torrance, *The Ground and Grammar of Theology* (Belfast: Christian Journals, 1980), 75.
7. Hawking, *A Brief History of Time*, vi.
8. Carl Sagan, 'Introduction', *ibid*, x.
9. 'To talk about the implications of science for theology at a scientific meeting seems to break a taboo. But those who think so are out of date. During the last 15 years, this taboo has been removed, and in talking about the interaction of science and theology, I am actually moving with a tide which is threatening to wash us away in a flood of publications.' [PT Landsberg, 'From Entropy to God?' in *Thermodynamics: History and Philosophy*, edited by K Martinas, K Ropolyi, and P Szegedi (Singapore: World Scientific, 1991), 380.]
10. '[The scientist] has scaled the mountains of ignorance; he is about to conquer the highest peak; as he pulls himself over the final rock, he is greeted by a band of theologians who have been sitting there for centuries.' [Robert Jastrow, *God and the Astronomers* (New York: WW Norton, 1978), 116.]
11. 'It may seem bizarre, but in my opinion, science offers a surer path to God than religion.' [Paul Davies, *God and the New Physics* (New York: Simon & Schuster: 1983), ix.]
12. 'If we do discover a complete theory . . . (t)hen we shall all, philosophers, scientists, and just ordinary people, be able to take part in the discussion of the question of why it is that we and the universe exist. If we find the answer to that, it would be the ultimate triumph of human — for then we would know the mind of God.' [Hawking, *A Brief History of Time*, 175.]

13. Sharon Begley, 'Science Finds God', *Newsweek*, 20 July 1998 and Kenneth L Woodward, 'How the Heavens Go', *Newsweek*, 20 July 1998.
14. Major centres include Center for Theology and Natural Sciences (Berkeley), Center for Theological Inquiry (Princeton), Chicago Center for Science and Religion (Chicago), The Pascal Center for Advanced Studies in Faith and Science (Ancaster, Ontario), Christians in Science (Perthshire), Ian Ramsey Centre (Oxford), Vatican Observatory (Vatican), and European Society for the Study of Science and Theology (Sweden).
15. Notably the chairs and lectureships on science and religion established in Princeton, Cambridge and Oxford in the 90s.
16. The full title of the Templeton Prize is: Templeton Prize for Progress Toward Research or Discoveries about Spiritual Realities. The Templeton Laureates who have been actively engaged in science-religion dialogue are Thomas F Torrance (1978), Ralph Wendell Burhoe (1980), Sir Alister Hardy (1985), James I McCord (1986), Stanley L Jaki (1987), Carl Friedrich von Weizsacker (1989), L Charles Birch (1990), Paul Charles William Davies (1995), Ian Barbour (1999) and Dyson (2000), Arthur Peacocke (2001), John Polkinghorne (2002) Holmes Rolston III (2003) and George Ellis (2004).
17. Theologically speaking, this dialogue, though breaking new grounds in the past three decades, is a continuation of a long established tradition of engagement between the two since at least the rise of modern science in the seventeenth century. Interaction with science has always been high on the theological agenda. On the one hand, the rise of modern science took place within the Christian culture. One the other hand, the history of Christian theology since the Enlightenment is also a history of the development of modern theology in responding to the impact and challenges of modern science.
18. 'Religious Studies: A (Star)bridge to Nowhere [editorial]', *Nature* volume 362, number 6419 (1 April 1993): 380.
19. 'Letters to the Editor', *The Independent* (20 March 1993), quoted by Michael Poole, 'A Critique of Aspects of the Philosophy and Theology of Richard Dawkins', *Science and Christian Belief*, volume 6 (April 1994): 41.
20. Colin A Russell, 'The Conflict Metaphor and its Social Origins', *Science and Christian Belief*, volume 1, number 1 (1989): 5.
21. It is instructive that the study was commissioned by *Nature*.

22. Abraham Pais, *The Genius of Science: A Portrait Gallery of 20th-Century Physicists* (Oxford: Oxford University Press, 2000)
23. See for instance, the translation of 1 Timothy 6:20 in King James Version (1611) 'Keep that which is committed to thy thrust, avoiding profane and vain babblings and oppositions of science falsely so called.' and in Revised Standard Version (1946) 'Guard what has been entrusted to you. Avoid the godless chatter and contradictions of what is falsely called knowledge.'
24. Among the greatest scientists in the twentieth century supporting the 'steady state theory' of the universe are Albert Einstein and Fred Hoyle.
25. Hawking, *A Brief History of Time*, 50. SW Hawking and R Penrose, 'The Singularities of Gravitational Collapse and Cosmology', *Proceedings of the Royal Society of London*, A314 (1970): 529–48.
26. *Ibid*, 136. JB Hartle and SW Hawking, 'Wave Function of the Universe', *Physical Review*, D28 (1983): 2960–75.
27. 'At this singularity, space and time came into existence; literally nothing existed before the singularity, so, if the Universe originated at such a singularity, we would truly have a creation *ex nihilo*.' [John D Barrow and Frank J Tipler, *The Anthropic Cosmological Principle* (Oxford: Clarendon, 1986), 442.]
28. Hawking, *A Brief History of Time*, 172.
29. Ibid, 135.
30. *Ibid*, 136.
31. *Ibid*, 134.
32. *Ibid*, 138.
33. '[Quantum] theory has, indeed, two powerful bodies of fact in its favour, and only one thing against it. First, in its favour are all the marvellous agreements that the theory has had with every experimental result to date. Second, and to me almost as important, it is a theory of astonishing and profound mathematical beauty. The one thing that can be said against it is that it makes absolutely no sense!' [Roger Penrose, 'Gravity and State Vector Reduction' in *Quantum Concepts in Space and Time*, edited by Roger Penrose and CJ Isham (Oxford: Clarendon Press, 1986), 129.]
34. Hawking, *A Brief History of Time*, 139.
35. For a fuller treatment of Hawking's purely instrumental character of cosmological model, see, William Lane Craig, 'Design and the Cosmological Argument', in *Mere Creation: Science, Faith*

and Intelligent Design, edited by William A Dembski, (Downers Grove, Illinois: InterVarsity Press): 346–51. Craig rightly observes that the 'force (of quantum gravitational cosmological models) in obviating the need for a Creator depends entirely on (i) the plausibility of a realist construal of such theories and (ii) a physically reductionistic understanding of time.' (*Ibid*, 348)

36. Hawking, *A Brief History of Time*, 174.
37. *Ibid*, 175.

Part Three

Living Creatures: The Buddhist Perspective

Shih Chao-Hwei

Abstract

This article utilises the principles of Buddhist doctrine to define life, and to introduce the characteristics, meanings, and prospects of living beings.

Creatures come in many varieties; mankind is just one among many. All creatures have similar natures. Egocentric emotions and intellects produce desire and vexation. Desire and vexation give rise to an assortment of 'karma', including the 'karma' of behavior, language, and consciousness. Good actions obtain happy rewards and evil actions obtain retributions of suffering. The circle of life and death revolves endlessly, and is unable to stop for even a moment.

Furthermore, of all creatures, human beings alone have three remarkable capabilities: rationality, morality, and will. Therefore humanity becomes the key to improving or debasing the quality of life. Depending on the three remarkable capabilities, humans may attain the Buddha's achievement.

Today abortion is being performed in excess. Therefore this article will look at the human embryo (fetus) to analyse whether it is the equivalent of a person? Does life begin with the combination of a sperm and an ovum? Can we rely on the scientific definition that human life begins after an embryo has grown fourteen days? Does an embryo have the perception of happiness or suffering while it is in its primary stages?

In the conclusion of this article, on the premise that all living beings are equal, the author expounds the essentials of life-protection, that is pratītya-samutpāda—madhyamā-pratipad (to follow the middle course, to accomplish to the best of one's ability).

This essay, divided into four sections, attempts to explicate the meanings of 'life' according to Buddhist principles.

1. Section I aims at giving a definition of 'life' and a succinct account of its characteristics, meanings and prospects according to Buddhism.
2. The purpose of Section II is to give an account of the common characteristics of all forms of life (that is, all kinds of living beings).
3. Section III offers an account of the value and specific characteristics of human beings.
4. Section IV focuses on the discussion, from the Buddhist perspective, of the ethical controversy relevant to human embryos. Due to the development of biotechnology, abortion has become increasingly convenient. People pay more attention to the utilisation of human embryos (foetus).

Definition

Life, in Buddhist terminology, is called *sattva*. It literally means things that are possessed of life, that is, creatures. Of course, it represents not only human beings but also all other kinds of living beings that are possessed of affection and consciousness.

> Master Yin Shun, in explaining 'creatures', points out that, Sattva symbolizes affection, wisdom and activity. According to this explanation, to say that a 'creature' has spiritual activity is the same as saying that they have a passion for life. All creatures, from ants to human beings, exist in every moment in the torrent of life, which has affection as its basis. Creatures have this inclination for affection, or the realization of affection, as the basis of life. However, due to the irrationality of their impulse and their propensity toward environment and self, they can hardly free themselves from these bondages in order to achieve the tranquillity of mind without burden.[1]

Creatures have a passionate attachment to their lives. This kind of attachment is called *atma-sneha* (ego desire) or 'attachment to self'. It becomes *mama-kara-sneha*, (attachment to what I have) when expanded in space. It is a kind of attachment to 'what I have' or 'what I belong to' (that is, 'attachment to surroundings'). Such a kind of attachment can be prolonged in time. It can instinctively give rise to a strong desire for the 'subsequent being' of life, a desire able to give life a rebirth immediately after its death. This cycle of death and rebirth revolves endlessly without cessation. We call this kind of attachment *punar-bhava-sneha* (attachment to one's life after death).

The principles of 'dependent-arising' and egocentrism

The occurrence of all phenomena is actually a process of the fusion, mutation and dispersion of cause-and-effect. The fusion of cause-and-effect gives rise to the phenomena. The mutation of cause-and-effect results in the change of phenomena. The dispersion of cause-and-effect causes the phenomena to disappear. This process of fusion, mutation and dispersion is called *pratitya-samutpada* (dependent-arising). Under the concept of dependent-arising, all phenomena are affected by cause-and-effect to change ceaselessly without rest. This is the principle of 'all products are impermanent'.

As all phenomena arise from the fusion of cause-and-effect, life cannot remain forever unchanged and exist independently. Therefore, there is no true 'self' at all. This is the principle of 'all phenomena are empty and selfless'. Under the mutation of cause-and-effect, everything does not only grow forever but also die forever. When something grows, it steps toward death at the same time. This is the principle of '*nirvana* is peace'.

Despite of the principles mentioned above, *atma-sneha* and *mama-kara-sneha* result in the formation of the mentality of *avidya* (lack of enlightenment) or *atna-moha* (self ignorance). To say that a person is in a state of self-ignorance is not the same as saying that he does not know anything at all. Rather, it means that he cannot experience the principles of dependent-arising, of everlasting change and of no self. The state of self-ignorance causes life to be possessed with a firm stubbornness, which regards ego as the centre of everything. Such a kind of stubbornness is called *atma-drsti* (self view). It also causes life to pay more attention to itself than to be concerned with others. This kind of behaviour is called *atma-mana* (self pride).

Vexation, action and suffering form a ring without beginning or end

With ego as their centre, attachment, view, pride and ignorance develop gradually. Such a development causes the three aspects of life—knowledge, affection and consciousness—to be greatly distorted. Therefore, life can hardly experience and comprehend the real, permanent nature of dependent-arising. As a consequence, life cannot help misconceiving as 'self' those physical and mental elements resulted from the fusion of cause-and-effect. This misconception has the effect that life becomes egocentric. It faces its situation and deals with other people and things with attachment, view, pride and ignorance. Besides, it also misconceives the impermanent nature of life and everything surrounding it as permanent. Under such a circumstance, life is encouraged to generate certain wrong expectations. It may wish itself to be immune from illness and death. It may wish other people would satisfy its desire. It may wish it could enjoy all kinds of happiness without any suffering. Once its wishes are not fulfilled, all kinds of suffering will naturally arise. All suffering, as mentioned in the canons, can be concluded into eight kinds: birth, old age, disease, death, association with the disliked, separation from the liked, not getting what one wishes and the uproar of the five aggregates. The first four kinds are suffering related to physiological processes. The fifth and sixth ones are suffering aroused by one's relationship with society and others. The seventh one is a result of one's relationship with one's surroundings. The last one acts as a conclusion of the substance of all different kinds of suffering. The uproar of the five aggregates relates to one's physical body and mental state, causing life to fall into the cycle of existence. Thus all kinds of suffering arise.

Creatures always misconceive impermanence as permanence, and no self as self. To face themselves and their surroundings with such attitude would do no good to their ignorance. On the contrary, their desire is intensified in prosperity and so is their hatred in adversity. Desire, hatred and ignorance constitute together as the root of worries, from which all kinds of worries (vexation) arise. These worries in return force life to commit all kinds of bad physical actions, bad verbal actions and bad mental actions, that is, behaviour, language and thinking in a negative sense. Even when good physical actions, good verbal actions and good mental actions have the chance to grow, they are unavoidably contaminated by 'attachment to self' and 'attachment to what I have'. Creatures thus are deprived of the chance to arrive at the realm of Purity. Under the principle of 'action and the appropriate result of action', creatures can acquire the fruit of happiness if they have committed good actions in their lives. Otherwise, they can only bring upon themselves the fruit of suffering.

Life is not without happiness. The practice in Buddhism is exactly a kind of teaching to direct us to avoid suffering and acquire happiness. The teaching can ultimately lead us to find an exit for life. However, if the creatures cannot give up the inappropriate attitude mentioned above, they still find themselves trapped in the emotion of worrying about worldly gains and losses even though they have already acquired the fruit of happiness. Under the influence of the mutation of cause-and-effect, the creatures' mood of happiness and the world of happiness in which they exist will change accordingly. The possibility of change compels those creatures who come short of understanding impermanence and no self to fall into endless worries. This kind of worry incurred by the lack of enlightenment is called 'suffering of change'. Therefore, from the perspective of Buddhism, the more one can curtail his desire and undertake altruistic business, the more one can enjoy the fruit of happiness. If one can reach the realm of completely understanding no self, one can definitely attest to the happiness of freedom—the kind of happiness acquired only when one is freed from being cast into the cycle of existence.

With ego as the centre, vexation, action and suffering form a ring without beginning or end. 'Attachment to self' is the motivating cause of the change of life. It enables life to have a rebirth immediately after its death. This cycle of death and rebirth is without cessation. The vexation and action brought forth by 'attachment to self' will in turn serve as the material causes, which are embodied in various forms of suffering and happiness. These material causes also contribute their effort to make possible the change of life. Generally, the forms can be classified into 'five migrators'—gods, human beings, hell beings, hungry ghosts and animals.[2] This chain of life is endless. Only when one has enough wisdom to understand 'the absence of self in 'dependent-arising', can one correct inappropriate attitudes like attachment, view, pride and ignorance and get rid of all worries in order to achieve freedom. The one who can reach such a realm is called *arhat* (demigod).

Criterion for moral concern: sentience

As mentioned above, Buddhism considers all creatures as 'life'. Human beings are not endowed with the divine nature of being made like gods. As made clear in Buddhist canons, human beings are possessed of a superior function (to be elaborated later) because they surpass other living beings in the aspects of knowledge, affection and consciousness. In spite of that, other kinds of living beings are not regarded as tools for the human beings to accomplish their goals. Therefore, divinity or rationality cannot be taken as a criterion to exclude other kinds of living beings, like animals, from our concern.

In some aspects, Buddhism comes close to the thinking of 'animal liberation' raised by Peter Singer. Singer makes use of sentience as the criterion for moral concern. He advocates, in abiding to utilitarianism, seeking the greatest utility for life, animals included. According to Buddhism, life has the extremely vigorous instinct of yearning after living and fearing death and that of questing for happiness and avoiding suffering. Therefore, as a life form possessed of moral perception, human beings should make use of sentience as a criterion to include into their moral concern for all sentient beings. It is as important that human beings should express their concern about those sentient beings from the standpoints of the sentient beings. This is why Buddhism adopts 'protection for living beings' as the spirit of its norms.

As egocentrism is an instinct of life, why should human beings have to show their concern about others? Why should they have to care about others' situations? The answers to these questions can be found in my writings: *Buddhism Ethics* and *Buddhism Normative Ethics*. In my books, I make use of three veins of reasoning to explain the answers in detail—'the way to achieve Buddhahood', 'relevancy in the phenomenon of dependent-rising' and 'equality in the nature of dependent-arising'.[3]

Common characteristics of life

Under the principles of dependent-arising, we can experience, even in the deepest thinking, that all creatures exist because of cause-and-effect. They lack the permanent substance that decides their own existence. In other words, all creatures are equal at the level of dharma. What make them different are the phenomena of characteristic, physiology, mentality and environment and others. The kinds of cause-and-effect that bring forth creatures vary from one to another. Consequently, it is not strange that there exists an immense diversity among creatures.

As mentioned above, 'protection for living beings' includes all creatures as the object of moral concern, not only human beings. With regards to the subject of expressing moral concern, we cannot help confining it to human beings. Only human beings are asked to abide by the teachings conveyed in Buddhist ethics. It is also because human beings can continuously elevate themselves in moral praxis. By means of their assiduous effort to break away from self-stubbornness and their practice of altruistic deeds, human beings can overcome personal desire and personal interest to sublimate humanity to achieve divine nature. This explains why only human beings can accomplish freedom and Buddhist nature. What makes them different from other living beings is exactly this superb value, which can be set off in moral praxis.

Buddhism takes all creatures as the object of its concern. Human beings can become the subject to express more concern. They are not chosen by Buddha to do so. Actually, it is due to the good actions or deeds they have committed in their previous life. Because of their good actions or deeds, they can enter a migrator state, as when they were cast into the cycle of existence after their death. Therefore they are possessed of certain superior conditions that other living beings have no access to. These conditions are not endowed by heaven. Neither do they arise without causes. Rather, they arise according to the dependent-arising principle. Moreover, all living beings stand the same chance to enter into migration in the same way, through the cause-and-effect generated by good actions. The right to enter a migrator is not a privilege assigned to certain specified living beings. Quite to the contrary, it opens a door for all living beings.

This essay, following Master Yin Shun's essay 'Humanity', introduces separately the characteristics common to human beings and other living beings and those that make human beings different from other living beings.4 Through this introduction, we can understand why we should take all creatures as the object of ethical praxis and confine the subject of this praxis only to human beings. As human beings, what are our advantages and weaknesses in undertaking ethical praxis? How can human beings make use of their advantages? How can human beings overcome their weaknesses? To answer these questions involves delving into Buddhist practice and deserves discussion in a separate essay.

Human beings are part of the collective of creatures, so they are apt to bear some common characteristics with other living beings. Among these characteristics, only three of them will be focused on in this essay.

All creatures depend on food
'Food', in Sanskrit *aharah*, means benefit and grow. Both human beings and other living beings, in order to prolong their lives, have to rely on the incessant supply of nutrition to sustain the growth of their body and mind. Buddha's saying serves as a reaction to the belief 'to achieve freedom by means of asceticism' advocated by his contemporary, Nigantha Nataputta. The fallacy of asceticism is discussed in my *Buddhist Ethics* (48–9). In the age of Buddha, those ascetic monks had themselves lived in hardship, thinking that by doing so they could get rid of the bondages of material desire and accomplish spiritual freedom. After his renunciation, Buddha tried practicing self-mortification for six long years. Later he found that such a practice is futile and unhelpful in accomplishing freedom. After that, he

accepted a supply of milk by a shepherdess to maintain his body. When he was in good condition, he accomplished Perfect Enlightenment under the *bodhi* tree. The ascetics laughed at him of accepting the milk, regarding such an act as unjustified. In this case, Buddha gave an account of the basic element for creatures to live—food. He further pointed out that food is an indispensable element for those who intend to accomplish freedom. In *Samyuttanikaya* Buddha says:

> There are four types of food that can benefit creatures. They make the living beings in the world imbibe them and thus grow up. Which four? They are (1) *kabaligkarahar*, (2) *phassakarahara*, (3) *mano sajcetanakarahara* and (4) *vijjanakarahara*.[5]

'Food' here does not refer to ordinary food only. It is used in a wider sense to signify everything that enables creatures not only to sustain and prolong their lives but also to enlarge their bodies and grow. There are four types of food.

The first food is *kabaligkarahara* (coarse food). *Kabaligkarahar* can also be translated as 'periodic food'. Usually we have several meals everyday. Creatures, especially those in the desire realm, need to have periodic food to sustain their lives. More than that, the food should be taken in fixed amounts at fixed times. Taking too much food makes one become ill. Taking too little food makes one feel hungry. The ascetics regard material supply as a hindrance to practice. They fail to know that periodic food can benefit one's body. More important, it can also benefit spirit indirectly. Only when one is in a good condition can he have a healthy spirit. Even though one is possessed with the ability to practice meditation, it still stands the possibility that he may die from practicing meditation too long without taking periodic food. The concentration in practicing meditation and the wisdom of understanding dependent-arising are the necessary conditions to accomplish freedom. However, if one is too weak in body and mind due to undernourishment, he can hardly achieve concentration and wisdom.

The second type of food is *phassakarahara* (food of touch). The six senses—sight, hearing, smell, taste, touch, and mental sense—have to develop into the six consciousnesses correspondingly in order to realise the six objects—visible form, sound, odor, taste, tangible object and phenomena. This process of realisation is called 'contact'. The harmonic fusion of sense, consciousness and object will give rise to a pleasant feeling, 'pleasant impression'. If the fusion is not in harmony, an unpleasant feeling will arise, 'unpleasant impression'. Food of touch mainly refers to pleasant impression—such as breath, massage, bath, sitting and sleeping, comfortable dwelling place. The feeling of happiness generated by pleasant impression can benefit life and promote health. As for unpleasant impression, such as fatigue after exercise or pain caused by injection or operation, it can also be considered as food of touch in that it can promote health and cure illness.

The third food is *mano sajcetanakarahara* (food of mental thought). Mental thought refers to desire and will, that is, hope. Hope is an extremely vital element for creatures to keep on living. If one has not the least intention to live, he will not be able to live. On the contrary, a strong desire to live often produces an unimaginable curing effect to patients with incurable diseases. Patients on the verge of death often prolong their life for a certain time in order to see their family or relatives for the last time. Moreover, it is not unusual to witness aged people suddenly lose their enthusiasm to work after retirement. They age faster and their health worsens quicker as they suddenly lose their hope. Whether one has food of mental thought or not can certainly cause him to behave in entirely different ways.

Master Yin Shun gives a further analysis in *Introduction to Buddhism*. Sometimes this desire and will is very minute. It is a kind of sub-consciousness. Although it does not appear very often, it is adamantine and violent. After one dies, one still desires a rebirth. This desire is called, as discussed above, *punar-bhava-trsna* in Buddhism. It is this kind of desire that makes possible the endless revolution of life and death. This desire can be expressed in other forms. Some may hope that they can enter the eternal heaven. Some may hope that their families can go on proliferating forever. The former is a religious desire while the latter a mundane one. All human beings hope that their families can keep on proliferating. Even animals bear with such a desire. For the creatures of lower class, their proliferation is made possible only because of their basic instinct rather than a precise conscious desire. For human beings, the motivation to have a proliferation of their families is quite different. The time for the children to be independent is comparatively longer. Before their independence, they have to rely on their families. The needs for living are complicated. For the human beings to grow up, they require the protection from and cooperation of the same specimen. Therefore, their desire of proliferation is much stronger. This motive to proliferate can also be counted as food of mental thought.[6]

The fourth food is *vijjanakarahara* (food of consciousness). *Vijja* does not refer only to consciousness but also sub-consciousness. In Buddhism it is called *ca*, which means the kind of sub-consciousness that grasps body and mind to correspond to ego. '*Soadanasya vijjana* gives rise to name and form.' This statement is a vital part of the dependent-rising principle concerning creatures.

'Name' refers to mind. 'Form' refers to matter. When used together, the two terms signify the mind and the body as a whole for creatures. Before it gets away from desire, *soadanasya vijjan* will not stop grasping. Once it leaves this mind and body, it immediately grasps another one. We can take as an example how a monkey jumps from a tree to another tree. After it loses hold of a branch, it grasps another branch at once. This function, that death of one stage will give rise to an embryo of mind and body of the next stage, is called *pratisamdhi samtati* (to feel an embryo and continue) in Buddhism.

To take human beings as an example, death is the beginning of another stage of life. Because of the grasp of *soadanasya vijjan*, there will be the fusion of sperm and ovum (that is, fertilisation). From then on, mind and body as a whole are given a shape. Due to the grasp and benefit of *soadanasy vijjana*, body and mind grow gradually in the mother's womb. After leaving the womb, body and mind as a whole continues to grow until it becomes an adult. Until the moment of death, *soadanasy vijjana* continues this process of grasping body and mind. It keeps on absorbing all beneficial materials into itself—'to make others become self,' to enable body and mind to become an energetic individual whole. Under such a circumstance, the process of metabolism proceeds naturally without cessation. Metabolism can enable different organs to operate smoothly to imbibe automatically all nutrition good for life (oxygen, water, sugar, fat, protein and so on) and get rid of those useless materials (carbon dioxide, stool, urine and sweat and so on). As to other harmful conditions, the nervous system and immunity of ours can take the responsibility to prevent, defend and eliminate those 'enemies'. It is because of the grasp of *soadanasy vijjana* that the body can grow and enlarge, without falling into decay. Once *soadanasy vijjana* gives up grasping, the body will become a corpse and fall into decay.

From the above discussion, it is evident that the four kinds of food are essential to the creatures in prolonging their lives of a stage. Among the four, food of mental thought and that of consciousness are the decisive factors for the prolongation of life of a stage and the endless revolution of life and death.

According to Buddhism, the lives of creatures can be divided into three realms, *trayo dhatavah*. They are *kamadhatu* (desire realm), *rupadhatu* (form realm) and *arupyadhatu* (formless realm). In desire realm there still exists sexual desire. Only a body deprived of desire can exist in form realm. Formless realm consists only of mind in contemplation. Creatures in desire realm require all four kinds of food. Creatures can exist in form realm only by means of meditation. Thus they are deprived of food of touch such as sex. They rely on meditation for food. However, they still cannot escape from the delicate food of touch like feeling well both physically and mentally. Even the creatures in form realm and formless realm, if they have not accomplished freedom, require food of mental thought like the will to live and food of consciousness like feeling an embryo to continue.

Egocentrism
Egocentrism is a characteristic common to all creatures and the root of their life and death. Following the discussion of the substance of life, an additional discussion of egocentrism is presented in this section.

All creatures are mutually dependent. Furthermore, the phenomena that constitute the elements of body and mind of creatures arise continuously one after another. They are not mutually exclusive. The phenomena arising are not permanent, independent or real. We can name these characteristics of phenomena as *asvabhava* (non-inherent existence) or *zunya* (void). Void in its highest sense does not mean 'nothingness'. In fact, it refers to the fact that all things, including the existence of the fusion of cause-and-effect, do not have what we may call their original self or real being.

However, in the course of the fusion of cause-and-effect, all creatures become individual entities. Separation exists between oneself and others. The reason is that the creatures are not enlightened and not able to be aligned with the nature of equality inherent in phenomena. This is also the reason why body and mind can exist as an individual entity. As an individual entity, a creature has deep-rooted egocentrism. Thus creatures of higher class have undergone an evolution. Various supply and transportation systems for their organs as well as the nervous system are developed. In Buddhism the properties ascribed to body and mind are broadly divided into five categories: *rupa-skandha* (form), *vedana-skandha* (feeling), *samjja-skandha* (discrimination), *samskara-skandha* (compositional factors) and *vijjana-skandha* (consciousness). They are usually referred as *pajcaskandhah* (five aggregates) in Buddhism. Form refers to the matter aspect of body and mind. Feeling refers to the function of receiving and feeling suffering and happiness. Discrimination refers to the function of forming concepts and language from images. Compositional factors refer to the function of making decisions and executing them. Consciousness refers to the function of the mind to govern all mental activities. The whole, in which the fusion of five aggregates takes place, appears to be united on the surface but is actually complicated inside. Egocentrism instinctually and strongly misconstrue the whole, where the five aggregates gather together, as a real, independent entity.

Whenever there is 'self', there is 'other'. Egocentrism causes creatures to be unable to treat themselves and others equally. It is often the case that creatures treat themselves better than they treat others. At the extreme, for the sake of their lives and the expansion of their interests, creatures will harm others. Because of egocentrism, creatures will unavoidably distort their understanding of the things happening in this world even though they intend to know those things. Buddhism makes use of the term *avidya* (ignorance or blindness) to name the kind of egocentrism caused by one's ignorance of the truth that dependent-arising is a non-inherent existence. Ignorance is the fundamental characteristic of all kinds of worries. In all activities of cognition contradictory to the mentioned truth, we can witness the involvement of ignorance in them.

From the root of worries, ignorance, egocentrism develop numerous kinds of worries. The three major kinds are attachment, view and pride. Some may add the prefix 'self' to them—*atma-sneha* (self attachment), *atma-drsti* (self view), *atma-mana* (self pride) and *atma-moha* (self ignorance), that is, *avidya*. Attachment, view, pride and ignorance are four kinds of *nivrtavyakrta*. The term is used to refer to things and actions that can be regarded as neither good nor evil. Egocentrism causes creatures to act according to their own instinct, so their actions are neutral. However, their actions may become a hindrance to the attainment of perfect wisdom and to the accomplishment of freedom. These actions may also develop further worries.

To enable the endless revolution of life and death, all creatures need to rely on the kind of attachment to life after death generated by egocentrism. The existence of a creature in a certain migrant is decided by the action-influence inspired by the creature. However, the good or evil actions committed are caused by various kinds of worries unfolded by egocentrism. Under such a circumstance, egocentrism decides directly the creatures' endless revolution of life and death by being cast into the cycle of existence. It also decides indirectly the suffering and happiness that the creatures come across in the process of being cast into the cycle as well as the migrators into which they are cast.

Desire of attachment
The root of attachment is attachment to self. We name it ego desire. Creatures always attach themselves to their lives. They can easily find excuses for their faults. This ego desire is the most fundamental and the strongest of a creature's ties to self. We call the tie between ego and self 'attachment to self'. Because of ego desire, all the things creatures do are for their own benefit, even to the extent where they have to sacrifice other creatures. The creatures do not only express a strong attachment to this life but also that of the next. Ego desire can be expanded to become 'attachment to what I have' or 'attachment to surroundings'. 'Attachment to what I have' is the kind of attachment expressed in one's deep concern and care of what one has or what one belongs to—body and mind, family members, hometown, country and religion. In spite of that, they do not care much about other people and their belongings. 'Attachment to surroundings' is a desire for external things and environment. To sustain body and mind necessitates the support of environment and the supply of external things. 'Attachment to self' drives the creatures, for the sake of maintaining their own bliss and happiness, to become attached to external things and environment.

The two most violent desires of attachment are food, on which one depends, and sex, by means of which one can proliferate. In Buddhism 'food' does not signify only ordinary kinds of food or drink but is used in a wider sense to refer to the four kinds of food as discussed above. Sex for human beings refers to sexual desire. Not all creatures are possessed of sexual desire (for example, creatures in form realm or formless realm). Even some creatures in desire realm are devoid of sexual desire, on the condition that they have accomplished practicing the meditation of form realm and formless realm. Meditation bears the function of freeing creatures from the bondages of desire. Another example can be found in a kind of lower class creature in the desire realm. This kind of creature reproduces by means of autogeny. As for hell beings and hungry ghosts, they do not have the least intention for any sexual desire since they are under severe suffering. As made clear by the explication, sexual desire can be considered as a common characteristic of most creatures, human beings included.

To take human beings as an example, since they differentiate themselves into male and female, a man and a woman need to couple each other for proliferation of descendents. Although babies born from sexual desire do not know what it is, they are not yet completely cut off from the potential desire of attachment. This state of attachment is described as *anusaya* in Buddhism. A*nusaya* is a kind of fundamental worry hidden deep in the heart and has only a very weak function. It begins to grow by following other creatures' actions. This explains why boys have somewhat of an Oedipus complex and girls an Electra complex. When they grow up, they are mature enough to initiate sexual desire. Marriage is a product of human civilisation to enable human beings to be satisfied with sexual desire.

Characteristics unique to human beings

The discussion of characteristics unique to human beings in this section is developed from the characteristics common to all creatures. The discussion begins with the negative aspects of humanity.

Negative qualities of humanity
Food, drink and sex are human beings' major desires. They bring great happiness to human beings. At the same time, they also bring great suffering to them in that the 'attachment to what I have' is usually expressed as possession and predation, acts that result in scarcity or destruction.

According to the nature of the conflicts, Buddhism divides conflicts mainly into two types—'conflict due to view' and 'conflict due to desire'. The former refers to a kind of conflict initiated due to different viewpoints. The latter refers to when one, in the process of satisfying his desires, clashes with others because of differing interests. For creatures, their conflicts are limited to conflicts of desire. In comparison to greed, vainglory, yearning for power and the accumulation of human wealth, other creatures' desires are much easier to satisfy. The conflict that arises from the desires of human beings is far more serious. Their desire, like a devil, expands limitlessly. What they plunder from other creatures are of numerous kinds, ranging from creatures' bodies to their hard labor. Some creatures may even become objects for enjoyment. A human being's goals go far beyond what they need for survival. Therefore, the tension of their conflicts due to desire is violent enough to push them down to the abyss of evil.

Conflicts of viewpoints exist only among human beings. They may quarrel among themselves without any compromise because of different opinions. Furthermore, they may also expand their opinions to become ideologies that may lead to a massive slaughter of people. Both the preaching of religions and the spread of ideologies begin with a good will, hoping to lead people to accept truth and to bring forth the greatest bliss. However, once a certain ideology becomes absolute, its supporters will insist what they advocate is the only truth. All other beliefs, to them, are heterodoxies. Thus, because of their fervor to save the world, the supporters will even kill all the people holding different beliefs from theirs. Only in human society can we find the kind of disaster of killing fellow members of the same community due to a conflict of views.

Animals are possessed of instinct to propagate, and towards the simple custom of the succession of generations. They need not come across the problem of differentiating good actions from evil ones because they lack the ability to reflect. They have no artificial restriction and emendation or adjustment of norms, which can be completed only by reflection, to follow. No wonder they do not have the sense of guilt that results from bad language or action. Therefore, attachment, view, pride and ignorance that act according to instinct cannot be considered as good or evil in Buddhism. This is why the Buddhists call those four elements *nivrtavyakrta* as discussed above.

These four elements act merely according to instinct. They are neither good nor evil. On the basis of this consideration, a cow that eats grass is not possessed of the merit of being a vegetarian. For the same reason, a tiger that eats a man does not commit an evil action by killing people. In spite of that, they cannot escape from being cast into the cycle of existence because they may become a hindrance to the attainment of perfect wisdom and the accomplishment of freedom. At the same time, they would not be elevated or downgraded to a certain migrator because their acts are committed merely according to instinct. Unlike animals, human beings commit good or evil actions according to their good or evil consciousness so they cannot avoid facing the fruition of suffering or happiness. Therefore, the crux of being elevated or downgraded to other migrators is possible in the world of human beings. On the one hand, human beings are capable of committing extremely evil actions that cause them to be sunken to the migrator of hell beings. On the other hand, by means of developing their knowledge, affection and consciousness to the highest extent, human beings can be rewarded with the fruition of entering into the migrator of human beings and that of gods. They may even be rewarded the achievement of accomplishing freedom and Buddhahood.

Superb qualities of human beings
Because of their developed knowledge, affection and consciousness, human beings become outstanding among the creatures. Their superb qualities, in Buddhism, are divided into three types.[7]

The first superb quality is the development of human intelligence. *Manas* can be translated as consciousness or mind. Human beings can differentiate all kinds of phenomena. They can remember the past, anticipate the future and realise the present. It is because their consciousness is possessed of the ability to think and contemplate. The highly developed conscious movements of human beings may cause them to commit sinful actions; but, on the other hand, it enables them to bring forth refined civilisation.

Among all the creatures, the thinking of human beings is the most highly developed. Modern scholars find out that, in the course of the evolution of human beings, the most obvious change of them is their skull capacity. Human brains became larger over time. They represent the development of human intelligence. Such a development is the crux for them to develop their biological nature into a cultural one. As a result of the evolution of human brains, human beings come into possession of powerful memory and thinking ability, which enable them to develop social organisations, to invent and produce weapons and to make use of language and words. The cultural nature of human beings is accordingly developed and changed.[8] Frankly speaking, the progress of human civilisation is the consequence of the human accumulation of past experiences to inspect the present and develop the future.

According to Buddhism, creatures are possessed of inborn wisdom. Bees can make honey. Ants can make a nest. Spiders can make webs. Their ability to do so is a kind of inborn intelligence. Only the inborn wisdom of human beings can be developed into higher intelligence after learning. Besides inborn wisdom, there is also a kind of wisdom that can be acquired through assiduous practice. Animals may also be possessed of a little bit of such wisdom. Yet their control is far less than that of human beings. On the basis of their instinct, human beings learn gradually. They can learn different kinds of language, knowledge and techniques to invent things or systems for their benefit. This capacity to learn is exclusively a characteristic of human beings.

The kind of powerful memory and thinking ability unique to human beings is exactly the foundation of their realisation of ethics. Buddhism even makes use of it to instruct nirvana wisdom that enables human beings to seek the mystery of human life and to quest for complete emancipation.

The second superb quality is that of the self-awareness of morality. According to Buddhism, it is because of their possession of *hri* and *apatrapya* that differentiates human beings from animals. As stated in *Vijnaptimatratasiddhi-sastra*:

> What is *hri*? It is the nature of *hri* to rely on the effort of self and Buddhism to revere virtuous, learned persons and to respect Buddhism. Its function is to offer solution to those without

hri and terminate evil actions . . . What is *apatrapya*? It is the nature of *apatrapya* to rely on various mundane efforts—morality, law, public opinion and so on—to despise cruel persons and dispel evil actions. Its function is to offer a solution to those without *apatrapya* and terminate evil actions.[9]

Hri is to respect truth and self. *Apatrapya* is to respect public opinion, law and custom. *Hri* is self-disciplined. *Apatrapy* is externally-disciplined. *Hri* is an act of approaching goodness. *Apatrapya* is an act to dispel evil. The inner mindfulness of goodness and the external norms as well bear the same function to terminate evil actions. To be sure, this driving force can also enable human beings to force themselves to approach goodness. Only when one is possessed of *hri* and *apatrapya*—the self-awaresness of approaching good and getting away from evil—can one be qualified as a human being. Of course, dogs also have the virtue of protecting their masters faithfully. Cats may have placid, elegant appearance. However, the dogs' virtue and the cats' appearance are different from human virtues generated from self-awareness.

Human beings can differentiate right from wrong and good from evil. Sometimes, they are prevented from performing good deeds because of the strong influence of worries. They may even be driven to commit evil actions. Yet they will somehow feel uneasy. Such a kind of feeling is caused by the influence of *hri* and *apatrapya*. Gangsters and murderers, because of being 'polluted' by environment and social conduct, gradually become numb in self-awareness and do not have any sense of uneasiness in face of all the evil actions they have committed. However, there still exists the possibility for them to repent of what they have done and to strive for reform, once the cause-and-effect is mature and the mind of *hri* and *apatrapya* emerge. We can see prisoners who are sentenced to death, unwilling to recollect their sinful life, are willing to donate their organs in order to contribute their last effort to society.

As discussed above, other creatures act according to their own instinct. They can hardly avoid coming into conflict with others for seeking food and companionship. As they are driven by basic instinct, they lack the sense of self-awareness. Therefore, they will not suffer grave degeneration. This is why hell beings, hungry ghosts and animals seldom degenerate because of committing evil actions. On the contrary, human beings are different. As they are possessed of the moral sense of self-awareness, they know what *hri* and *apatrapya* are. Or they may commit evil actions purposely, without feeling any sense of *hri* and *apatrapya*. Human beings—especially those who follow Buddhist teachings—would suffer degeneration when they degenerate. They would also try their utmost to advance if they intend to advance. Even when they suffer degeneration, they can still generate the force of dispelling evil and approaching good so as to repent and move away from evil. This is a human characteristic. It explains why human beings become the crux of the elevation and degradation in five migrators.

Morality comes from self-awareness. It is not the instinct whereby they cannot help doing it. It is the thought that, though we have the choice of not doing it, we have to do it; otherwise, we would feel uneasy. This brief explanation evidences the value of morality. As to moral conduct without thought, it can only be regarded as the fruition of morality. The virtue of creatures in the migrator of gods is far more excellent than that of human beings. Yet we can still witness more of their degeneration than their strife for advance. Their moral conduct is inspired by the goodness they attained in the former existence. Besides, there is no cause-and-effect to induce them to commit sinful actions. Quite different from creatures in the migrator of gods, human beings have to try their best to stand firm, to accept suffering and to dispel evil if they want to abide to moral conduct. Obviously, it is more difficult for human beings to abide to moral conduct than the creatures in the migrator of gods.

Human beings can realise and differentiate the various kinds of relationships existing between father and son, elder brother and younger brother, husband and wife, themselves and their relatives and friends, and teacher and student. Because there is the sense of *hri* and *apatrapya* in them, human beings can establish appropriate ethical norms and try their utmost to have sexual intercourse within the restriction of ethical norms and to avoid incest and adultery. To be sure, there are limitations to having family as the base of ethics and morality. Nevertheless, the kinds of relationships existing in a family can still be regarded as the beginning of human morality. The order of the various kinds of personal relationships signifies that human beings maintain a more intimate relationship with some and a less intimate one with others. With the most intimate relationship as the centre, the order of the kinds of personal relationships radiates from more intimate relationships to the least intimate one—from family to clan to hometown to country and then to all living things. This is the Confucians' idea of 'starting with a close relationship with family, then enlarging it to be kind to all people and finally to love all things'.[10]

The third superb quality is the perseverance of mind. In Buddhism the world in which we exist is called *sahalokadhatu*. *Saha* means 'endure', 'able to endure', and 'can be endured'. The dwelling place of creatures able to endure all kinds of suffering is called *dhatu*. Human beings exceed all other creatures in their ability to endure hard work. Once human beings are aware that what they do is meaningful, they will endure without hesitation whatever difficult situation they encounter.

'*Sattva*', which can be translated as 'a passion for life', is another name for creatures. The word bears with it the signification of 'intrepid' and 'fierce'. In a modern sense, it means 'full of life-force'. In Buddhist Scriptures, *sattva* is compared to the hardness of diamond. It is to say that the ambition of creatures is as hard as diamond, going ahead bravely without looking back. The vitality of human beings is of the supreme one. 'Diligence relies on desire of wish which in turn relies on faith.' Instinct is not the sole cause that enables human beings to become fierce and intrepid. The faith that one is aware of gives rise to desire, and desire to devotion and diligence. It is this kind of devotion and diligence that enables one to generate dauntless determination and perseverance to endure suffering and hardship. One's potentiality thus can be brought to play to the full to attain his goal. Of course, human beings very often abuse the desires of wishes. In this case, they may adopt whatever means they can in order to achieve their ambition. However, such an astounding will-force is at the same time indispensable to those who intend to pursue self-sacrifice and altruistic Buddhist practice.

From humanity to Buddhahood

The three superb qualities of human beings discussed above will emerge when one's knowledge, affection and consciousness are brought into play in fullness. In these three aspects—development of intelligence, self-awareness of morality and persistence of will, human beings are superior to all other kinds of creatures, even those in the migrator of gods. Therefore, human beings should make use of these advantages and seek advance.

There is a hint of Buddhahood within the three superb qualities of human beings. If one can expand and purify theses qualities, he can also become a buddha. A buddha is necessarily possessed of three characteristics—great wisdom, great compassion and great sublimity. Great wisdom refers to the correct and perfect enlightenment accomplished by a buddha. It is a kind of wisdom accomplished when a buddha is still in the category of creators, by means of gradually purifying fallacies and nourishing purifying wisdom. Great compassion refers to a buddha's sympathy for all creators. It is a kind of sympathy expressed in identifying with the subjects. Such a kind of sympathy can only be accomplished through the purification of ones' strong inclination to the attachment to self and the attachment to what he has or what he belongs to. Great sublimity is a characteristic that differentiates a buddha from creatures. It is a kind of sublimity unique only to buddhas. Great sublimity consists of ten forces of a buddha and four fearlessnesses.[11]

In Buddhist Scriptures, a buddha is often praised as the 'lion's roar'. The figure of speech means that Buddhist teachings can subdue all other kinds of heterodox sayings without defeat, just as a lion's roar can terrify all other animals. The kind of fearlessness is not only found in Buddha's teachings but also in his actually taking the great burden, with the spirit of fearlessness resulted from his great sublimity and great bravery, to seek salvation for the creatures. This kind of fearlessness is a result of his accomplishment of going through Buddhist practice, a kind of practice characterised by great wisdom and great compassion.

The ability of human beings is limited however. Buddhism does not place its emphasis on external redemption. On the contrary, it teaches human beings how to enhance and glorify their ability and character.

To say that Buddha awakens creatures under a delusion is the same as to say that Buddha gives help to them. He teaches them how to overcome the sense of powerlessness brought forth by limitations by undertaking practice to develop or strengthen the three kinds of superb ability and character. That Buddha regards it is possible for human beings to go directly from humanity to Buddhahood is a great affirmation of the unlimited potential of the subject of actions.

A discussion of the status of embryos

Life cast into the cycle of existence can come to the human world only in one of the four forms: the viviparous, the oviparous, the water born or the metamorphic. The viviparous have to be nurtured inside the mother's body and come out of it only when they are mature enough. The oviparous are nurtured in the mother body for a period of time and then egested outside of it. They emerge from eggs only when the process of incubation is completed. The water born come into shape after the fertilisation of ova outside the mother body. Those creatures, which resort to parthenogenetic propagation, also belong to the water born. The metamorphic do not need to undergo fertilisation but come out suddenly according to the influence of their actions in previous life. Most of them can be found in the migrator of gods or that of hell beings.

Due to sexual discrimination, women's liberation and development and research in the life sciences, induced abortion becomes more and more abused. The research on stem cells can be taken as one of the examples of such an abuse. There are four major ways to obtain multi-functional stem cells for research: (1) to obtain embryo tissues after women have miscarriages or induced abortions; (2) to obtain superfluous embryos after ectogenesis; (3) to obtain embryos produced by means of the transfer of cell nuclei from a human body and (4) to obtain embryos produced out of gametes donated for the purpose of research. Except for the third way, the other three ways are apt to be accused of seizing the lives of embryos. An investigation of the ethical meaning of human embryos and the ethical controversy about induced abortion, according to the viewpoint of Buddhism, will be presented below.

The controversy over the status of embryos
Can an embryo be regarded as a human being? Does it have the completed form of a human being? Should it be included, in law, under the protection of human rights? Regarding these issues, religionists and scientists bear entirely contradictory views.

According to the viewpoint expressed clearly in Genesis, God creates human beings, making them in his image. Therefore, human beings are endowed with an incomparable 'divinity' that other animals are devoid of. Since human beings are touched by 'divinity', any medical treatments resorting to terminating human lives artificially are totally prohibited by the Vatican, whether it is through abortion, euthanasia or the screening of embryos during artificial insemination. However, when the mentioned measures are applied to animals, the Vatican does not raise any objections in that such applications are not involved in an infringement of 'divinity'. Following this line of argument, if it is proved that 'an embryo is a human being', then its divinity is beyond doubt. Similarly, if the statement cannot be proved, then embryos can only be regarded as animals, and the killing of them will not involve an infringement of 'divinity'.

Other than identifying the uniqueness of human beings from the theological viewpoint of creation, non-Christians opposing the utilisation of embryos may resort to teleology to prove the existence of intrinsic value unique to human beings. As they claim, human beings are the ends but not the tools in that they are born with rationality and its accompaniment—moral awareness. They are moral agents. (In fact, it is not difficult to consider this claim as another view of 'divinity'.) However, such a claim needs to have the belief that 'an embryo is a human being' as its presumption.

However, it is hard to say if embryos can be included into human beings with moral awareness. The argument about moral awareness, as pointed out by Peter Singer, father of animal liberation, can also be applied to infants, mentally retarded people, or those suffering from Alzheimer's disease.[12] In following the logic of their argument, not all supporters of teleology will stand firm in opposing the utilisation of embryos. The discussion evidences that Christians are more consistent in insisting their opposition against the utilisation of embryos because they include all human beings into the scope of 'divinity'.

Supporters of the law of utilitarianism in teleology—to seek the greatest benefit for the most people—may come at quite diversified results in the controversy over 'animal rights'. On the one hand, we can have viewpoints like Peter Singer's: the affirmation of equality between animals and human beings, and the resolute opposition against the utilisation of animals. On the other hand, other supporters agree to utilise animals for the sake of benefiting the most people. Similarly, in the face of controversy over the stem cells of embryos, they can agree, following the argument in teleology, to seek the most benefit by protecting embryos. On the contrary, following the same argument, they could also agree to utilise embryos in order to benefit the most patients. To put into concrete quantification 'the greatest benefit to the most people' for comparison and reference, at the technical level, is extremely difficult.

Scientists doing research on stem cells of embryos and even foetuses, on the basis of liberalist viewpoints and biological consideration, would definitely deny that embryos are to be regarded as 'human beings'. The reason is that they cannot be seen to have human form yet so they should not have the right to enjoy the same moral protection that those with human form do. Opponents refute such an argument from the perspectives of 'potential' and 'continuity'. They contend that fertilised ova, at the moment of fertilisation, have already acquired the potential to develop continuously without cessation and to grow up to become human beings. On the ground of this contention, they should be granted the right to enjoy the protection of human dignity. This contention, however, still cannot succeed in persuading those in favor of the utilisation of embryos to give up their standpoint. For the development of embryos to become human beings necessitates the assistance of numerous conditions. Chen Ying-chien uses a metaphor to explain the case:

> Every citizen stands a possibility to become a president . . . but not everyone can enjoy the numerous kinds of special protection as a president does. Every student of law stands a possibility to become a judge or even a grand justice. However, in the process of his becoming a grand justice, he needs to meet with many conditions.[13]

Chen's logic of explanation bears a similar logic to the statement: Human beings are possessed of the potential to achieve Buddhahood, but not everyone is possessed of Buddha's mysterious reward body adorned with achieved virtue.

The Warnock Committee in England suggests that embryos can be utilised for research within a fortnight of the fertilisation of ova since the development of the embryos then is still at the diploblastic stage (the pre-embryo stage). Embryos at this stage are only biological cells. They are devoid of nervous system and cerebrum so they lack the senses and feelings that enable one to have the sense of morality unique to human beings. To utilise embryos at the diploblastic stage produced by external fertilisation for research and clinical treatment, therefore, should not be regarded as an act opposed to ethical morality. This viewpoint has been generally accepted by scientists all over the world.[14]

The status of the embryo from the Buddhist viewpoint
Religions (including both Catholicism and Buddhism) generally regard the moment that an ovum is fertilised as the starting point of the birth of a new life. The destruction of, under such a circumstance, means the killing of a new life. Therefore, the separation, the research and the application of embryo stem cells acts contradictory to ethical morality. With regards to this issue, Buddhism is able to lay aside the controversy of whether an embryo is a human being, and adopt the notion that 'all creatures are equal' to defend its standpoint. It can emphasise that, whether an embryo is a human being or not, once it is a life, the utilisation of it is an act to commit the moral evil of killing.

Is it right that an embryo within a fortnight of fertilisation need not be regarded as a life? Is it right that an archenteron nurtured outside the body need not be regarded as a life? When is the starting point of the life of an embryo? Can it be fixed on the fifteenth day after fertilisation? If the answer is positive, it is just like fixing brain death as the ending point of a life. The act of fixing the starting point and the ending point of a life is deliberately designed to operate in coordination with medical technology. No wonder the act incurs a widespread controversy.

From the viewpoint of Buddhism, the ego desire and the influence of actions in self induced life to undergo many stages of birth. This phenomenon is called 'flowing and returning' or 'cycle of existence'. Attachment refers to the ego desire. It is a kind of deep-rooted and obstinate attachment to self. This attachment to self is the primary motive for a life to undergo a birth. The actions or deeds committed by a life without beginning are countless. However, those mature deeds will become the secondary motive for a life to undergo a birth, deciding the form in which a life is born and the migrator into which it is cast. In other words, ego desire is the motivational cause and the influence of actions is the material cause.

The starting point of a life, as stated in Buddhist Scriptures, begins at the moment when the fusion of a sperm and an ovum takes place. The issue of when a life begins is explicated in detail in *Muulasavraastivaada Vinaya*, *Maharatnakuta Sutra* and *Yogacarya Bhumi Sastra*.[15] A summary of the account in these three Scriptures is given here for the convenience of discussion.

For normal gamogenesis, a female is pregnant only when all three causes coexist: paternal cause, maternal cause and the appeal to have a child. As to parthenogenesis, like amoeba, paramecium or the technique of cloning, the coexistence of the three causes is not a necessary condition. A whole and individual new life can be produced directly through the division of a body or the transfer of cell nuclei from a human body.

For normal gamogenesis, when there is the coexistence of the three causes, creatures ready to enter the embryos will see, in *antara-bhava* (the intermediate state of existence between death and reincarnation),[16] their parents (either human beings or all kinds of animals) having sexual intercourse. At this moment, a desire of coming close to their parents will be generated inside those creatures. At first, an illusion is generated inside them when they see their parents' sperms and ova. They by then will regard illusion as reality. They do not know that it is their parents who are having sexual intercourse. Instead, they think that they are having sexual intercourse with their parents. Their illusion induces them to generate the sensuous craving for attachment. If they are going to be born as female, they will have sensuous craving for having intercourse with their fathers and getting rid of their mothers. On the contrary, if they are going to be born as male, they will have sensuous craving for having intercourse with their mothers and getting rid of their fathers. The account here may offer an explanation of where the Electra complex and Oedipus complex come from.

Having such a sensuous craving for attachment, creatures ready to enter embryos can only see the partner they want to have intercourse with. Therefore, they will come closer and closer to their parents until they can see only their parents' reproductive organs but not their whole bodies. There they are captured. In other words, they enter the wombs.

When the father and mother reach their climax, each of them will release a drop of dense pure blood, that is sperm and ovum. The two drops after fusion, the fusion of the sperm and ovum, will stay in the mother's womb to become one, just like a cooked meal is congealed. By that moment, the intermediate state of existence between death and reincarnation will come to an end. The consciousness of those creatures has already stayed in the continuity of the bond of rebirth. A new stage of life has by then begun. The period of the first seven days after the moment of fertilisation is called *kalala*. From then on, due to the function of the embryo and 'all organs and the four great seeds' (the multi-functional stem cells prior to their separation into specific systems and organs) accompanying it, roots (organs) like eyes will develop one by one.

Kalala arises from the mutual dependence of *rupa* (matter), *citta* (mind) and *caitasa* (the attributes of the mind). This mutual dependence enables the embryo to be immune from decay. Matter and mind coexist and go through all situations together. At the same time, they grow up and enlarge equally. Obviously, *kalala* is the earliest abode of the mind and its contents. The moment when fertilisation takes place, the mind and its contents already existed. This moment, therefore, can be regarded as the starting point of a new stage of life.

A creature entering into an embryo undergoes eight stages in the womb. An elaboration of the eight stages can be found in *Yogacarya Bhumi Sastra*:[17]

1. *Kalala*: The term can be translated as congelation and smoothness. It refers to the first seven days after fertilisation.
2. *Arbuda*: The term can be translated as pimples. It refers to the period within the second seven days (fourteen days) after fertilisation. At this time, the shape of the embryo is like a pimple. (Kalala and arbuda are periods within fourteen days after fertilisation, which is the time limit to legally obtain the stem cells from embryos.)
3. *Peshi*: The term can be translated as the condensation of blood or tender meat. It refers to the period within the third seven days (twenty-one days) after fertilisation. In this period, the shape of the embryo is like the condensation of blood.
4. *Ghana*: The term can be translated as congelation and thickness. It refers to the period within the fourth seven

days (twenty-eight days) after fertilisation. The shape of embryo becomes firm. It is possessed of body and consciousness. The eyes, ears, nose and tongue have not yet developed.
5. *Prashakha*: The term refers to the period within the fifth seven days (thirty-five days) after fertilisation. The lump of meat begins to grow. The limbs and the physical body begin to be seen.
6. The stage of hair and claws: This refers to the period within the sixth seven days (forty-two days) after fertilisation. In this period, hair and claws can be seen to appear.
7. The stage of roots: This refers to the period within the seventh seven days (forty-nine days) after fertilisation. The embryo is possessed of organs like eyes, ears, nose and tongue.
8. The stage of form: This refers to the period after the eighth seven days (fifty-six days) after fertilisation. The growth of the body is completed.

If the creatures entering into the embryos happen to be human beings, they will stay in their mothers' wombs for two hundred and twenty-six days. By that time the growth of the embryos is completed. After that, they continue to stay in their mother's wombs for four more days before they are given birth. This is the perfect way for embryos to stay in the wombs. The birth of babies that stayed in the wombs for only eight to nine months can also be regarded as perfect. However, it is not extremely perfect. The birth of babies staying in the wombs for only six to seven months is a kind of premature birth. It cannot be regarded as perfect. There may also be some deficiencies in their health.

As ordinary people often obstinately attach to themselves, what they have and what belongs to them, a sense of self-pride will certainly generate in them. As a consequence, they will place more emphasis on themselves than on others. Therefore, the saints believe that, due to one's self-stubbornness, different kinds of suffering will occur in his life. As to creatures that are still in embryo form, they would only have the feeling of *aduhkhasukha-vedana*, the state of experiencing neither pain nor pleasure because their sensory organs for sensing suffering and happiness have not been developed yet.[18] In this respect Buddhism and medical science bear the same view. One can have the ability to sense suffering or happiness only when the systems and sensory organs in an embryo have fully developed and operate in coordination with causes and effects in the environment that bring forth those feelings.

Although it is made clear in Buddhism Scriptures that embryos at the earliest stage are not possessed of the ability to sense suffering or happiness, it does not mean that the utilisation of embryos needs not be considered as an act of killing. (Can embryos be regarded as human beings? Are they possessed of the intrinsic value of human beings? We can lay aside the controversy over these issues here for a moment.) People in a coma are also unable to sense suffering or happiness; however, to terminate their lives is still considered committing the evil action of killing. The destruction of embryos is of no different.

The dilemma that ethical choice faces
Following the above explication, the Buddhist viewpoint of embryo life can be summarised as follows. A specific stage of life of the viviparous arises from the coexistence of paternal cause, maternal cause and parent-child cause. The immediate cause for creatures entering into embryos is their own sexual desire. From the Buddhist viewpoint,

sexual desire is neither good nor evil. However, it can act as a hindrance to attaining truth. Sexual desire comes from ego desire and ignorance. On the basis of this viewpoint, we can hardly prove that there is a touch of 'divinity' in human lives. Are the lives of embryos possessed of any sense of purposefulness, not just that of instrumentality? The answer is undoubtedly positive. The expectation of an embryo to live on can no longer be counted only as the subjective wish of father and mother. Rather, a stronger expectation comes from the instinct of self-attachment of the creature entering into the embryo.

Self-attachment can still exert strong influence even if the self is in the state of experiencing neither pain nor pleasure. It enables life to undergo the continuity of the bond of rebirth. It also enables the embryo in the womb to maintain the mutual dependence between matter and mind and to remain in a state of growing and enlarging, without falling into decay. Destroying embryos is sure to be less able to arouse a sense of empathy in human beings than killing animals, since people can hardly witness the destruction themselves and have no way to identify themselves with the embryos.

Because of the reason mentioned above, Buddhism is forced to face a dilemma. Nowadays, medical science utilises animals for experiment in a large scale. The fate of the animals utilised for experiment is so miserable that it can easily arouse the sympathy of human beings. The research on the stem cells of embryos may therefore be considered as an alternative so as to decrease the demand of animals utilised for experiment. Such a kind of message naturally forces Buddhism, which strongly advocates the belief of not killing any creatures, to face a dilemma in making an ethical choice.

How can Buddhist followers, who believe in the equality of all creatures rather than the 'divinity' of human beings, make an ethical choice?[19] Is it better to sacrifice the embryos at the earliest stage, as they are not able to sense and feel? Or, is it better to sacrifice the animals? However, they are real and lively. They are able to sense. They can also wear different kinds of expression according to the pain and joy they sense.

To be sure, Buddhist followers adhering strictly to the discipline of not killing would choose not to sacrifice embryos or animals. To sacrifice either of them is immoral. The intrinsic value of life, including the life of embryos and that of animals, does not come from 'divinity' as claimed in theology. Neither does it come from its rationality or self-awareness of morality. Rather, it comes from the irreplaceable subjectivity of each life itself. No life form, animals included, would allow others, in order to achieve their own ends, to take it as an instrument or to force it to sacrifice itself involuntarily. On the basis of this consideration, the mentality of Buddhist followers is inclined to abide to the obligation of not killing even one innocent creature.

Conclusion: The practice of following the middle course

As discussed above, the Buddhist viewpoint of life is built on the principle of dependent-arising. On the one hand a creature has to face the impermanent change of life and death. On the other hand, there does not exists an independent self. If one does not have a thorough understanding of impermanence and selflessness, various kinds of sadness and worries, as a consequence of the flowing and returning of vexation, action and suffering, would naturally occur in his life. If one can undertake more altruistic deeds without selfish-ness, his life can enjoy more bliss in. If one can have a thorough understanding of impermanence and selflessness, his life can enjoy the bliss of accomplishing perfect freedom.

Under the principle of dependent-arising, all creatures are mutually dependent on others and equal in *dharma*-nature. As they are possessed of the sense of perception, they will similarly intend to approach happiness and life, and get away from suffering and death. Therefore, we need to consider the benefit of all kinds of life (not just the life of human beings) on the basis of equality. Passively, people can avoid killing any creatures. Actively, they can endeavor to protect them.

Whether embryos can be regarded as human beings is still subject to controversy. However, it is definite to say that they are living beings. For the same reason, induced abortion should be avoided.

The Buddhist viewpoint of life respects life's instinct to approach life and to get away from death. This is why followers of Buddhism place emphasis on the action of protecting life in practice. However, it is impossible for lives to avoid hurting others or being hurt. In reality, people are often forced, among all kinds of harmfulness, to choose a less harmful one. People may be forced to choose between continuing to utilise animals for experiment and allowing restricted research on the stem cells of embryos. What is their choice, if they are forced to choose either the animals or the embryos? People are hard put to make a choice even though they take into consideration the perspective of emotion. On the basis of empathy, is it possible for them to entirely neglect the numerous patients in need, who can sense suffering and happiness? How about those who take part in physical experiments? How about the miserable situation in which animals are utilised for experiments? If we put deep thought into these questions, should we defend, allowing no conciliation, the embryos at the earliest stage, which are incapable of sensing suffering or happiness?

The discipline of not killing can be taken as another example for our discussion. It is Buddha's subjective wish not to have any creatures killed. However, can this discipline be carried out completely in reality? Even those Buddhist disciples, who adhere strictly to the discipline of not killing, cannot avoid killing germs and parasites when they breathe, drink, eat or receive medical treatment. Even those who abide strictly to vegetarianism cannot prevent farmers from killing creatures when they plant their vegetables and fruit, when they open up barren lands for farming and when they spray pesticides. Even in a situation they can exercise their free will, Buddhist disciples with moral ideals still cannot completely avoid killing. In the face of society and the benefits of different groups, the room for one to exercise his free will in a public sphere is much smaller.

Buddhist disciples with moral ideals, even though they cannot completely avoid killing, should persist in devoting the rest of their effort to protecting life. In the public sphere, should Buddhist disciples give up the rest of their influence once the enactment of laws or the adoption of policies cannot completely meet their ideal? When encountering public issues, what we should choose is not the moral mysophobia of non-intervention but forcible intervention. Though the laws enacted about animal protection may be far from our ideal, we should not give up the chance of exerting even a little bit of influence. It is better for us to affect the quality of the laws gradually and slowly with our merciful ideal of not killing than to give up our effort in doing so entirely.

Obviously, at the level of ideal, we can stick fast to the norm of not killing, allowing no discount of it. However, at the level of praxis, Buddhism needs to have a philosophy of action. Even Buddha is not exempt. On the one hand, he insists on not killing. On the other hand, due to the restriction of begging alms, he accepts the three kinds of 'clean' flesh—when a monk has not seen the creature killed, has not heard of its being killed for him, and has no doubt thereon.

This is the wisdom of the practice 'to follow the middle course', which can be taken as a philosophy as action. I once gave it a definition: Under finite cause-and-effect conditions, we make the comparatively best choice without consideration of our own interest. Under the principle of dependent-arising, there exists a continuity of life and death without cessation. In encountering such a phenomenon, if one intends to put into practice the ideal of life protection, he needs to abide to the practice 'to follow the middle course' as the principle of praxis. To try one's best to achieve the comparatively best effect is the principle of praxis to protect life in reality.

End Notes

1. Master Yin Shun, *Introduction to Buddhism* (Taipei: Zheng wen Press, 2003), 43–4.
2. In *Vātsīputrīyas*, the five migrators are enlarged to become six migrators by including the category of demigod. The classification of six migrators becomes popular later for *Mahayana*.
3. Shih Chao-hwei, *Buddhism Ethics*, third edition (Taipei: Fa Chieh, 1998), 75–86; *Buddhism Normative Ethics* (Taipei: Fa Chieh, 2003), 84–93.
4. Master Yin Shun, 'Humanity' in *Buddha in the World* (Taipei: Shui Shang Hang Press, 1956), 75–97. My discussion in this section is an elaboration of Master Yin Shun's essay. The order of the headings in that essay has been changed for the sake of the development of my discussion here.
5. *Samyuttanikaya*, Book 15, volume 2 (Taisho edition), 101.
6. Yin Shun, *Introduction to Buddhism* (Taipei: Zheng Wen Press, 2003), 72.
7. For the division, see *Abhidharma-mahavibhasa-sastra*, Book 172, volume 27 (Taisho edition), 867. For the explanation of the three types of qualities, see Master Ying Shun's 'Humanity' and 'The Path for Human Beings to Accomplish Buddhahood', in *Buddha in The World* (Taipei: Shui Shang Hang Press , 1956) 88–94 and 132–3. See also *The Way to Accomplish Buddhahood*, annotated edition, 48–9 and *Introduction to Buddhism Dharma* (Taipei: Zheng wen Press,1982) 50–4.
8. Chuang Ying-chang *et al*, editors, *Cultural Anthropology*, Book 1 (Taipei: National Open University Press, 1991), 100.
9. *Vijnaptimatratasiddhi-sastra*, Book 6, volume 31 (Taisho edition), 29.
10. The Former Part of 'Jin Xin', in *Meng Zi*, 45.
11. The 'ten forces of a buddha' is used to subdue external devils in order to enjoy peace and stability both physically and spiritually. They are (1) knowledge of sources and non-sources, (2) knowledge of actions and their fruitions, (3) knowledge of the divisions of the eighteen constituents, (4) knowledge of varieties of inclinations, (5) knowledge of superior and non-superior faculties, (6) knowledge of the paths leading to all forms of cyclic existence and solitary peace, (7) knowledge of the concentrations, liberations, and meditative absorptions, and knowledge of others' afflictions and others' non-contamination, (8) knowledge remembering earlier lives, (9)

knowledge of death, transmigration and birth and (10) knowledge of contaminations and their extinction. The four fearlessnesses represent the absolute confidence in performing deeds that can benefit both self and others. They are (1) fearlessness with respect to asserting that I am completely and perfectly enlightened, (2) fearlessness with respect to asserting that the contaminations have been extinguished, (3) fearlessness with respect to asserting that the contaminations have been extinguished and (4) fearlessness with respect to teaching that the obstructions are to be ceased.

12. Peter Singer, *Animal Liberation*, Chinese edition (New York: Ecco, 1996) 64–5.
13. Chen Ying-chien, 'The Restrain of the Research on the Stem Cells of Human Embryos', in *Essays of The Third International Conference of Life Ethics* (Taiwan: National Central University Press, 1991) H-I-11
14. Chiu Hsiang-hsing, 'Several Ethical Issues of the Research on the Stem Cells of Human Beings', in *Essays of The Third International Conference of Life Ethics* (Taiwan: National Central University Press , 1991), H. 7.
15. Among the Buddhism Scriptures translated into Chinese, an elaboration of the starting point of a life can be seen in the following Scriptures: *Muulasavraastivaada Vinaya*, Book 11, volume 24 (Taisho edition), 253–6), *Maharatnakuta Sutra*, Books 56 and 57, volume 11 (Taisho edition), 328–333) and *Yogacarya Bhumi Sastra*, Book 1–2, volume 30 (Taisho edition), 282–5. In *Yogacarya Bhumi Sastra*, it is mentioned that the account in it has its origin in *Fo Shuo Ru Tai Jing*.
16. *Antara-bhava* exists only for creatures in the realm of sensual desire and those in the world of form and material. The Sarvastivadin insists that there is the real existence of antara-bhav while the Vibhajyavādins and the Ma*ahasamghika* deny its real existence.
17. For details of the eight stages that an embryo need to undergo in the womb, see *Yogacarya Bhumi Sastra*, Book 2, volume 30 (Taisho edition), 284–5).
18. *Yogācārabhūm-śāstrai,* Book 2, volume 30 (Taisho edition), 282b.
19. Why are all creatures equal? For the details of a discussion concerning this issue, see my *Buddhism Ethics*, chapter 2 (Taipei: Fa Chieh, 1995).

What Is Life—Current Scientific And Philosophical Perspectives

Frank Budenholzer, SVD

Abstract

The phenomenon of life is considered from both a scientific and philosophical point of view. From the point of view of science, life involves metabolic processes for the utilisation of energy as well as some form of hereditary reproduction. The organism must also in some sense be set apart from its environment, have a certain 'selfness' and autonomy. Philosophy is in no way a substitute for doing science. Rather from a consideration of the basic nature of human knowing, a certain understanding of the nature of the known can be obtained. From the philosophical point of view, the living organism is an emergent phenomenon—a new unity-identity—whole integrating otherwise coincidental manifolds of chemical processes (BJ Lonergan, 1992, *Insight: A Study of Human Understanding*, 286, 477). Issues such as the physicalism versus vitalism debate, supervenience and the possibility of 'test-tube life' will be considered. The paper closes with comments on the importance of the question of the nature of life for the religion-science dialogue.

Introduction

What is life? *Life* seems to be one of those things that we all know more or less what it is, but seem quite at a loss to define it. A quick look at the definition in the *Oxford English*

Dictionary seems to back up this statement. '*Life*—The condition or attribute of being alive; animate existence; Opposed to *death*'. While we recognise that sometimes it is hard to know for sure if something is alive (a coral, a virus, an animal or plant near death), we generally are quite confident in our judgments of the presence of life.

One of the reasons for this 'feeling for life' is that we ourselves are living beings. We experience ourselves as living unities in relation to an environment. We feel a kinship with other living things and dread the loss of life, which we call death. Because life is the basic fact and condition of our being human, we also use the word in many metaphorical and analogical senses to describe the exuberance that we feel about many things. This exuberance can vary from the mundane, 'She was the life of the party', to our deepest religious experiences, 'I am the resurrection and the Life (Jn 10:24)'.

But while life seems to evade simple definition, it is clearly something that can be studied through the methodologies of the physical and life sciences, primarily biology and chemistry. This study already has its roots in pre-Christian times (think of Aristotle's writings on biology), but has seen its greatest flowering in the last 100 years with the developments in physiology, genetics, biochemistry and molecular biology. Biologists and those in related disciplines are gradually teasing out the mechanisms and processes by which life differs from non-life.

Many in the biological community would argue that the question 'what is life' is simply a biological question for which we either already have or soon will have rather complete answers. What possibly can the philosopher bring to the discussion? To ask this question dredges up a whole raft of questions upon which there is little consensus. It involves the classical philosophical questions of the possibility of human knowing and the nature of human knowledge. More recently, such questions have re-emerged in the somewhat different context of the philosophy of science. What are the goals of the physical and life sciences? What does science have to tell us? Does science in some sense describe the 'real world'? And finally, what is the relationship of philosophy to science? Is philosophy primarily a way to tidy up scientific statements and language, as some of the earlier analytic philosophers would seem to suggest? Or does philosophy provide a sort of 'separate window' on the world, which can then be brought into dialogue with the results of the physical and life sciences?[1]

In the course of this paper, some of these questions will be dealt with in at least an indirect manner. However, it is not my intention to spell out a full philosophy of science or philosophy of biology. To clarify matters, let me make some comments on my personal philosophical starting point. These points will be made with minimal argumentation. For those interested in the background I would suggest consulting the author who has had the greatest impact on my own thinking, Bernard Lonergan. For my own slant on Lonergan's thought and especially how it relates to problems in the contemporary physical and life sciences, you may wish to consult my own papers listed in the bibliography.

(1) Both the physical and life sciences and philosophy are, in a generalised sense, empirical.[2] Both science and philosophy begin with experience. Philosophy begins with the experience of the human person in the process of knowing and deciding. Science begins with either the direct or indirect experience of the material things which science studies.

(2) This experience of either myself or the things around me is only the first component of human

knowledge. Knowledge implies further questions coming out of that experience and the answering of those questions in a reasonable and coherent way. A true increment in knowledge is had only when the adequacy of those answers is confirmed in judgment. Knowledge implies a triple cord—experience, understanding and judgment.[3]

(3) The special role of philosophy, especially in relation to the sciences, is to experience ourselves as knowers, to understand ourselves as knowers and finally to judge whether our understanding of ourselves as knowers is correct or incorrect. In this sense, philosophy has its own role that cannot be simply subsumed under the sciences. It is not because philosophy gives us some 'super-view', but because philosophy examines human knowing and, for better or worse, knowing is the only way we know things.

(4) So far so good. What we have said seems reasonable and would even have its points of contact with later linguistic philosophy.[4] There is, however, a further step, which is clearly more difficult. Does the nature of human knowing tell us anything about the nature of what is known? Kant's preliminary answer was 'yes', but then he realised that the *a priori* categories fatally prejudiced the possibility of true knowledge. All we can know with certitude is the phenomenal world, the deeper noumenal world remains, at best, obscure. Lonergan's answer to the same question is a clear, but limited affirmative. The structure of human knowing reveals something about the structure of the real.

This is not the place to unpack this assertion. But let me give an example where everyday science makes the same kind of assertion, the way we ask questions already tells us something about the way we presume things really are. When I teach elementary quantum mechanics, I tell my students that the time-dependent wave function describing a particle is a function of space and time, in one dimension we write $\psi = \psi(x, t)$. Why a function of x and t? Maybe another choice of variables would be better? OK, check it out. But why use a functional relationship at all? I would suggest that it is because the things physics studies are intelligibly related and that mathematical functions is a good way to represent those intelligibilities. (We could conceivably use geometry the way poor Galileo did before the development of algebra. But most would argue that there is an intelligible isomorphism between the geometric and algebraic ways of expressing the relationships.) Some philosophers of science would suggest that this is the reason why a denial of scientific realism is the only course. I would suggest, and I think most scientists would agree, that we are justified in presuming intelligible relationships at least between some variables. In other words, we make presumptions about the nature of reality based on the way we know.

Lonergan describes this isomorphism between cognitional structures and the object of our knowing in terms of 'heuristic structures'. The nature of human cognition tells us something about the nature of what is known?

(5) If knowing is all we have, then we should be very careful to limit our knowledge to what we can know —nothing more and nothing less. Knowing is about experience, understanding and judgment. The reality of things is of them as experienced, understood and judged. Lonergan's nemesis is that most of us tend to truncate our knowing to the level of experience. Or to put it in other terms, we make the criterion of reality our ability to imagine it or what we might call a 'hard sense of reality'. Our knowledge begins with experience, but the real is ultimately verified intelligibility.

Enough of this for now, lets get back to the question of this paper, 'What is life—current scientific and philosophical perspectives'.

Life from the point of view of the life sciences

The life sciences obviously have a great deal to tell us about the particulars of living systems, but what do they have to tell us about the more general question, 'what is life?'

In general the life sciences have been extremely successful in explaining more complex entities in terms of what are usually referred to as more basic entities. Thus the macroscopic phenomenon of reproductive inheritance is explained in terms of the laws of genetics and basic units referred to as genes, which in turn is explained by the chemistry of DNA and associated molecules, which is explained in terms of the chemistry of large polymers, and so down the line. Erwin Schrödinger in his 1944 classic *What is Life* stated the basic presupposition of many scientists very clearly,

> How can the events in *space and time*, which take place within the spatial boundary of a living organism, be accounted for by physics and chemistry?
>
> The preliminary answer, which this book will endeavor to expound and establish, can be summarised as follows:
>
> The obvious inability of present-day physics and chemistry to account for such events is no reason at all for doubting that they can be accounted for by those sciences.[5]

Schrödinger wrote this statement in 1944 before the discovery of the structure of DNA and the many subsequent advances in molecular biology and biochemistry. Sixty years later one would be hard pressed to deny the chemical and physical basis of all living systems. But is biology just chemistry? Is there something about life that goes beyond the chemistry?

Most biologists and biochemists would probably argue for some variety of *physicalism*.

> *Physicalism* claims that all living things are physical objects. If you take an organism, no matter how complex, and break it down into its constituents, you will find matter and only matter there. Living things are made of the same basic ingredients as non-living things. The difference is in how those basic ingredients are put together.[6]

The physicalist stance is usually contrasted with what is called *vitalism*. Definitions of *vitalism* vary, but in general they argue that living beings require something more than just the right combination of molecules and atoms.[7] Henri Bergson referred to this something more as the *élan vital*, a 'vital force' responsible for the dynamism seen in evolution.[8]

We will later comment further on the physicalist-vitalist dichotomy. However, as mentioned above, most biologists would argue for the physicalist account of life. But all would agree there are problems. One way to approach these problems is to ask a simple question. If biology is really just chemistry and physics, then can all biology be fully explained in chemical or physical terms? This is the so-called problem of epistemological reductionism. Can statements made in the science of biology–physiological explanations, evolutionary theory, ecology, whatever–be fully reduced to statements in chemistry or physics?

In some cases it may be true that a biological explanation is fully reducible to a chemical or physical explanation. For example, such and such an illness is always due to a defective gene at such and such a position in the DNA of the human person. However, most situations are not so simple. Take for example the concept of evolutionary fitness.[9] The particular biological and chemical trait that makes for fitness in one organism will be very different from that in another organism. And even the same organism under different environmental pressures, may have a different genetic make up that we would describe as fit. Clearly there is no one-to-one mapping from biology to chemistry to physics. Examples could be multiplied at will.

This situation is logically referred to as *supervenience*. *Supervenience* implies a non-symmetric hierarchy of explanation. Properties at the lower level are presumed to determine the higher-level properties, but not vice-versa. Higher-level properties do not determine lower level properties in a deterministic way. A certain genetic trait, with its corresponding physical trait, determines the fitness of a particular animal. However, the biological trait of fitness can be embodied in innumerable ways in various animals and in various environments.[10]

Supervenience allows a more nuanced understanding of physicalism and also indicates why the higher-level sciences such as biology or psychology are important, even in an essentially reductionistic account of living things. The well-known theologian Nancey Murphy argues that the concept of supervenience allows for a 'non-reductive physicalism'. Her main concern is whether the human mental states can simply be reduced to neuro-biology. However, similar arguments would hold on the relationship of biology to chemistry or chemistry to physics.[11] As a logical concept that helps clarify explanatory relationships at various levels, it seems uncontroversial. Whether it can bear the weight of allowing a truly 'non-reductive' physicalism when considering the relationship between conscious states and the neurological substrate or between living and nonliving things is a more controversial question.[12]

The question of what is the 'something more' that distinguishes life from non-life (or more importantly for us, the human from other animals) will not go away. The problem with vitalism is that it seems too much like a magic something added to chemical system to make it come alive. Biologists are slow to accept it because it seems almost by definition to be outside the gamut of their investigation.

A concept that is used with increasing frequency in theoretical biology and in philosophy is that of *emergence*. It is a slippery concept, but its proponents want to recognise that there are really new things that emerge without denying the physical and chemical basis of living things and of human persons.[13]

The root of the concept of *emergence* is the perceived complexity of the universe we inhabit. Complex things exist that are on the one hand based on lower level things (molecules are made of atoms) but at the same time involve a clearly defined subset of all possible variations at the lower level. This rule of limitation is described by Harold Morowitz as a 'pruning rule' or 'pruning algorithm'. The most commonly given example of this pruning algorithm is the *Pauli Principle*[14] which allows the emergence of the periodic table and chemistry from a much larger possible range of subatomic entities.[15] It is suggested that the emergence of life must involve similar 'pruning algorithms'. What constrains the chemistry in a living cell such that only a certain subset of possible chemical behaviors are present in living systems?[16]

On a physicalist understanding, emergence would seem to simply point to the appearance of new entities through a re-arrangement of the component parts. These new entities are explained by concepts that supervene on lower levels of explanation. Molecules are a certain arrangement of atoms that allow a new class of entities to be studied. This new emergent science (chemistry) has many explanatory concepts that are not simply in one-to-one correspondence with the concepts of atomic physics. Chemical concepts such as valence, reactivity and isomerism supervene on the lower level atomic and physical concepts. However, on this understanding of emergence, ontological priority is still given to the smallest element. Many, though not all, would presume that the lower levels completely determine the higher-level emergent properties.

There are problems with this simple physicalist understanding of emergence. One problem is 'Where to put the pruning algorithm?' To what level should we assign the capacities that allow integration at a higher level–to the lower level or the higher level? For example the Pauli Principle is often cited as the principle that allows the emergence of the periodic table, which is basic to chemistry and ultimately biology. Does the need to deal with higher-level entities lead to an 'enlargement of the lower-level science'?[17] Is the Pauli principle, which allows the formation of atoms, a basic property of sub-atomic matter or an emergent property of chemical systems? The position argued in this paper is that (a) there are truly emergent properties that can only be understood at the higher level of integration and (b) to learn at what level a certain scientific principle is active is primarily a question for science to determine.

There are also emergent phenomena that seem difficult to understand in the pure physicalist framework – life on the level of organism and cognition and consciousness on the level of the human person. Terrence Deacon, a physical anthropologist now at Berkeley, is concerned with the development of the human mind.[18] He argues for three categories of emergence.[19] The first level involves the emergence of higher order collective properties, which can be explained in terms of the component parts. Using statistical thermodynamics, the properties of liquid water can be explained in terms of the collective properties of the water molecules. Second-order emergence adds in a feedback mechanism that will amplify certain properties and diminish others. Oscillating chemical reactions and developments studied in chaos theory would come under this rubric.

First-order emergence is essentially independent of time. In second-order emergence, the emergent properties are a function of time and in more complex (chaotic) systems, the longer the period of time, the less the possibility of predicting future states of the system. The third category of emergence adds development and/or evolution to the second category. Information at one level of development is 'remembered' and acted upon in such a way that it may either be amplified or lost, with the resulting divergence of new types of entities. Evolution is the primary example of third-order emergence. Because of the global nature of the evolutionary process, except in very controlled experiments, it will be impossible to predict the products of third category emergence. As is often noted, neo-Darwinian evolutionary theory is explanatory but in most cases not predictive. This is in contrast to the properties of liquid water, which can, in principle, be determined from a study of the collective properties of H_2O molecules.

So what is life? As suggested above this is primarily a scientific question. First of all, essentially all scientists would agree that it is the result of an extremely complex process, what we might call layered third-category emergence. And what are the unique properties of living systems as opposed to other complex systems? This again is a scientific question. Schrödinger in his 1944 lectures stressed the order that is maintained in living organisms despite the randomness of physical processes. He had only vague hints of DNA and RNA and so suggested a-periodic crystal structures as the basis of the stability and evolutionary development of living things. His lectures are an amazing, if still vague, prediction of what molecular biology would bring to light during the second half of the twentieth century and right up until our own time.

Beyond the tension between stability and the possibility of evolutionary development, organisms require an energy processing mechanism. This is usually referred to as *metabolism*. For essentially all living systems, bacteria to human beings, the key molecule in this complex process is usually identified by a three-letter acronym— ATP (adenosine triphosphate). But just as DNA by itself explains very little but is at the heart of a very complex web of chemical reactions, so ATP is at the heart of the complex chemical processes usually referred to as the 'metabolic pathways'[20].

Stuart Kaufmann, a theoretical biologist and complexity theorist, while recognising the tremendous strides that have been made in biochemistry and molecular biology agues that a real answer to the question 'what is life' still alludes us. Kaufmann understands living things as 'autonomous agents'. 'An autonomous agent must be an autocatalytic system able to reproduce and to perform one or more thermodynamic work cycles'.[21] The definition essentially retains the two key notions in the above paragraphs, reproduction and metabolism. But to this it adds the concept of 'autonomous agent'. There is a certain 'selfness' in any living thing. Living things are unities that are somehow separated from their environments and can thus develop in unique ways.

Kaufmann then asks if there are laws for the emergence and evolution of biological systems, somehow analogous to the Pauli principle in chemistry. In his most recent book he suggest four candidate laws for the construction of a biosphere.[22] We will not review these suggestions here, but only note that they are attempts to understand the constraints (pruning algorithms) that allow the emergence of living things from their chemical precursors.

What does philosophy have to tell us?[23]

So far much of what we have said seems to be more science than philosophy, even if it is not the detailed science that is moving forward in laboratories all over the world. The title of this paper suggests that we consider philosophical as well as scientific perspectives.

I suggested earlier that at least one of the purposes of philosophy was to consider the very process by which we can know anything at all—DNA, ATP, autonomous agents, etcetera. Is any of this stuff really true? How do we know it is?

There are many good philosophers who would deny the possibility of really knowing the truth of modern biology. They doubt not only the possibility of knowing whether current theories are true, but even the possibility of there being any kind of process by which incorrect or incomplete understandings can be improved upon.[24]

Given this situation, can philosophy give us some clue about what we can know and what we can't? Many of those with a scientific bent have argued that sense knowledge is the one thing that is common to all of us – if we can all agree on certain sensible phenomena there is some hope of saving objectivity. The problem, of course, is that science, whether physics, chemistry or molecular biology, is not just about sense knowledge but also about very complex understandings and equally complex ways of verifying these understandings.

Here I now return to the five points I made at the beginning of the article, which outlined my personal philosophical starting point. Knowledge is based on the triple cord of experience (both experience of the 'outside' world and experience of myself), understanding that experience and finally judging on the adequacy of that understanding. Each level calls forth the next. The process of knowing is all we have and we affirm it even in the denying the possibility of knowledge. For even the most adamant relativist will argue that his particular understanding of the nature of reality is somehow verifiable.

Science is an extremely complex web of knowledge where much of what we know is dependent on other areas of science. This web-like nature of scientific knowing imparts a tentativeness to scientific knowing that is not present in common sense knowing. However, when all is said and done, science does tell us something about the real world. During the last 50 years humankind has gained real knowledge of the mechanism of living things.

But what does it mean to say that I know something? Does it mean we have a picture, something like a photograph? Does it mean we use some kind of inner model to correlate various sense impressions? Lonergan's work reveals that when we say we know about subatomic particles, quarks, strings, atoms, molecules, metabolic pathways, and other objects of scientific knowledge we are simply answering questions and then doing our best to verify that those answers are correct. In saying this we are broaching a topic, which sets Lonergan's thought apart from our normal intuitive feelings about knowing. Because all of our knowing begins from experience, we tend to make experience—a sense of hardness or imaginability—the criterion of reality. But what scientific practice reveals is that the criterion of reality is verified intelligibility, nothing more and nothing less.

Now what does this have to do with biology? If the imaginability of certain objects of knowledge is the criterion of their reality, then the smallest pieces will have ontological priority. A next step is often to presume these smallest components (quarks, strings or whatever) completely determine the reality of larger things. We are left with a strong mechanistic determinism.[25] Ontological priority is given to the smallest chunks of matter, which determine the nature of all complex systems. This kind of thinking is behind the 'physical monism' which is presumed by most to be implied by contemporary physics, chemistry and biology.

But what is the alternative? Who could deny that physics is the basis of chemistry and that chemistry is the basis of biology and that biology is the basis of human psychology? Are we to return to vitalism, the idea that 'something new' is added for life to emerge from non-life or for the human person to emerge from the biological matrix?

To answer this question we must ask about the nature of the tiered levels of reality that are the objects of our science. As argued above, all knowing, at least in the universe in which we live, involves a triple cord: experience, understanding and judgment. We experience data, whether size, shape, weight, color, etcetera. From this experience we seek to gain understanding. We may seek to understand the way things operate either in an explanatory mode (things in relation to each other) or in a descriptive mode (things in relation to us). In the explanatory mode, we are ultimately seeking to understand the basic laws of physics, chemistry, biology and so on. We also attempt to understand things—unity, identity, wholes such as atoms, molecules, living organisms, or human persons, which we experience and ultimately understand in their oneness. Finally, we may attempt to understand the complex arrangements of things in both space and time—what Lonergan refers to as 'schemes of recurrence'. Such schemes of recurrence would include everything from our solar system, to social and economic systems to the complex artifacts of human ingenuity. However, not all understandings are correct, whether of scientific laws, our understanding of the nature of the things that make up our universe or complex schemes of recurrence. Ultimately our knowing requires verification in judgment.

To describe the properties of things and events, Lonergan uses the technical term 'conjugates'. 'Experiential conjugates are correlatives whose meaning is expressed, at least in the last analysis, by appealing to the content of some human experience.'[26] Colors and tastes, as well as the categories of descriptive science such as anatomy or geology, are examples of descriptive conjugates. 'Pure (or explanatory) conjugates, on the other hand, are correlatives defined implicitly by empirically established correlations, functions, laws, theories, systems.'[27] Explanatory conjugates since they involve things in relation to each other, are implicitly defined by the equations and explanatory networks of the sciences.

Lonergan defines the notion of a thing 'as an intelligible, concrete unity differentiated by experiential and explanatory conjugates'.[28] Things exist on various levels and are the unities, which are explained—subatomic particles, atoms, molecules, cellular organisms, sensitive organisms, human persons that can transcend themselves in knowing and loving. Science knows each level through the descriptive and explanatory conjugates correlative to the thing under study. The criterion of reality of both conjugates and things is simply their verified intelligibility.

Each level of reality has its own set of explanatory conjugates, which are the particular subject of the science of that level—physics, chemistry, biology, sensitive psychology, etcetera. No set of conjugates or any level of things is more real than any other. The real is verified intelligibility at whatever level one is operating. Having said that each level is equally real is not to deny the clearly verified conclusion of levels of reality. At each level the random conjugates of the lower level are unified in a higher integration. Chemistry systematises what would be merely coincidental events on the atomic level allowing the emergence of an autonomous science of chemistry. Biology is an autonomous science integrating what would be merely coincidental events on the level of chemistry. The integration of coincidental manifolds at a new level does not take away the autonomy of the lower levels. The reality of the biological organism includes the conjugates of chemistry and physics. Because of this, the most exciting areas of science will be the cross disciplinary areas—molecular biology, chemical physics, etcetera. Here science attempts to understand how those lower level conjugates are systematised at the new level.

As noted above, a thing for Lonergan is an 'intelligible, concrete unity differentiated by experiential and explanatory conjugates'.[29] Experiential conjugates refer to the properties of the thing in relation to the knower, while explanatory conjugates refer to properties implicitly defined by scientific laws and correlations, which consider things in relation to things. Lonergan then makes use of the traditional categories of potency, form and act. In keeping with Lonergan's starting point of cognitional analysis, these three are related to each other, as are experience, understanding and judgment. Thus central form refers to the intelligible unity of a given thing, while conjugate form refers to the intelligibility of its properties (that is, conjugates). Central and conjugate act refer to the in-principle verifiable existence of the thing itself (central act) or of the properties of the thing (conjugate act).

With these definitions we are now ready to define 'emergence'. Lonergan defines emergence as the process where 'otherwise coincidental manifolds of lower conjugate acts invite the higher integration effected by higher conjugate forms'.[30] For example, on the level of subatomic physics there exist things such as protons, electrons and neutrons. Lower conjugate acts here refer to the existing properties of these things on this level. These conjugate acts are intelligible and this intelligibility is in accord with what Lonergan describes as both classical and statistical laws of physics. However, there exists a basic randomness, which on one level a physicist might describe as a collection of random particles or events and Lonergan describes as a 'coincidental manifold'. However, given the right set of initial circumstances, in other words the right probabilities, from this random situation (what Lonergan calls 'coincidental manifolds of lower conjugate acts') there may emerge a higher integration with its own conjugate forms. What is the nature of these emergent entities?

Here Lonergan distinguishes between two levels schemes of recurrence and new things. As noted above, schemes of recurrence refer to intelligible systems that circle in on themselves. If A occurs then B occurs, if B occurs then C occurs, and so to the point that A recurs and the circle begins again.[31] Lonergan likes to use the example of the planetary system. Somehow in the development of our corner of the Milky Way, there emerged a group of planets that orbit around our sun. The recurring pattern of the orbits leads to the emergence of a degree of stability in what otherwise would be random movement. Examples of schemes of recurrence are essentially infinite—from the subatomic through the artifacts of human industry to human society and economics. In the emergence of schemes of recurrence, new conjugate forms will arise. We can describe the mechanics of the solar system, the nature of phase changes in chemistry, the symbiotic relationship of plant species or the nature of business cycles in economics. Yet, as can be seen from the examples given, schemes of recurrence are ontologically reductive. Given the right circumstances, the classical and statistical laws governing the elements of the scheme will allow us to predict the nature the scheme of recurrence.

But besides the emergence of new schemes of recurrence, there is also the fact of the emergence of truly new things—things now used in Lonergan's technical sense. As we have noted above Lonergan defines the notion of a thing 'as an intelligible, concrete unity differentiated by experiential and explanatory conjugates'.[32] In what many consider one of Lonergan's more puzzling chapters, he argues that there are no things within things. This seems to be at odds with atomic and molecular theory of matter, which is now part and parcel of contemporary science. To understand we must return to our understanding of the real as verified intelligibility. An animal is a concrete unit, whose basic conjugates are the subject of zoology. The lower level conjugates of atomic physics (atomic mass and number, electronic structure) are integrated at the new level of chemistry. And the conjugates of chemistry (valence, reactivity, etcetera.) are integrated at the level of the biological. Thus an animal, say a rabbit, is a unity which each of the various levels of matter are integrated in this unity, identity whole of the rabbit. On the level of bodies, of course the rabbit has various organs—heart, liver, brain, etcetera—but these are all integrated in one living unity, the rabbit. Terms like respiration and metabolism refer to this unity-identity-whole that is the particular rabbit.

Above I noted that when talking of schemes of recurrence, or more simply when talking of simple aggregates, the new properties (conjugates) that emerge are in principle reducible to the lower level properties. I can explain the movement of the planetary system solely in terms of the laws of physics. However, when we speak of the emergence of new 'things'—atoms, molecules, bacteria, animals, persons—'the higher integration effected by higher conjugate forms' is indicative of a new central form, a new center of intelligibility.

What is life?

So what is life? From the point of view of science, we argued life must involve metabolic processes for the utilization of energy and some form of hereditary reproduction. The organism must also be set apart from the rest of the world, a certain 'selfness' for which Stuart Kaufmann coined the term 'autonomous agents'. This is not meant to be an exhaustive definition. Other characteristics could be added, for example, a system far from equilibrium, which obtains its sustenance from the environment, or we could add laws similar to those suggested by Kaufmann and alluded to above.

From the point of view of philosophy life is a higher integration of chemical conjugates with the corresponding emergence of a new central form and a new unity—the living organism. As a higher integration of chemical conjugates, the laws of chemistry remain in tact. To understand the organism, one has to know chemistry, and for that matter atomic physics and subatomic physics and on down the line. But at the same time the organism is a unity, identity, whole, unifying the chemistry under higher level biological conjugates such as metabolism and reproduction. The nature of these conjugates is a matter for the sciences to explore. Philosophy will not provide a short cut.

And where does this put us on the physicalism-vitalism continuum discussed earlier? I would suggest that neither alternative will do. Physicalism, at least in most of its forms, is dependent on what Lonergan calls the myth of 'knowing as looking'. For something to be real, beyond the somewhat Spartan categories of verified intelligibility, the physicalist adds the criterion that the real must be analogous to the objects of sensation. In this scenario ontological priority is given to the smallest particles—little solid chunks—and the hierarchy of complexity that the sciences reveal is simply due to increasingly complex combinations of the fundamental building blocks. My contention is that at each new level there emerge truly new unities that integrate the lower level conjugates.

Vitalism is mistaken in that it more or less presumes the physicalist interpretation—the real is ultimately comprised of little chunks of matter—and then finds itself at a loss on how to explain living things. So at the last minute an unimaginable 'vital force' is added. The suggestion here is that at each level there emerge new unities that integrate the lower level conjugates. The new central form is not an extra something added to a set of lower level building blocks, but rather the central reality of the integrated unit.[33] There exist on these various levels different categories of things and these categories imply both experiential and explanatory conjugates at the level at which they are understood. Thus there are the relatively autonomous sciences of sub-atomic physics, atomic physics, chemistry, biology and sensitive psychology. At any level, including the macroscopic level of sciences such as physiology and anatomy, the criterion of the real is not ultimately the ability to experience the organism as a unity but verified understanding of the organism as a unity.

Having said the above, I should add that there is a sense in which physical monism is correct. Abstaining for the moment on the subject of the human mind and human intentionality, the various levels of things are all material. Their materiality consists not in their ability to be felt or imagined—what does it mean to 'feel' a quark or a string?—but in their being individuated objects in space and time.[34] The nature of space and time are primarily physical questions currently understood in terms of the theories of special and general relativity.

The emergence of a new thing requires a subtle interplay of classical and statistical laws. The term Lonergan uses for this engine of emergence is 'emergent probability'. Given the right set of conditions, there will emerge new schemes of recurrence and new things. The only way to understand the details of the process of emergence is to do the interdisciplinary science—in the case of living things, molecular biology is the key to understanding the emergence of life in terms of the chemical conjugates.

A question that is often asked is whether scientists will be able to create life forms in the laboratory. My own belief is that sooner or later, scientists will be able to tweak probabilities so that a living thing will emerge from the chemical matrix. This has already been accomplished twice with viruses.[35] Scientists still argue whether viruses can be described as living things. They do not seem to fit the definition quoted from Kaufmann above. But they are very close to being living things and while the simplest bacteria are far more complex, all indications are that sooner or later living things will be 'created' in the laboratory from organic starting materials.

Religion, Science and Philosophy.

This paper was originally presented at the conference 'Cosmology—Religion and Science in Dialogue'. What does all this have to do with the religion and science dialogue? First it must be stated that the really key question for the religion-science dialogue is the nature of the human person. All religious traditions are concerned with the human person and his or her relationship with ultimate reality. Believers in the monotheistic traditions share the belief that the human person is created in the image of God. Christians believe that the person Jesus is God incarnate—God among us. In one sense what has been presented here is preparatory for the larger question of the nature of the human person and what is referred to in many religious traditions as the human soul. But to say that this work is preparatory is not to say that it is not important. The human person is also an emergent reality. Just as there is an autonomous science of biology, there also exist autonomous sciences of the human person. But also just as a complete understanding of life must include an understanding of the lower level conjugates of chemistry and physics, so a complete understanding of the human person requires an understanding of the lower level biological, chemical and physical conjugates.[36]

Thus the answer to the question 'what is life' provides the framework for what Christians would call theological questions. Human persons are part and parcel of the material world. They are emergent entities of this world and not just some sort of spiritual beings acting out their lives on a material stage. Christians believe that God entered this material world in the person of Jesus. As emergent unities—and not just a clever combination of the basic constituents—human persons stand apart and, in a sense beyond that of the individual organism, are autonomous agents. Our dignity is to know and love and to be known and be loved as the emergent unities that we are.

End Notes

1. Nicholas Maxwell, *The Human World in the Physical Universe: Consciousness, Free Will, and Evolution* (London: Rowman and Littlefield, 2001).
2. Joseph Flannagan, *Quest for Self-Knowledge: An Essay in Lonergan's Philosophy* (Toronto: University of Toronto Press, 1997), 268.
3. Bernard Lonergan, *Collection: Papers by Bernard Lonergan, SJ* edited by FE Crowe SJ (New York: Herder and Herder, 1967), 230.
4. Joseph Fitzpatrick, 'Lonergan and the Analytical Tradition' Second International Workshop, Regis College, University of Toronto, august 1–6, 2004.
5. Erin Schrödinger, *What is Life? :The Physical Aspect of the Living Cell (with Mind and Matter and Autobiographical Sketceterahes)*, (Cambridge: Cambridge University Press, 1967 [1944]), 3–4.
6. Elliott, Sober, *Philosophy of Biology. Dimensions of PhilosophySeries* edited by Norman Daniels and Keith Lehrer (Oxford: Oxford University Press, 1993), 22.
7. *Ibid.*
8. *Ibid.*
9. *Ibid*, 57–87; Ansgar Beckman, Hans Flor, Jaegwon Kim, editors. *Emergence or Reductionism: Essays on the Prospects of Nonreductive Physicalism.* (Berlin: Walter de Gruyter, 1992), 119–38.
10. Sober, *Philosophy of Biology,* 73–77
11. Nancy Murphy, 'Non-reductive Physicalism: Philosophical Issues' in Warren Brown, Nancy Murphy and H Newton Malony editors, *Whatever Happened to the Soul? Scientific and Theological Portraits of Human Nature* (Minneapolis: Fortress Press,1998), 129–31.
12. Donald H Wacome, 'Reductionism's Demise: Cold Comfort' in *Zygon: Journal of Religion and Science.* volume 39, no 2 (June): 321–37.
13. Beckman *et al, Emergence or Reductionism.*
14. The Pauli Principle is a basic principle of quantum statistics. "When the labels of any two fermions are exchanged, the total wave function changes sign. When the labels of any two identical bosons are exchanged, the total wave function retains

the same sign." While seeming quite abstract, it is this principle that allows the existence of complex structures such as atoms and molecules. Peter Atkins, Paula de Julio, *Adkins' Physical Chemistry* 7th edition (Oxford: Oxford University Press,2002), 385.
15. Harold J Morowitz, *TheEmergence of Everything* (New York: Oxford University Press, 2002), 54—57.
16. *Ibid*, 76.
17. Ernan McMullin, 'Biology and the Theology of the Human' in Philip R Sloan editor *Controlling our Destinies: Historical, Philosophical, Ethical and Theological Perspectives on the Human Genome Project* (Notre Dame: IN: Notre Dame University Press, 2000), 373.
18. Terrance W Deacon, *The Symbolic Species: the Co–evolution of Language and the Brain* (New York: WW Norton and Company, 1997).
19. Terrance W Deacon, 'The Hierarchic Logic of Emergence: Untangling the Interdependence of Evolution and Self-Organisation' in Bruce Weber and David Depew editors *Evolution and Learning: The Baldwin Effect Reconsidered* (Cambridge, MA: MIT Press, 2003); Arthur Peacocke, 'Emergence, Mind and Divine Action: the Hierarchy of the Sciences in Relation to the Human Body–Brain–Mind' in *The Palace of Glory: God's World and Science* (Adelaide: ATF Press, 2005), 100.
20. Morowitz, *The Emergence,*70–77.
21. Stuart Kaufman, *Investigations* (Oxford: Oxford University Press, 2000), 49.
22. *Ibid*, 160.
23. Much of the material in this section is taken from my earlier article: Frank Budenholzer, "Emergence, Probability and Reductionism" *Zygon: Journal of Religion and Science* volume 39 number 2 (June 2004): 339–56.
24. See Arthur Fine, 'The Natural Ontological Attitude' in *The Philosophy of Science*. Richard Boyd, Philip Gaspar and JD Trout editors. (Cambridge, MA: MIT Press, 1991), 261–77.
25. Bernard Lonergan, *Insight: A Study of Human Understanding. Collected Works of Bernard Lonergan,* volume 3 (Toronto: University of Toronto Press, 1992(1957)),153–4.
26. *Ibid*, 102.
27. *Ibid*, 103.
28. *Ibid*, 280.

29. *Ibid.*
30. *Ibid*, 477.
31. *Ibid*, 141.
32. *Ibid*, 280.
33. *Ibid*, 505.
34. *Ibid*, 50.
35. Jeronimo Cello, Paul V Aniko,Wimmer Eckhard, 'Chemical Synthesis of Polio Virus c: Generation of Infectious Virus in the Absence of Natural Template' *Science* volume 297, issue 5582(August 2002); ,Hamilton O Smith, Clyde A Huchison III, Cynthia Pfannkoch, J Craig Venter, 'Generating a synthetic genome by whole genome assembly: ϕX174 bacteriophage from synthetic oligonculeotides'. *Proceedings of the National Academy of Sciences USA,* volume 100, number 26, (2003):15440–45.
36. Frank Budenholzer, 'Christian Philosophy, the Natural Sciences and Human Dignity' *Second International Lonergan Workshop,* Toronto. [An earlier version was presented at the *International Conference on Christian Philosophy and Human Dignity*'Fu Jen Catholic University, Hsinchuang, Taiwan, December 13–15, 2002.]

Part Four

Matter And Spirit In Taoism

John B Chuang

Abstract

In this article, the ideas of Body and Spirit in early Daoism are examined from two aspects. First, this study explores the ideas of body and soul in Western philosophical anthropology, and secondly tries to understand the context of Body and Spirit in pre-Taoism (the period before the Qin and Han dynasties). The section on early Daoism mainly discusses texts of four Daoist books: *Tai Ping Jing*, *Lao Zi Xiang Er Zhu*, *Bei Dou Jing*, and *Nan Dou Jing*. In other words, the ideas of body and soul in philosophical anthropology, the view point on body and spirit from the pre-Qin period to the Han dynasty, and the view point of Body and Spirit in early Daoism will be discussed. The results of this research indicate that the points of view on body and spirit in Chinese and Western cultures come to a consensus to some extent—they are not totally different. However, it is important to note that the ideas of body and spirit in early Taoism and in ancient China are not completely the same.

Not many scholars devote themselves to studying body and spirit in Daoism. Even fewer scholars study the two concepts in early Daoist scriptures.[1] When referring to philosophical anthropology, this essay focuses mainly on the work of Thomas Aquinas (1225–1274), the *Philosophical Anthropology* of FF Donceel, SJ and the

Dictionary of Western Philosophy of W Brugger. As to the discussion of the concepts of body and spirit prevalent before the Qin and Han dynasty, the focus will be placed on *Zuo Zhuan* (*Zuo Qiuming's Commentary on* Spring and Autumn Annals), Confucian, Mencius and Xun Zi of Confucianism, in addition to Lao Zi, Zhuang Zi, Lie Zi and Huainan Zi of Daoism. In clarifying the two concepts adopted in early Daoism, the discussion will be limited only to four scriptures: *Tai Ping Jing* (*Classic of the Highest Peace*), *Lao Zi Xiang Er Zhu* (*Xiang Er's Commentary on Lao Zi's Book of Dao and its Virtue*), *Nan Dou Jing* (*Scripture of South Dipper*) and *Bei Dou Jing* (*Scripture of North Dipper*). For a comparative study of these concepts from the perspective of philosophical anthropology, the essay is divided into three sections: the concepts of body and soul in philosophical anthropology, the concepts of body and spirit before the Qin and Han dynasties, and discussion of body and spirit in early Daoism.

The concepts of body and soul in philosophical anthropology

As Western philosophy has developed and been amended continuously, there are quite a lot of discourses on philosophical anthropology. The purpose of this section is to understand the concepts of body and soul as discussed in philosophical anthropology and, with this understanding as a basis, to examine the concepts of matter and spirit found before the Qin and Han dynasties, and in early Daoism, in China. Therefore a discussion of the following aspects is necessary: the properties of soul and body, the complementary relationship between body and spirit, the origin of body and spirit and what happens to them after one's death.

The properties of body and soul

Thomas Aquinas argued that the soul is incorporeal, subsistent and incorruptible. For Aquinas a human being is composed of matter and form, in other words, corporeal substance (body) and spiritual substance (soul).[2]

The soul is simple not only because it is only a part of an object, but because it is an object undivided. The notion Aquinas follows means that the soul is indivisible. That the soul is immaterial means that it cannot extend in space. Although the soul does not rely on a body to perform its actions such as thinking and judging, it is in need of the cooperation and help of the latter. Thus the body becomes the site in which spiritual activities are substantially expressed.

According to Donceel, an outstanding scholar of philosophical anthropology, the soul is characterised by the following properties: (1) it is an immaterial entity (in other words, it is a spiritual entity);[3] (2) It is self-subsistent; (3) it is simple and indivisible; (4) it is eternal; (5) it can activate body; (6) it is possessed of intelligent and volitive functions; and (7) it is an incomplete entity.

In Western philosophical anthropology, the body is characterized by the following properties: (1) It is corporeal; (2) it is non-subsistent; (3) it is material and divisible; (4) it can accomplish humans' potentiality; (5) it decays in this life (however, it is inclined to unite with soul in an afterlife); and (6) it is an incomplete entity.

As soul and body are characterised by their unique properties, what then what is the relationship between the two?

The complementary relationship between body and soul

Both Aristotle and Aquinas argue for the theory of 'substantial union'. They both claim that the body itself is not a complete entity, since it is not self-sufficient or self-subsistent. It needs the cooperation of the soul in order to act. Neither is the soul a compete entity. However, the soul can activate body. In spite of that, it needs the cooperation and help of body if it intends to perform any actions.[4] This theory relies on hylemorphism and the concept of 'actualisation and potentiality' for its theoretical foundation.[5] Aquinas applies this theory to the soul and body of humans. Soul is form while the body is matter.[6] A human being can become a complete entity only when his soul and body are unified.

Moreover, Aquinas asserts that a human being does not have more than one soul. Plato argues that there is more than one soul in a body because he views the soul as a dynamic force inside body. Both Aristotle and Aquinas opposed Plato's viewpoint. They contend that the relationship between soul and body is one between form and matter. 'It cannot be said that several important souls to unite together to form a body.' Neither can it be said that it is body that makes the soul and body a unity to become a whole. 'Therefore we have to come to such conclusion: What we call sensitive soul, intellectual soul and nutritive soul are actually referred to the same soul. There is only one soul in quantity' (ST 1, 76, 3).

For Aquinas, since there exists such a close relationship between body and soul, how does philosophical anthropology understand the origin of body and soul? Furthermore, how does it understand the destination of body and soul after one's death?

The origin of body and soul and their destination after one's death
For the sake of convenience, the discussion of body and soul is divided here into two parts: the origin of body and soul, and body and soul after one's death.

a. The origin of body and soul

Aquinas holds that the 'human soul can only come from God's creation as it, consisting of not any material components, cannot "grow" from material' (ST 1, 118, 2). According to Donceel, the birth of soul can be explained by the viewpoint of 'continuous creation'. The human soul is created out of God's will and the cooperation of parents. However, the soul can be revealed only when the embryo develops to the stage that all the human organs are ready and, most important of all, when cerebral activities begin to appear. This argument can be supported by the example of twins coming from the same egg (Donceel, 440–445).

Generally speaking, the view of soul in philosophical anthropology can be related to the origin of body and soul in three propositions. These are: (1) The human soul is created by God from nothing; (2) after God creates human beings, God keeps on creating, with the parents' cooperation; and (3) the view of indirect spiritualisation is adopted: a baby is endowed with a soul only when its organs and cerebrum are ready.

b. The body and soul after one's death

Aquinas' hylemorphism is different from Aristotle's viewpoint. He regards that, after one's death, the metaphysical unity is not separated. Because the separation of body and soul denotes the incompleteness of a man, Aquinas proposes the concept of 'the eternal wholeness of humans'. As he has to abide to the Catholic tradition, he is more inclined to rely on a 'binary union' to understand the issue. Therefore he holds that the separation of body and soul is not completed at the moment of one's death. Soul is in an unideal state temporarily. Since it is the nature of a soul to desire a body, it will unite with the glorious body when it is the time of the resurrection.[7] He concludes that 'when they are separated, soul [and body] maintain an appropriate existence. Even more, it is possessed of the trait and tendency to unite with body' (ST 1, 76, 1).

Karl Rahner states that human soul can leave the finite past behind and break through the limitedness of body in order to have a direct and wide contact with the whole universe. What Rahner points out is exactly what the traditional conception has advocated since Aquinas' time: After resurrection, the soul (form) retains a transcendental relation to the body (matter). On the basis of Rahner's observation, it is not far-fetched to affirm that the relationship between body and soul, after the resurrection, is not contingent or transient (Donceel, 439).

Concepts of body and spirit before the Qin and Han Dynasties

The aim of this section is to examine how the ancient Chinese thinkers, especially those before the Qin and Han dynasties, regarded the concept of body and that of spirit. Three aspects of the issue are singled out as the focus of the discussion here: (1) the properties of *hun* (celestial spirits, souls), *po* (terrestrial spirits or souls) and body; (2) the complementary relationship between body and spirit; and (3) the origin of body and spirit and what happens to them after one's death.

The properties of hun, po and body
    a. The properties of *hun* and *bo* in ancient times
In ancient China, both heart and *shen* (spirit of the heart) were regarded as *qi* (life energy). The earliest discussion can be seen in *Zuo Zhuan* of Zhou dynasty. In the book, it is recorded that it is Zi Chan, a minister of a small kingdom called Zheng, who first discussed heart and *shen*. 'When a baby is given birth, it is *po* that is produced first and *hun* later. This kind of *hun* and *po* can strengthen day by day. They do not remain changed after birth. If we use abundant

and exquisite things for the body, *shen* and *hun* can thus be strengthened. Even *shen qi* and *jing* (vitality) *qi* become clear.' *Po* is not used to refer to body. Zi Chan argue that 'The *hun* and *po* of a man are attached to his body'.[8] However, scholars of later ages misunderstood that *hun* and *po* were used to refer to spirit and body respectively. Thus *po* is wrongly regarded as the same as body.

Before the Qin dynasty, *hun* and *po* were used individually to signify two kinds of spiritual forces—one governs thinking and the other body.[9] *Hun* is a kind of *qi*. It is generated by *po*. *Po* is also a kind of *qi*, not the body itself.[10] According to the study of Wang Tzung-yu, the notion of '*jing qi*' appeared first in ancient China, then followed by Zhuang Zi's '*qi xue*' (study of *qi*). The notion of '*yuan* (primordial) *qi*' did not appear until early Han dynasty.[11] Therefore, the concepts of *hun* and *po* should be ascribed to the concept of *jing qi*, which insists that the spirit of a man is constituted by *jing qi*.

b. The nature of body and spirit in Daoism

Lao Zi (460–380 BC) does not have much to say about body and spirit. In the book known after his name, *Lao Zi*, it is stated that a human person is the product of the neutralisation of *yin qi* and *yang qi*.[12] The human should conserve the *qi* of *hun* and *po* and make them as submissive as babies. Otherwise, *hun* and *po* will be separated (*Lao Zi* 10). Lao Zi pays special attention to the nourishment of the *qi* of *hun* and *po*. He declares that the followers of Daoism will not be afraid of poisonous snakes and wild animals. Their tendons and bones may be soft and weak, but their limbs will be strong and powerful. What the followers manifest is the state of the cultivation of *jing qi* to its highest possible potential (*Lao Zi* 55). *Jing qi* or spirit, according to *Lao Zi*, can be strengthened. Moreover, this conception of spirit lays the seed for the development of the belief that *hun* comes from the *yang qi* of heavens while *po* from the *yin qi* of earth.

Before Zhuang Zi (369–286 BC), the words '*jing*' and '*shen*' were widespread in mainland China. It is Zhuang Zi who uses the two words together to express his thought.[13] In comparison with Lao Zi, Zhuang Zi has a more balanced view on the concepts of body and spirit. He uses the words '*shen*', '*jin*', '*jin shen*', '*shen qi*', '*hun*' and '*hun po*' to express the concept of spirit. At the same time, he uses another series of words like '*xing*' (body), '*xing ti*' (body), '*xing hai*' (skeleton), 'ear' and 'eye' to express the notion of the body.

In the Western Han dynasty, the king of the vassal state Huai Nan, Liu An (179–122 BC), presented the book *Huai Nan Zi* (*Book of the Prince of Huai Nan*) to Emperor Wu. This book still retains the traditional notion of *jing qi*, agreeing that *jing shen* (spirit) of a man is *jing qi* and both *jing* and *shen* are *qi*. It also differentiates clearly between spirit and body, regarding spirit coming from the heavens and body from earth.[14]

This edition of *Lie Zi* includes not only the past, incomplete edition of the book but also many viewpoints from people in the Qin and Han dynasties. In the book we can find the argument that all things are composed of the three elements—*qi*, *xing* (body) and *zhi* (material). The spirit of a man is constituted by *qi*, or to be more specific, the light, clear and dissipating *qi* that comes from heavens. As to body, it is composed of body and material. In other words, it is constituted by the turbid and congregate *qi* that comes from earth.[15]

c. The nature of *hun*, *po* and body in Confucianism

Confucius (551–479 BC) scarcely touches on the study of human beings or human nature. He has few remarks on the structure of body and soul. From Mencius onwards,

Confucianism starts to call spirit as 'big body' or 'heart'. As to body, including those sensual desires, it is called 'small body' or 'body and skin'. 'Live' and 'body' are words used to stand for life.[16]

For Mencius, the nature of *qi* is rather vague. It is inclined to come close to spirit though (*Mencius*, former part of 'Gong Sun Chou').

The book *Li Ji* (*The Classic of Rites*) records the thought of the interval between Qin and Han dynasties (221–206 BC). In the chapter of 'Ji Yi' of the book, the relationship between *qi* and *po* is outlined. So is the relationship between *shen* (spirit) and *gui* (ghost). It is clear that *hun shen* and *po gui* are not of the same kind.[17] Here the *hun* of a man is closely related to *shen qi* and his *po* is formed by the essence of ghost.[18] Simply speaking, both *hun* and *po* are spiritual entities.

d. The interpretation of '*hun*' and '*po*' in Han philology
In *Shuo Wen Jie Zi* (a character dictionary), Xu Shen (100 AD) of Eastern Han dynasty interprets *hun* as *yang qi* and *po* as *yin qi*. Duan Yucai, in annotating '*po*', points out that when a man is dead, his body will decompose and decay.[19] Judging from Duan's annotation, it is obvious that *hun* and *po* are self-subsistent. They do not rely on a body to exist. By employing the concepts of *hun* and *po* evident in Gao You's annotation of *Huai Nan Zi*, together with Xu's and Duan's interpretation of the two terms, Guo Guanghung asserts that, in China *hun* and *po* are viewed as spirit or soul before the Han dynasty. This view is different from the one advocated by the scholars of the Jin and Tang dynasties. For the sake of dealing with the two kinds of souls, *hun* and *po*, those scholars interpret *po* as body or 'body *po*', a view which is far remote from the original tradition of China.[20] In other words, in pre-Qin times, *hun* and *po* are used to refer to spirit.[21] Until Zhu Xi of the Song

dynasty, the two concepts of spirit and body are clearly differentiated from each other. He asserts that '*Qi* is also called *hun*. Body is also called *po*'.[22] Zhu's assertion causes Chinese nowadays to misunderstand that the concepts of *hun* and *po* of ancient Chinese are the same as those held by people in the Jin, Tang and Song dynasties.

From the above discussion, we can derive several properties for the concepts of *hun* and *po* popularly adopted before Han China. (1) They are incorporeal, immaterial and spiritual. (2) They are self-subsistent and self-sufficient (for example, *hun* can exist even without body). (3) They are simple and indivisible. For example, the description 'clear and dissipating' used in *Lie Zi* signifies that spiritual entity is pure. Unlike material entity, spiritual entity does not condense in a particular place. Therefore, it is indivisible. (4) They are imperishable. Since Confucian, the folk belief that man will become *gui* (ghost) or *shen* (a spirit) has been widely accepted by Confucian scholars and nearly all the people. Such belief implicates that *hun* and *po* are imperishable even after one's death. (5) *Po* can manage body. As it is a kind of *yin shen* or *yin qi*, it is the spiritual force that governs body. Its property is different from that of soul in the Western philosophy to activate body. (6) *Hun* is possessed of intellectual function since it is the spiritual force that governs thinking.

Three properties can be derived for the concept of body before Han China. (1) It is corporeal. (2) It is material and divisible. (3) It decays in this life. It is possessed of the propensity to unite with soul in an afterlife.

The complementary relationship between body and spirit

As to the nourishment of body, the notion of immortality is only vaguely mentioned in *Lao Zi*. This is the first Chinese document from which we can learn such notion.[23] Lao Zi regards that, for one who really attains Dao, the death of his body does not mean the real death of him but his return to Dao. In this way, he is endowed with longevity (see *Lao Zi* 33).

Mencius, a Confucian scholar, advocates that human body is composed of heart, *qi* and body. Heart is the centre which manages and controls the human person. Its level of importance is far above that of body. In between these two levels, there is *qi*, which is the medium of spirit and body. The whole body is infused with *qi* governed and guided by heart (*Mencius*, former part of 'Gong Sun Chou' 11). His contemporary, Xun Zi (313–326 BC) has already used the two words '*xin*' and '*shen*' individually to express the concepts of body and spirit. He claims that heart governs *shen ming*, which governs body in return.[24]

The survey of the basic view of the relationship between body and spirit before Han China attests to the complementary relationship between *xing*, *jing* and *shen*. In other words, the human person can live a long life only when the complementary relationship between body and spirit is maintained.

The origin of body and spirit and their destination after one's death

The origin of spirit and body
The views of the origin of body and spirit before Han Chin can be categorised into four types. These are: (1) The body comes from *jing shen* (spirit). Spirit comes form Dao. Dao is the wellspring of body and spirit (*Zhuang Zi* 'Zhi Bei You'). (2) Both Lei Zi and Huai Nan Zi hold that spirit comes from heavens and body from earth (*Huai Nan Zi* 'Jing Shen Xun'). Nevertheless, no discussion about the unity of body and spirit is offered. Moreover, there is no attempt to find out the final cause of these two items. (3) Confucianism, as evidenced in *Li Ji*, regards that *hun*

comes from the essence of *shen* (spirit) while *po* from that of *gui* (ghost). (4) Zi Chan considers that *shen hun* comes from *po qi* (*Zuo Zhuan* 'King Zhao' 7). Besides being different from one another, all these four views are quite remote from Western anthropology in regarding the origin of body and spirit.

The hun, po and body after one's death
After discussing the concepts of *hun* and *po*, Zi Chan states that, after one's death, they can attach to the body of someone else ((*Zuo Zhuan* 'King Zhao' 7).

In the *Lao Zi*, a Daoist scripture, it is argued that some people can refine their bodies to the extent that the bodies can become immortal. An immortal body is necessary for one to achieve immortality. Such view becomes the foundation of the later development of Daoist concept of immortality. Zhuang Zi contends that the life of a man depends on the coagulation and dissipation of *qi* (*Zhuang Zi* 'Zhi Bei You').

Another Daoist, Lei Zi, regards spirit will leave body after one's death. After then, it will return to heavens and earth, the place where it originally comes from and the abode where it originally lives.

Confucius has litte to say about the spiritual entity after death. His students almost have no impression of his discussion of the issue (*Analects* 'Shu Er' number 20). Nevertheless, at least, he uses the notions of *gui*, *shen* or *gui shen* (ghost and spirit) to describe the *hun* of the dead ancestors ('Xian Jin' number 11). The notion of *gui* used in the *Analects* refers to the *po qi* after one's death, and that of *shen* the spirit or *hun shen* after one's death. *Gui* and *shen*, therefore, are not comparable to divinities and God in Western thought. Being unable to know the real meaning of the notions, many people often misunderstand Confucian's sayings here.

Gui and *shen* are also mentioned in *Yi Zhuan*. 'The wandering *hun* begins to change, so we can know about the situation and condition of *gui* and *shen*.' In the Han dynasty, it is the dominant view in the documents that *hun* and *po* will be separated from body and return to heavens and earth respectively. Such a view of *hun* and *po* suffices to explain the reason why we found in the number three Han tomb in Mawandui at the same time a drawing on a piece of silk—a dead person ascending to heavens, and one on thick bamboo tablet—a dead person descending to earth. The same view is explicated clearly in the chapter 'Jiao Te Sheng' of *Li Ji*, a work contemporary with the tomb. Body and spirit will be separated once a person is dead. *Hun qi* (spirit) will return to Heaven while body and *po qi* to earth.

The Confucian view of *hun* and *po* after one's death still exerts influence on Chinese civil society nowadays—*hun* ascends to heavens and *po* returns to earth. A man comes back as a ghost after his death. After the ceremony of the consecration of the tablet, the ghost is turned to a spirit. It becomes ancestor's spirit and is prepared for entering the rank of ancestors. In the later sacrifice ceremonies, he will be worshiped as ancestor god.

The concepts of body and spirit in early Daoism

The literature of early Daoism on the concepts of body and spirit is quite copious. The discourse is to be examined from three aspects: the properties of spirit and body, the inseparable relationship between body and spirit in this world, and the origin of body and spirit and their relation to each other after one's death.

a. Properties of spirit and body

The view of body and spirit of early Daoism is to be understood with the help of three writings: *Tai Ping Jing*, *Lao Zi Xiang Er Zhu*, *Nan Bei Dou Jing*.

The notion of *jing shen* (spirit) happens frequently in *Tai Ping Jing*. It is sometimes referred to as *shen jing*.[25] The two words are also used separately as '*jing*' and '*shen*'. Another term '*hun shen*' is also used with the same meaning. In *Tai Ping Jing*, it is stated that there are three kinds of *qi* in human body. They are *shen* (clestial *qi*), *jing* (terrestrial *qi*) and *qi* (human *qi*) (*Tai Ping Jing* 728).

According to the study of Wang Tzung-yu, god in body mentioned in *Tai Ping Jing* has three characteristics. (1) God in body is *jing qi*. Basically, god in body is the *shen* gathering in human body. Its nature is actually *jing qi*. Later Daoism regards that '*jing* is the primordial vitality of life; *qi* is referred to the circulation of energy; and *shen* can dominate the god of heart'.[26] (2) God in body is a god who is in charge of punishment. In a narrow sense, god in body is a personal god who has image, behavior, thinking and emotion and is in charge of punishment. The thinking that spirit can be in charge of punishment reflects the combination of the traditional concept of *jing qi* and that of the mutual inspiration between heavens and man prevalent in the Han dynasty. (3) God in body is a god of organs. On the basis of the two properties mentioned previously, there develops the concepts of god of five viscera and gods related to specific organs such as god of head and that of four limbs. For Daoism, the human body is perceived as a sacred microcosm. This perception is the origin of the Daoist thought that god in body can reside in the organs of human body. Human body is a faithful duplication of heavens and earth. Consequently, gods of heavens and earth can exist in human body. This thought is actually an extension of the concepts that heavens and earth is the macrocosm for human body to model after, and the latter is the duplicate microcosm of the former.[27]

Two more properties, besides the ones discussed above, can be attributed to god in body. (4) God in body can be strengthened or weakened according to the human will. There are both virtuous and evil gods in body. The strengthening or weakening of them is resulted from the righteous or wickedness of the human person. (5) There are both virtuous and evil gods in body. In *Tai Ping Jing*, there is the remark that 'body is in charge of man's stepping towards death while spirit man's stepping towards longevity' (716). Evil gods and human body are possessed of the property to guide man towards death. On the contrary, during the pull and drag between life and death, spirit still guide man, with its utmost effort, towards life and even the quest for longevity.

Properties of hun and po in Nan Bei Dou Jing

Zhang Daoling is allege to have initiated the writing of two Daoist scriptures of the Han dynasty, *Nan Dou Jing* and *Bei Dou Jing*. Daoism followers of later stages added their viewpoints to them and completed the compilation of the two books.[28] In the text it is claimed that a woman has to receive simultaneously the *qi* from the North Dipper and that from the South Dipper in order to become pregnant. Both the genuine *qi* descending from the North Dipper, or *po*, and that from the South Dipper, or *hun*, are *shen* or spiritual entities. The formation of such a conception is the result that Daoism had inherited from the midland the pre-Qin concepts of *hun* and *po*. People in the pre-Qin period generally believe that man is generated by the *yin qi* and the *yang qi* of heavens and earth. *Yang qi* becomes *hun*. *Yin qi* becomes *po*. *Hun* governs thinking and ideas of man. *Po* governs body actions of man. Both *hun* and *po* are spiritual forces.[29]

Livia Kohn (1956–) has been studying *hun* and *po* for many years. She realises that death for Chinese is the separation of two essential souls. They are exactly the same souls that enable the formation of a living being. *Hun* is the sprit soul that is originated from heavens while *po* is material soul that belongs to earth.[30] Another scholar, Kristofer Schipper, regards that what is mentioned as *shen* or *shen ming*, both of them with the meaning of god, in ancient Chinese religion are far remote from divinities and God in Christian. *Shen* in China refers to the celestial soul that ascends to heavens after one's death. He makes a comparison of the three pair of terms frequently used in the ancient past—'*jing shen*', '*hun po*' and '*gui shen* (ghost and spirit)'—in a table to illustrate the relationship between them. '*Jing shen*' is categorized to be used in cosmology; '*hun po*' in physiology; and 'ghost and *shen*' (god) in religion or theology.

Table for a comparison of *jing shen*, *hun po* and *gui shen*

	Cosmological	Physiological	Theological
Higher level	*shen*	*hun*	*shen*
Lower level	*jing*	*po*	*gui*

Source: Kristofer Schipper, *The Taoist Body* (Berkeley: University of California Press, 1993), 33–6.

To sum up, there are seven properties that can be ascribed to the concept of spirit of early Daoism. (1) It is incorporeal, it is an immaterial, spiritual entity. (2) It is self-subsistent. Spirit is said to be capable of traveling out of body. (3) It is complex. Daoism's view of spirit differs not only from the Western view of soul but also greatly from the popular concept of *hun shen* before the Qin and Han dynasties, a concept that emphasizes on the simple and indivisible nature of spirit. (4) It is eternally imperishable. Daoism also touches upon the subject that one may become *gui* or *shen* after his death. Such a conception embeds in it the implication that spirit is imperishable. (5) It manages body. *Po* is a spiritual force that governs body. This concept is an inheritance of the traditional view prevalent in the pre-Qin period. The Daoist belief of god of five viscera is not in accordance with Chinese ancient tradition. (6) It is possessed of intellectual and ethical functions. For example, *hun* is used to refer to intellectual function. In additional to intellectual function, the gods in charge of punishment inside human body reveal that spirit is possessed of volitive and ethical functions. (7) There are both virtuous and evil gods, for instance, three-corpse-god and seven *po*. The seven *po* are in fact seven filthy ghosts. Out of the three *hun*, two of them entice man to commit evils. Both the dichotomous view of spirit and the concept of the existence of evil gods in human nature are not found in Chinese ancient tradition and Western philosophical anthropology. There is a discrepancy between the Chinese and the Western tradition. The concept of *hun po*, in both Daoism and the pre-Qin period, does not consider the property of incomplete entity that usually characterizes the discussion of soul in Western philosophy. Perhaps god in body can be regarded as a complete entity. However, the existence of several gods inside human body is not in accordance with Aquinas' contention that human body cannot be composed of numerous important souls.

As to the concept of body of early Daoism, four properties can be ascribed to it. (1) It is corporeal. (2) It is material. (3) It decays in this life. (4) Evil gods are possessed of the property to lead man to death.

The affinity between body and spirit in this life
Daoism places much emphasis on the importance of the inseparability between body and spirit. Such conception, with the concept of the matter and spirit of *qi* as its theoretical foundation, is rendered as a necessary condition of the belief that man, after achieving immortality, can fly up to heavens with mortal body and becomes a *xian* (an Immortal). Under such a circumstance, the concept of 'the body and spiritual *qi*' serves indirectly as the theoretical and practical basis for one to achieve immortality to become an Immortal with his mortal body.[31]

Daoism proclaims that man ought to control *hun* and *po* so as to suppress his wickedness and evilness, to maintain good health, to be excused from casualties and finally to become an Immortal. If one 'loses' his *hun* and *po*, he will become slow both in thinking and in action.[32] The external alchemy of Daoism quests for the capability of the mortal body to fly or the immortality of body. As to the internal alchemy, it is in pursuit of the unity of body and spirit to achieve nothingness or the immortality of spirit. Although their goals are not quite the same, both external and internal alchemy, in fact, are resulted from the theoretical extension of the affinity between body and spirit.

As observed from the above discussion, the view of the relationship between body and spirit as revealed in the scriptures of early Daoism can be summed up as two points. (1) There exists a complementary relationship between *qi* (body *qi*), *jing* and *shen*. In other words, those scriptures advocate that body and spirit are in a complementary relation. This view is close to the traditional view prevalent before the Qin and Han dynasties. The nourishment of body can result in sanity and is helpful to the nourishment of spirit. The nourishment of spirit can enable man to live a long life. On the contrary, "the loss of *hun* causes one to become slow in thinking and action. When his *shen* perishes, it is inevitable for one to age and die. (2) If one can preserve his *hun shen* for his whole life, he can become an Immortal and his body does not perish. The belief that it is possible to achieve the immortality of both body and spirit makes Daoism a distinct religion from others.

The origin of body and spirit and their relationship after one's death

What is the viewpoint of early Daoism about the origin and destination of body and spirit? We can investigate this issue from two aspects: the origin of spirit and body, and their relationship after one's death and deliverance

The origin of spirit and body
That there are three kinds of *qi*—*shen*, *jing* and *qi*—is stated explicitly in *Tai Ping Jing*. The former two are the fundamental elements of *shen*. The third one is the basic principle of body. *Shen* (celestial *qi*) and *jing* (terrestrial *qi*) come from heavens and earth respectively. *Qi* (human *qi*) is generated from the neutralization of celestial *qi* and the terrestrial one. As to human body, it is originated from human *qi* or body *qi* (*Tai Ping Jing* 728). However, in another part of the scripture, it is asserted that certain kinds of spirit are generated from the *qi* of four seasons and five elements (292).

For early Daoism, the body and spirit of the human person come from the nature and the cosmos. Such a view is totally different from that in Western philosophy. For Western philosophy, the body and spirit of man come chiefly from the supernatural God, with the assistance of the cooperation of parents.

The relationship between body and spirit after one's death and deliverance
Tai Ping Jing proclaims that the human person has only one birth and one death. Except the Immortals, man stands no chance to resurrect. 'All people have to die. This is not a case to be overlooked. Man has only one death . . . Man resides between heavens and earth. All men have only one birth. They cannot resurrect. Only those who can attain Dao can resurrect. They become *shijie xian* because they can resurrect after death" (*Tai Ping Jing* 298). '*Shijie*' (deliverance by means of the corpse) means that a man can undergo metamorphosis after his death. His outer shell (corpse) is still there, yet his spirit has already become an Immortal.[33]

As to the concept of life after one's death, we can observe from *Bei Dou Jing* that Daoism is under the influence of Buddhism as early as in the period of the Eastern Han dynasty. Daoism believes that when a person is dead, he or she is brought to the netherworld for a trial first. Then they undergo a transmigration to become a domestic animal, a beast, a bird or an insect (*Nan Bei Dou Jing* 264). Tung Fang-yuan finds out that the 'three *hun*' belief in Taiwan Daoism and among the common folk is affected by Confucian and Buddhism. There exists a clear cleavage between this belief and the 'three *hun*' concept of traditional Chinese Daoism.

An intrinsic problem can be found in the thoughts about human beings in Daoism. There exists a contradiction between the peculiarity of practicing to become Immortals and the generality of the limited transcendence in life. In fact, only few people can master the knack of practicing to become an Immortal.[34] Such contradiction may be resolved by realizing that there is no mention of the concept that 'all people can become Immortals' in the scriptures of early Daoism. There is also another contradiction.

On the one hand, it is asserted in the scriptures of early Daoism that a person can have one birth. On the other hand, it is stated a person can undergo transmigration to obtain rebirth again and again. Li Feng-mao attempts to reconcile this contradiction. He points out that, from the North Song dynasty onwards, priests of Daoism have been undertaking to relieve the souls of the death from purgatory through religious rituals.[35] However, Li's suggestion can only solve the problem that most people cannot become Immortals. It offers no help to the contradiction between 'no rebirth' and 'obtaining rebirth again and again through transmigration'.

Conclusion: The consensus of and difference between Chinese and Western concepts of body and spirit

There is a consensus among early Daoism, the sages before Han China and Western philosophical anthropology in regarding the discussion of soul. Both soul and *hun po* are incorporeal. They are non-material spiritual entities. They are also self-subsistent and imperishable. They are possessed of intellectual and volitive functions.

Both philosophical anthropology and ancient Chinese thought propose that the soul is simple. Their view differs greatly from the view of Daoism in that the latter proposes a complex spiritual entity. Because of its proposal, Daoism of later stages asserts that the spirit of human beings comprises of numerous virtuous gods and evil ones, with the implication that those gods in *hun po* are individual complete entities.

As to the concept of body, early Daoism, the sages before Han China and Western philosophical anthropology admit that it is corporeal and material. It decays in this life but will unite with soul (spirit) in afterlife to form an inseparable unity. Their presentation of the concept may be different. Yet the common viewpoints that they share still reveal their concern and expectation of the destiny of human beings. Nevertheless, we should notice that the divergence between the two concepts is not yet integrated—the concept of the inseparability of body and soul after one's life as well as the dichotomy of body and soul.

From the perspective of the relationship between body and spirit, philosophical anthropology, the sages before Han China and even early Daoism all agree that they are complementary to each other. Thus both the nourishment of spirit and that of body are regarded as of the same importance. Consequently, the stereotype that Daoism stresses only the nourishment of body is cast into doubt. The greatest divergence between the Chinese view and the Western one is that Western philosophical anthropology advocates the concept of binary union while the Chinese emphasises the complementary relationship between *xing* (body), *jing* and *shen*. Moreover, Western philosophical anthropology is able to utilise the systematic concepts of hylemorphims and 'actualisation and potentiality' as its theoretical foundations. On the contrary, Chinese Daosim lacks any systematic, theoretical foundation to support their contentions.

Western philosophical anthropology regards that the final cause of soul is the supernatural God and its intermediate cause the parents. Different from Western philosophical anthropology, sages before Han China and early Daoism mainly propose nature as the origin of soul. There are also other suggestions. However, all of them have no direct discussion on the final cause. Both Lao Zi and Zhuang Zi hold that Dao is the final cause of all the things in the cosmos. Daoism of later stages, however, does not adopt the ontological system of the primitive Daoists. On the contrary, it values the constellations of stars in nature as the final cause. The shift of the final cause from Dao to stars causes the arguments of later Daoism to become less solid.

With regard to the destination of body and spirit after one's death, there is the consensus of the Chinese and Western views that body and spirit will be separated temporarily after one's death and the spirit will remain to exist. Both Daoism and Western philosophical anthropology believe that any person has the possibility of the resurrection. After the resurrection, the body and spirit will never be separated any more. They both also assert that after death the body and spirit will maintain a special kind of relationship with nature and the whole cosmos. The consensus derived from the discussion here may serve as the platform for a dialogue between Daoism and the Western thought.

As a whole, the Chinese and Western concepts of body and spirit are not totally different from each other. There exist not only a few consensus points between them. Surprisingly, the concepts of body and spirit of early Daoism are not entirely the same as those of ancient China. There are interesting motifs raised in this essay. Among them, one is the tension between the inseparability of body and spirit revealed in Daoist scriptures and the dichotomy of body and soul. Another is the comparison and dialogue between the concepts of body and spirit recorded in early Daoist scriptures and the concept of soul revealed in early Greek myths. These motifs deserve further investigation by the scholars.

End Notes

1. See Fu-shih Lin, 'An Outline of Daoism Studies in Taiwan from 1945–1995', in *Taiwan Association of Religious Studies Journal*, volume 5 (Taipei, April, 2000): 34–74. See also 'An Outline of Daoism Studies in Europe and America from 1950-1994,' in *Taiwan Association of Religious Studies Journal*, volume 6 (Taipei, September, 2000): 29–88.
2. Thomas Aquinas, translation by the Fathers of the English Dominican Province, *Summa Theologica*, volume 1 (New York: Benziger Bros, 1948), 363–9. Hereafter abbreviated as (ST I, 75, 1–6).
3. JF Donceel SJ, *Philosophical Anthropology* (New York: Sheed and Ward, 1967), 411. Abbreviated hereafter as (Donceel, 411). See also the translation of Donceel's work by Kuei-chieh, Liu, *Philosophical Anthropology* (Taipei: Chiu-liu Publications), 412. Abbreviated hereafter as (Liu 412).
4. Battista Mondin and MA Cizdyn, *Philosophical Anthropology: Man, an Impossible Project?* (Bangalore, India: Theological Publications, 1985), 237–41.
5. *Ibid*, 240.
6. W Brugger editor, Tui-chieh Hsiang translator, *Dictionary of Western Philosophy* (Taipei: Hua Hsiang Yuan Publishing Co, 1989). See number 37 for 'body-soul relationship' and number 350 for 'spirit'.
7. Luis Gutheinz, SJ, *Anthropology in Theology*, second edition (Taipei: Kuangchi Cultural Group, 1991), 219–20.
8. Yu Dsu, *A Collection of Annotations on Zuo Zhuan*, (rpt. Taipei: Hsin Hsing Book Co., 1973), 308. Also see Ying-shih Yu, 'The Development of After Death Worldview in Ancient China', in *United Journal*, 26 (September 1983): 83. Changyi Ma, *Zhongguo Linghun Xinyang* (Shanghai: Shanghai Arts Press, 1998), 35.
9. Teng-fu Hsiao, *Thoughts about Underworld and Celestial Beings in Pre-Qi and Han China* (Taipei: Wen Chin Publishing Co Ltd, 1990), 17–19.
10. Cheng-sheng Tu, 'From Longevity to Immortality: Change of Life Concept in Ancient China', in the *Bulletin of the Institute of History and Philology of Academia of Sinica*, volume 66, number 2 (June 1995): 444.
11. Tzung-yu Wang, 'God in Body in *Tai Ping Jing*', in the *Chinese Culture Journal*, volume 159 (January 1993): 72–3.

12. Pi Wang, *Annotation of* Lao Zi, Book II, Chapter 42 (reprinted Taipei: Taiwan Chung Hua Book Co, 1970), 5a. Abbreviated as (Lao Zi, 42).
13. Fu-kuan Hsu, *A History of Human Nature of China* (Taipei: The Commerce Press, Ltd 1969), 387.
14. You Gao annotates, *Huai Nan Zi*, ninth edition (Taipei: The World Book Co Ltd, 1991), 99. Abbreviated hereafter as (*Huai Nan Zi*, 'Jing Shen Xun').
15. Wan-shou Chuang annotates and trans, *New Translation of Lei Zi* (Taipei: San Man Book Co Ltd, 1989), 27, 51 and 59. Abbreviated hereafter as (Lei Zi, chapter of Tian Rui).
16. Xi Zhu, *Annotations of Four Books* (Taipei: Hua Lien Publishing Co, 1970), 170. Abbreviated hereafter as (Mencius, former part of Gao Zi, 15).
17. Ying-shih Yu, 'The Development of After Death Worldview in Ancient China', 86.
18. Hao Chen, *Li Ji Ji Shuo*, third edition (Taipei: The World Book Co Ltd, 1969), 260.
19. Yuchai Duan, *Annotation of* Shuo Wen Jie Zi (reprinted Taipei: Lan Tai Book Co, 1972), 439.
20. Guanghung Guo, 'Yin Shang Ren De Hunbo Guannian', *Zhongyuan Wenwu* 3 (1994). Journal collected in CJFD, disc number HIST9409, downloaded from PDF essay.
21. Teng-fu Hsiao, *Thoughts about Underworld and Celestial Beings in Pre-Qi and Han China*, 20.
22. Xi Zhu, *Zhu Zi Yu Lei*. Quoted from Pao-lun Hsueh, *Philosophy of Soul* (Taipei: Fu Jen University Press, 1994), 28.
23. His-tai Ching edition, *Daoism and Chinese Tradition Culture* (Taipei: Chinese Orthodox Press, 1996), 130.
24. Jing Yang annotates and Xianqian Wang explicates, *A Collection of Annotations of* Xun Zi (Taipei: The World Book Co Ltd, 1974), 265.
25. Ming Wang editor, *Tai Ping Jing Hejiao* (Beijing: Zhuanghua Book Co, 1960), 27. Abbreviated hereafter as (*Tai Ping Jing* 27).
26. Su-chun Cheng, 'Theoretical Construction of Daoist Life Education', *Fu Jen Religious Studies* volume 8 (winter 2003): 89.
27. Changyi Ma, *Zhongguo Linghun Xinyang*, 57.
28. Dengfu Xiao, *Modern Annotation and Translation of Nan Bei Dou Jing* (Taipei: Hsing Tien Temple Foundation for Culture and

Education, 1999), 25. Abbreviated in this essay as (*Nan Bei Dou Jing* 25). In this essay, *Taishang Shuo Nnandou Liusi Yanshou Duren Miaojing* is abbreviated as *Nan Dou Jing*; *Taishang Xuanling Beidou Benming Yansheng Zhenjing* as *Bei Dou Jing*.
29. *Ibid*, 71
30. Livia Kohn, *Daoism and Chinese Culture* (Cambridge: Massachusetts: Three Pines Press, 2001), 56.
31. Yijie Tang, *Daoism in Wei, Jin, and South and North Dynasty* (Taipei: Tung Ta Book Co, 1991), 349. Also see Chien-cheng Liu, 'Matter, Spirit and Life, Death: The Competition between Matter and Spirit in the Period of Wei, Jin, and South and North Dynasty' in *Chinese Culture Journal* volume 208 (July 1997): 37.
32. See *Nan Bei Dou Jing*, 95, 288 and 297.
33. Li Zhou, 'Pi Ruo Chantui, Jie Hua Tuo Xiang—"Shijie" Chuanshuo Toushi', in *Southeast Culture* volume1 (January 1996): 1. Collected in CJFD. Disc no. HIST9607.
34. Yu-hui Yang, 'Daoist Anthropology and its Intrinsic Contradiction', in *Monthly Review of Philosophy and Culture* 29 issue 5 (May 2002): 452–3.
35. Feng-mao Li, 'The Complex View of Hun Bo from the Perspectives of Fast Rite and Burial Rite and Custom', in *Rite, Temple Fair and Community: Daoism, Folk Belief and Folk Culture* (Taipei: Institute of Chinese Literature and Philosophy, Academia Sinica, 1996), 472.

Considerations Of The 'Soul' In Western Thought

Thomas Berg

Abstract

What is a human being? Western thought has posed this fundamental question for millennia; it continues to do so today. Over twenty-two centuries ago, Plato—through the mouth of Socrates in his dialogue with Alcibiades—proposed three possible answers to that question, namely: 'soul, body or both together, forming a whole'.

To this day, western thought continues to grapple with all three alternatives. They correspond rather succinctly to what have historically emerged as three rival conceptions of what it means to be a human being. The first answer corresponds to the Platonic tradition, the second to the approach of reductive materialism, and the third to the tradition engendered by Aristotle and Thomas Aquinas. For the purposes of this paper, I will understand the Platonic tradition to include any conception of the human person which is at root dualistic, that is, positing the soul as something substantial, inhabiting and using a body. By reductive materialism, I understand any number of contemporary philosophies of mind which in one way or another reduce mental events to physical events of the biological organism. Finally, by the Aristotelian-Thomistic tradition, I mean any view which holds the human being to be a *composite* of a soul and matter, soul being the life-giving principle and *substantial form* of the body to which it is intimately united, as Aristotle says, 'as the wax and the shape given to it by the stamp are one'.

What is a human being? Western thought has posed this fundamental question for millennia; it continues to do so today. Over twenty-two centuries ago, Plato—through the mouth of Socrates in his dialogue with Alcibiades—proposed three possible answers to that question, namely: 'soul, body or both together forming a whole'.[1]

To this day, Western thought continues to grapple with all three alternatives. They correspond rather succinctly to what have historically emerged as three rival conceptions of what it means to be a human being. The first answer corresponds to the Platonic tradition, the second to the approach of reductive materialism, and the third to the tradition engendered by Aristotle and Thomas Aquinas. For the purposes of this paper, I will understand the Platonic tradition to include any conception of the human person which is at root dualistic, that is, positing the soul as something substantial, inhabiting and using a body.[2] By reductive materialism, I understand any number of contemporary philosophies of mind which in one way or another reduce mental events to physical events of the biological organism. Finally, by the Aristotelian-Thomistic tradition, I mean any view which holds the human being to be a *composite* of a soul and matter, soul being the life-giving principle and *substantial form* of the body to which it is intimately united, as Aristotle says, 'as the wax and the shape given to it by the stamp are one'.[3]

The Western concept of 'soul' up to Descartes: Platonism vs Aristotelianism

From the time of Plato (born *circa* 428 BC) to the early fourteenth century AD, the Platonic and the Aristotelian-Thomistic views co-exist among Western philosophers. The latter tradition in particular, prior to the fourteenth century, is nurtured in a plasma of richly meaningful background issues. A *revolution* of thought beginning in the late fourteenth century and culminating especially in the thought of Sir Francis Bacon (1561–1626) and René Descartes (1596–1650) will profoundly and irreversibly disrupt background issues and precipitate the demise of the Aristotelian-Thomistic view. Let's now briefly explore this set of *background issues* as it developed prior to the fourteenth century, how it was revolutionised beginning in the early modern period, and how it precipitated the demise of the Aristotelian account. This will then leave us in a good position to explore the emergence of Descartes' anthropological dualism and its tremendous impact on our Western understanding of the 'soul'.

The background of an Aristotelian-Thomistic conception of the 'soul'
The four back-ground issues I mean to elucidate here are those of 'act and potency', 'matter and form', Aristotelian four-dimensional causality, and the teleological 'cosmos'. Lacking these, we really have little hope of understanding an Aristotelian-Thomistic account of soul. To do this, let me note a fundamental fact about our modern scientific mindset.

We take great satisfaction in knowing, for example, that water is reducible to hydrogen and oxygen, that our brain is just a complex system of cells made of molecules, made of atoms, made of quarks, and so on. The modern scientific mind asks *how* a thing is what it is, and is normally satisfied with asking that and nothing more.

Aristotle, the great naturalist and proto-scientist, didn't stop there.

He also asked *why* a thing is what it is? Why does it *become*? Why does it *change*? He asks why is there *being, becoming and change* at all? Such questions go beyond the realm of physical material accounts of *how* things are what they are. That's why Aristotle called answers to these questions *metaphysical*, 'beyond the physical'.

Nowadays, most people are baffled by both the questions and the answers of Aristotelian metaphysics. But to elucidate some of those questions and the ultimate answers Aristotle proposed is precisely my task now.

Act and potency, form and matter[4]
First, let's try to get our brains around the co-concepts of 'act and potency', 'form and matter'. To do this we must understand that the doctrine of 'act (or actuality) and potency (or potentiality)' is Aristotle's ultimate explanation of all that forms part of the real world around us. He needed an explanation *beyond* the 'elements' as they were known at the time (air, earth, fire and water). Beyond the elements, Aristotle held that the world *had to be* ultimately explainable in terms of *an underlying dynamic,* because only the dynamic communion of two fundamental dimensions of the real world could explain the great problem of *why* there is *change* in that world. Act and potency are *principles* (in Greek, *archai*) or ultimate starting points in accounting for the reality of *change*. They also constitute the very ground of Aristotelian-Thomistic metaphysics and anthropology. Let's see how Aristotle gets there.

In the first three books of the *Physics*, Aristotle takes on the great problem of change by first how the fact of change presents itself in reality. He was grappling with what appeared to be a great contradiction: change (and in a broader sense, all movement) appeared to be simultaneously a being and a non-being; and since this was intrinsically contradictory, it could not be the case. So change seemed to be at odds with intelligibility!

In *Physics* I, he resolves this difficulty by introducing the concept of *potentiality*. He does this by explaining that to understand nature we must get at its principles (*archai*) as in any science. He then goes on to reason toward three ultimate principles in nature: form, privation, and what he calls 'matter'—or the utter *potentiality* to become.[5] Hence, all change in nature could now be construed as the passage from potentiality to actuality:

- The underlying 'matter' (also known in the tradition as 'prime matter'[6]) is a pure potential to become. (And here we are not talking about something like 'dark matter' out there in the universe or plasma or anything of the sort; this is not 'matter' in any physical sense, but simply *the utter possibility of being something, without actually being anything*; the undetermined basis for some determination).

- The 'privation' sets in when the 'form' that had determined the matter previously leaves and is displaced by a new 'form'. (And here form does not mean shape, but rather 'intelligibility' and 'actual determination').

- Potentiality is always present as the underlying matter (the element of constancy); actuality is always present as some form, but forms can be present and cease to be present.

This is the only way for *change* to make any sense! There had to be an underlying something (matter) which remains constant, and an element that is versatile and mutable (form). Matter is potential to be and to become; the form 'in-forms' that matter, making it actually *be* something.

So there we have it: act and potency. In the Aristotelian-Thomistic metaphysics, then, all change and all becoming can be parsed into the interplay of these two co-principles of reality, the binary coordinates of all contingent entities. In living bodies, the dynamism of act-potency is played out by form and matter: form, the intelligible element, bears the role of actuality; 'prime matter' is the pure potential for becoming, un-actualised, open to be 'in-formed'.

Now, if that was hard to get your brain around, what follows is even harder: act & potency, or form and matter, are not separate *things*, separate *substances;* rather, they make a thing *to be* a thing, they make a substance *to be* a substance.

Here's how: Aristotle and Thomas certainly held that matter and form (potentiality and actuality) are distinct from one another. But here the tradition upholds a notion of distinction which is quite foreign to our contemporary scientific worldview, namely, the so-called real distinction '*in re*—within the thing'.[7] That is to say, these co-principles of reality are really distinct considered in themselves, but never *found* in reality by themselves. As an ultimate internal metaphysical dynamism, they together constitute the *res*, the whole, and underlie all of its particular development, change and movement. Were they not really distinct (but merely logically distinct), they would be useless to explain change as a process in which something is taken away (form) and something remains (matter). So, the principles of actuality/potentiality, form/matter must be *really* distinct dimensions bearing their own influence, but never discovered by themselves, *never existing apart from their corresponding co-principle.* Together they constitute two dimensions working together in a dynamism as ultimate starting points, distinct prior to any work of the mind, and together account for *one* fundamental reality.⁸ This notion of 'real distinction *in re*' is a condition *sine qua non* for understanding an Aristotelian-Thomistic account of the soul. As we will see, in the case of animate beings like ourselves, it is the form, in-forming prime matter, which gives us a body; it is the form (as what will be called substantial form) that makes matter be a living body.⁹

The four causes and the teleological framework of reality
As we have already seen, in Aristotle's view, underlying the realm of the physical is the realm 'beyond' the physical, the meta-physical, where we are to find the ultimate and final account of how things transpire in reality in terms of their most fundamental causes. Of these causes we have already met two: matter and form. Here we have to free up the notion of 'causality' from the primarily mechanistic sense in which we practically understand it, to understand causality simply as the ultimate 'why' and 'wherefrom' for what there is in the cosmos.

The doctrine of the causality exerted by matter and form is also known as the 'hylemorphism' or 'hylo-morphism' from the Greek, *hyle* (matter) and *morphe* (form). It could explain both the *numeric multiplicity* of beings within a species (for example, why millions of olive trees have existed in the world and not just one ideal Olive Tree), and substantial change from one species of a thing to another, as when an oak tree becomes ashes and smoke.

Now, on Aristotle's view, form proceeds in its development toward a natural end state of fullness. That is, form acts for an end: the 'oak form' present in an acorn pursues the state of full flourishing as an oak tree; the 'trout form' present in the trout minnow pursues the state of full flourishing as a mature trout, and so on. That all things act for their natural end is called the doctrine of 'teleology' (from the Greek *telos*, 'end'). This final end state of flourishing within a species or natural kind also exerts a causal influence on the metaphysical level: it is present as the goal and end-state toward which a form is inclined a dynamic tension.[10]

The fourth cause—the efficient—is doubtless more accessible to us. This is simply the kind of causality brought about by any agent, any actor or doer. Aristotle notes that final, formal, and efficient cause, in the realm of natural beings, can often coincide: it is clear that notionally form and end are in confluence: the form is not only the definition or the what-it-is-to be something, but also the end for which action takes place, the end at which nature aims in producing that thing. Further, in natural process the form is literally present in the efficient cause: man engenders man by possessing the form of man in himself.

An ordered cosmos
And now to the final background issue: the Aristotelian cosmos. He conceives of this cosmos and the natural bodies which constitute it (everything from galaxies to grains of sand) as existing within distinctive *kinds*, distinguishable as genus, species, and eventually individuals. Hence we have a conception of a cosmos as *ordered*.[11] This is a cosmos filled with natural 'forms', a universe pregnant with essences, meanings, 'logos'.[12] This constitutes what can be called a 'logocentric' conception of being, in which being is by its very nature intelligible and meaningful.[13] The ordered-ness of the cosmos, imbued as it is with its rich network of meanings and teleologies all arranged in balance and harmony, becomes normative for human societies as *physis* (the principle of movement in nature), *nomos*: (law in culture), *ethos* (right personal conduct

or virtuous behavior) and logos (ultimate meanings).[14] Persons, culture, the flow of development within species, the richness of natural kinds—all constitutes a marvelous whole, the fabric of meaning of which the human person finds him or herself to be a part.

Toward the demise of an Aristotelian-Thomistic conception of the 'soul': the rejection of the notion of 'form' in Western thought
Having finished out metaphysics lesson, we must now explore the historical and philosophical milieu in which the Aristotelian-Thomistic conception of the soul meets its demise. This is historically tied to developments which begin to appear in the thought of William of Ockham (1290–1348) and culminate in the thought of Francis Bacon and, most especially, that of Rene Descartes. With Ockham we see the beginnings of what will become an ever more ambitious reformulation and/or rejection of much of the preceding 'background' just discussed. Cutting right to the chase, we will see that the net outcome of the revolution launched by Ockham will be *the rejection of the notion of formal causality*. And this is how it happens.[15]

The first notion to undergo serious transformation is that of 'cosmos.' From its predominate position in the consideration of reality as organised and normative whole, pregnant with *logos,* manifest in culture as *nomos* and *ethos*, present in animate beings as teleological *physis,* the notion of cosmos is submitted to a gradual reduction to that of 'nature' as a collection of extra-mental objects vis-à-vis the knowing mind of the observing individual. The reduction will be complete in the thought of Francis Bacon, incarnation of the consummate inquiring 'self' who looks out onto the cosmos now conceived of as 'physical nature', the composite of 'objects' of scientific inquiry.

In this period, consideration of the 'real' is marked by a tension between the universal (*form*) and the singular (*singulum*), prominence gradually being accorded to the latter to the point at which, in the thought of Ockham, a veritable 'ontology of the singular' is articulated in contraposition to an ontology of the divine. Consequently, Western thought passes from the previously predominant view of one universal ontology of which human nature is a partaker and participant, to a separation of ontologies, one for the realm of the singular man, another (detached from the latter and beyond it) for the divinity.

In the realm of the singular, the *singular* dominates to the point that form is emptied of its metaphysical weight. The cosmos is not alive with forms, but with singular entities. Ockham sees forms as mere human constructs at best; not as profound metaphysical principles. Ockham's cosmos of the singular, in fact, gets along just fine without forms; their use is merely linguistic and they simply help us to communicate and organise our reality: a horse is a horse, not because it is in-formed by the natural form of horse, but because a culture has produced the term 'horse' and it is useful.

This also illustrates how the same period witnesses a transformation in our understanding of the nature and (we might say) 'vocation' of 'mind.' From a growing tension between mind as *conforming to, and receptive of*, the cosmos—knowing it by abstracting and sharing in the intelligible forms that comprise it—there emerges an ever more predominant understanding of mind as *productive* and *creative* of the real. Similarly, the fundamental conception of mind as 'entwined' with, and participating in, the real order or cosmos is slowly supplanted by the ever more predominant notion of mind as the *isolated observer* of nature. This sets the stage for the emergence of the category of the 'self' in later modernity. In this fashion, the knowing subject falls out of the framework of nature and becomes a detached, third-person observer, the autonomous referent of what-there-is, and especially autonomous moral referent, the self who also objectivises the body of others, as well as his own body.

In sum, the erosion of an understanding of *cosmos* as organised and normative whole, pregnant with *logos*, the growing ontological pre-eminence of the singular within metaphysics, the growing gulf between the mental and the extra-mental, and the evolving philosophical fixation on the self as detached and knowing subject all work together to undermine the entire notion four-dimensional causality, particularly the notion of formal causality on which the Aristotelian-Thomistic notion of soul hinges. The demise of that notion will be virtually complete, and the revolution in Western thought set in play by William of Ockham will reach its zenith in the thought of Rene Descartes.

From 'soul' to 'self': Cartesian dualism
Descartes' philosophical anthropology constitutes the intellectual death knell of an Aristotelian-Thomistic concept of soul which will effectively disappear from intellectual landscape of modern and contemporary Western philosophy (with the exception of those institutions, such as Catholic seminaries, which will maintain the tradition of Scholastic philosophy). Descartes' account of the soul likewise sets the stage for the rapid demise of the unworkable and intellectually unsatisfactory Platonic conception. Allow me to explain.

We must first recall Descartes' philosophical program: this was nothing less than the development of a method for arriving at an inscrutably certain body of true knowledge. To this end he develops *The Discourse on the Method*, published in 1637, and four years later in 1641, the *Meditations on First Philosophy,* a work which greatly expounds a number of key principles developed in the former. Though Jesuit trained and steeped in Scholastic philosophy from his youth, Descartes rejects the Aristotelian metaphysics and crafts a theory of human nature which obeys the logical consequences of that rejection which had already been set in play by Ockham and Bacon.

Following his intellectual forebears, in one swipe of the pen, Descartes does away with final causality. '[T]he species of cause termed final,' he writes 'finds no useful employment in physical or natural things'.[16] Why reject final causality? Why would Descartes (following Bacon) eliminate final causality from his metaphysics? Because both Descartes and Bacon assumed the truth of the denial of formal causality theoretically heralded by Ockham two centuries earlier. Now, if there are no natural forms out there, then quite clearly there could be no natural ends to be pursued because final cause only makes sense in conjunction with formal cause. In metaphysics, the two fall and rise together.

So this leaves a Cartesian metaphysics with only two kinds of causality, the material and the efficient. Lacking any notion of formal causality as that which in-forms and gives actuality to a purely potential 'matter' (prime matter), the latter necessarily undergoes an intellectual reification and is henceforth supplanted by the notion of *matter as physical body*. Efficient causality, in turn, undergoes a reworking and mutates into *mechanistic causality* which, since the time of Bacon, was the only notion of causality worth of the name.

In sum, by the time we get to Descartes, modern thought is dominated by the reduction of causality to the notion of mechanistic efficient causality, by the notion of 'thing' as bodily, substantial, separate unto itself, and by an understanding of reality parsed in terms of bodies working upon each other, all bodies really distinct and *separate* from each other. In Descartes' mind—and this is crucial—this is the *only* way of understanding 'distinction'. The Cartesian cosmos is a whole of objects (bodies) influencing each other in the manner of mechanistic causality—human body and human soul included. In such a worldview, there is no room for an Aristotelian-Thomistic understanding of soul as substantial form of the body. So, it is set aside.

How then, does Descartes, with his mechanistic metaphysics, account for the phenomenon of the human person, with his subjectivity, his thought, mind, consciousness, senses and bodily organism? He does it using the only tools he has. His starting point, as we know, is to affirm the radical, ontological priority and self-evidence of mind-thought as the unquestionably certain starting point for constructing an organic whole of certain and universal knowledge. From the certainty of his own thought, the 'cogito', he goes on to reason in the *Discourse*:

> From that I knew that I was a substance the whole essence or nature of which is to think, and that for its existence there is no need of any place, nor does it depend on any material thing; so that this 'me' that is to say, the soul by which I am what I am, is entirely distinct from body.[17]

Here we have the complete account the Cartesian person, complete with a nuanced and refurbished Platonic conception of soul. On the Cartesian view, the human person is a 'thinking thing' or soul (the *res cogitans*—non-extense, self-contained, unquantifiable) which *uses* an 'extended thing' or body (the *res extensa*—extended, measurable, quantifiable). And these two *separate* substances are caught up in a relationship of mechanistic causality. Such is the doctrine of Cartesian 'substance dualism'. As a theory of human nature, it was quite short lived and so untenable that it provoked the further demise of the Platonic conception of soul.

The Western concept of 'soul' from the post-Cartesians to the 'philosophy of mind' and John Searle

Substance dualism was short-lived because it was untenable and unworkable. How could there be any causal relationship between these two radically different substances? Descartes failed to supply an answer, and solutions such as Occasionalism[18] were veritable absurdities. The unanswered question of the causal relationship between the Cartesian ego and the Cartesian body engendered what today has become known as the mind-body problem: what is the relationship between mind and body? Or (more specifically), how the does the brain cause mind? The pursuit of a reasonable answer to the problem has been the aim of the philosophy of mind for the better part of the last five decades.

The eventual reaction to Descartes and his immediate aftermath was to jettison the notion of soul altogether along with Descartes' substance dualism—throwing out the baby with the proverbial bath water. Gilbert Ryle's derisive rejection of 'ghost-in-the-machine' approaches to understanding human personhood marked the intellectual itinerary of philosophy of mind which would endeavor to explain the mind-body or mind-brain relation entirely without recourse to anything approaching a classical conception of 'soul'. So, in truth—at least in terms of mainstream Western philosophy—talk of a 'contemporary understanding of the soul' is almost an oxymoron. There is no *contemporary understanding of the soul* other than understanding it as a component of a now discarded premodern psychology.

Time does not allow here to examine in any detail the intellectual itinerary of the philosophy of mind. I will limit myself to say that in grappling with the mind-body problem, and in dominating academic philosophy in the Anglo world for the past five decades, the philosophy of mind has generated a nest of fascinating questions and a plethora of literature. Out of the fray have emerged several quite entrenched stances or schools of thought.[19] Of all the philosophers of mind, however, John Searle, the Mills Professor of Philosophy at UC Berkeley, is today arguably the most compelling.

Searle can be described as a non-reductive materialist.[20] That is to say, he invites us to accept the 'obvious facts' about our mental life, meaning to accept that mental phenomena are real and they have a causal influence on us (a position referred to as 'mental realism'). In so-doing, he has been accused of buying into Cartesianism. But on Searle's account, the acceptance of these facts does *not* entail Cartesianism. Rather, the facts of mental life (especially consciousness and intentionality) are reconcilable with the reality of neurophysiology, once we simply 'see'[21] that the former are nothing more than features of the latter, and caused by the latter in the manner that the hardness of an ice-cube is caused by the vibrations of H_2O molecules in a lattice-structure.[22] In a nutshell, Searle holds that the brain causes mind, not in the sense of mechanistic causality, but in the kind of causality which holds in a *system of properties*, particularly that which holds between microfeatures and macro-features of a system. Searle holds that the mind—and consciousness in particular—is simply a property or a 'feature' of the brain just as hardness is a feature of water molecules in a lattice structure.

Fundamentals of the Aristotelian-Thomistic account of the soul

If we have understood the preceding sections, we are now in a position to consider the Aristotelian-Thomistic account of the soul in greater detail. Let us here explore five of the central (and most poorly understood) features of that conception.

The human soul is the form of the body
In Book II of his *On the Soul*, Aristotle defines the soul as 'the form of a natural body having life potentially within it'.[23] Now, the affirmation that the soul is 'form' (*eidos*) with regard to the body must necessarily be understood from within the Aristotelian account of reality as ultimately explainable in terms of the fundamental ontological dynamic of potentiality (*dynamis*) engaged with actuality (*entelecheia*). Soul, therefore, understood as 'form' (*eidos*) of the body, is to be understood as 'actuality' or 'act'.[24]

To say that soul is the form of a body 'having life potentially within it' is to say that it is the form of a body which is so *ordered* (organised) so as to sustain life. Aristotle thus simplifies the definition to read 'the actuality of a natural organised body'.[25] Hence, Thomas will formulate his definition in Latin as *'entelechia corporis organici physici potentia vitam habentis'*[26] or more commonly *'actus corporis organici'*.[27]

A bit further on, Aristotle takes the fine tuning of his definition of soul one step further. He has given the name 'soul' to that in the body which is its actuality. He points out however, that actuality can be understood in two ways.[28] Certainly any organism displays myriad and virtually infinite kinds of actualities, from a heart beating, to neurons firing, to digestion, to the winking of an eye. However, at the basis of all of these there is an even more fundamental actuality, the most basic which is the very *act of being*, the most fundamental positivity—'is-ness'—of that organism, the very given-ness of it, its existence considered in itself. Which is to say, there must be, in the very make up of any living being, one fundamental starting point of all its activity—a first (primary, most fundamental) actuality that is the ground for all the secondary actualities (such as those just referred to). In any organism, 'soul' corresponds to this latter sense of actuality, which is deeper and more fundamental, and to which Aristotle refers to as the 'first degree' of actuality.[29] Consequently, his now more succinct definition of soul reads: 'the first degree of actuality of a natural organised body'.[30] So, from an Aristotelian-Thomistic perspective, the soul is the *being* of an organised body; soul is the *actuality* of an individuated and existent human nature present and living. This is the meaning of soul as *form* of the body.

The human soul is not something 'added' to an already existing body
Now, this means that soul is not something added to an already existent body; rather an organism is an organism in virtue of, and thanks to, the presence of soul (actuality). Soul is not one thing 'added' to or imposed upon or infused into an already in-formed, existing organism; rather soul is, by its essence, the very existence or actuality of that organism. St. Thomas is emphatic about this.[31]

The human soul is intellective and incorporeal
For Aristotle and Aquinas, to say 'human soul' is to say 'intellective soul'—and it is about as redundant as saying 'flying jet', for they held it to be immediately evident that it is the soul which thinks. If the soul is the first act of a living organism, then in the case of a human being, it is also the first starting point of thought. Now, while the tradition has come to understand that thought has an *extrinsic*

dependence on our physical organism (particularly the brain), it still upholds the *intrinsic independence* of thought from any organ. That is to say, in its essence, intellection does not depend on or take place through an organ, that it is intrinsically independent of the body.[32] Both thinkers affirmed, however, (unlike Plato) the extrinsic dependence of the soul/intellect on some bodily organ in order for thought to take place:

> The body is required for the intellect's action not as the organ through which such an action is carried out, but on account of its object. For a phantasm is related to intellect just as color is to sight.[33]

For Aristotle and Aquinas, intellection is only possible through recourse to 'phantasms', that is, those composed and stored sensory images of extra-mental singular objects, the product of a composition worked by the internal senses on the data received through the five external senses.

That external dependence does not cancel out the intrinsic independence of its operation. The operation of the intellect is intrinsically independent of an organ because that is the only way, on their view, that the intellect can do what it does. This, in turn, is tantamount to affirming that the soul in incorporeal. And here are the reasons they give.

The hallmark of human intellection is the intellect's radical openness to a virtual infinity of cognitions. Aquinas (following Aristotle in *On the Soul*, III) is wont to repeat that the soul—and consequently the intellect—is *quodammodo omnia*, 'in some sense all things'. Aquinas further explains that it is precisely this capacity of soul/intellect for a virtual infinity of cognitions which tells us that the soul must be non-corporeal, because:

that which can cognize certain things must have non of those things in its own nature because that which exists in it naturally would impede its cognition of other things . . . Therefore, if the intellectual principle were to contain within itself the nature of any body, it could not cognize all bodies.[34]

Accordingly, for Aristotle and Aquinas, human intellection—the very operation of the soul—is essentially incorporeal.[35]

The human soul is not a substance
Here we arrive at the unique and most valuable contribution of the Aristotelian-Thomistic understanding of soul. It is also the most misunderstood and misconstrued. Recall that Aristotle and Thomas give the name 'soul' to that co-principle within the human being which corresponds to the actuality. That is all it is. Hence, the contribution which is so crucial to our contemporary debate: *on an Aristotelian-Thomistic read, the soul is not a substance*.

We will be in a position to understand this if we have understood the following elements of Aristotelian metaphysics and anthropology:

- The fundamental metaphysical composition of existent entities, that is, their analyzability into the dimensions of potentiality/actuality;
- The name 'soul' applies *only* to the element of actuality;
- In the human substance, the role of potentiality is played out by a properly organised body capable of existence;
- This actuality *is* the very life-form of the resulting organised and *living* body.

Consequently, it is not the soul that is a substance, but the whole living human being, the *subject* of this particular existence in this particular living body. Soul by itself is only one dimension of that existing, substantial subject. Soul is only a part of the whole—a subsistent part to be sure—but only a part, a dimension.[36] Man is not given to us in experience (either of others or of ourselves) as *a body* and *a soul*. What is given to us in experience is the human being as embodied-immateriality or, if you will, *corporeal-spirit*. Beyond the distinction between soul and matter, there is a whole, a *fundamental unity*, for one is the *subject* of both, namely, the 'I' of our experience.

The soul-body communion constitutes one reality: the human person
Thus, the unity of the human being is best articulated as *the dynamism of soul-informing-body:* from two dimensions, one substantial reality. Here, we must not fail to grasp the dramatic difference between the Cartesian anthropology and the Aristotelian: on an essentially mechanistic view, we could not but understand Aristotle to be as much a dualist as Plato or Descartes, for we could *only* understand Aristotle to be talking about two *things:* psyche and soma, soul and body, form and matter, actuality and potentiality. Parse it as we might, in a mechanistic view, these will always necessarily be understood as really distinct and *separate* things.

In radical contrast, on an Aristotelian-Thomistic view, we can understand these dimensions to be present and in play in the ontological universe, indeed, really distinct, yet *inseparable* dimensions of *one* and the same entity. That is, inseparable dimensions constituting a unity. As Aristotle himself puts it:

> Unity has many senses (as many as 'is' has), but the most proper and fundamental sense of both is the relation of an actuality to that of which it is the actuality.[37]

The most proper sense of unity is that of the reality of actuality to potentiality. For Aristotle, that adds up to one reality, not two. Indeed, there are no two things to add, but only two dimensions to distinguish. They are, to be sure, really distinct, but not separate. Together, they constitute one reality. As I have insisted, the distinction '*in re*' between co-constitutive principles is essential for understanding the soul in the Aristotelian-Thomistic tradition.

Conclusion: Can science dialogue with Aristotle and Aquinas?

So why on earth should our colleagues in philosophy of mind and the hard sciences ever bother to muster the patience to dialogue with this tradition? For one simple reason, if I may be so naïve and so bold as to suggest it: an Aristotelian-Thomistic anthropology *might* be able to resolve the mind-body problem. Explaining *how* the tradition might accomplish this constitutes an intellectual challenge that must be met with utmost intellectual integrity and rigor. Here I have merely endeavored to point open minds in that direction.

I will insist, however, that the scientific mindset will only be able to engage the tradition if it is willing to countenance the possibility of non-physical causal pathways as part of the ultimate explanation of things; what is worse, science will have to seriously re-consider the legitimacy of the notion of formal causality.

Too high a price?

Perhaps. But the benefits for our shared understanding of human life, and human dignity as members of a world community may make the price well worth it. Now, John Searle has actually hit on something which suggests that my proposal may not be so incredible.

In *The Rediscovery of Mind*, he attacks one of the most fundamental and spectacularly counter-intuitive features of the predominant scientific worldview, namely that 'all empirical facts, in the ontological sense of being facts in the world, are equally accessible epistemically to all competent observers'.[38] In other words, Searle challenges the untenable position that the *only* facts about the world deserving of the name are those which are 'testable by third-person means'. As Searle rightly points out, this is clearly false. For example, we all take it (I assume) to be empirical fact that dolphins use sonar to navigate. Yet, no one in their wildest imagination could ever consider himself in a position to describe (from a third-person perspective) *what it feels like* qualitatively to be under the influence of sonar. The fact that such a datum is inaccessible to standard criteria of empirical verification does not render it any less an accepted empirical fact.[39]

So, there is already an acceptance within science for explanations which defy the standard empirical model of explanation. Now, it is only possible to admit the reality of mental life (in its dimensions of consciousness, intentionality and subjectivity) on similar grounds, for mental life too defies explanation on the standard model. So, if the contemporary scientific mindset in some sectors is seeing its way clear to accepting the causal influence of non-physical, epistemically subjective things such as mental states, I ask: why could it not go tout court, and readmit non-physical, formal causality into the privileged club of 'the real'?

The tradition, for its part, welcomes the vast and growing body of knowledge regarding the strict correlation between biochemical events in the brain and mental life.

If the soul is what Aristotle says it is—the first degree of actuality of a living organism, and that which actualises the bio-chemical manifold of the brain as a necessary, though insufficient, condition for mental life—then we should have no problem whatsoever with discovering the strictest correlation between brain events and mental events. Indeed, we should wonder at it and be fascinated by it—as would both Aristotle and Aquinas.

In conclusion, a renewed consideration of the notion of formal causality may render a more intellectually satisfying answer to the mind/body problem than materialists have proffered so far. If my understanding of Aristotle is correct, then endorsement of the Aristotelian hylemorphic conception of ontological composition commits us neither to substance dualism nor to property dualism.[40] Thinkers in the Aristotelian-Thomistic tradition have a way of maintaining mental realism and anti-reductionism without falling into dualism, while at the same time rejecting material monism. Indeed, the day may soon be coming when we understand and accept that understanding the human person as incarnate spirit, as a dynamism of soul-in-forming-body, is truly our best and only workable response to Alcibiades.

End Notes

1. Plato, *Alcibiades I*, 130a, Jowett translation.
2. 'Plato, however, since he claimed that sensing belongs to the soul alone, could claim that a human being is a soul using its body' (Thomas Aquinas, *S T*, I, q. 75, a. 4c, Pasnau translation).
3. Aristotle, *On the Soul*, II, 412b7. JA Smith translation in McKeon. All English renderings of Aristotle are taken from the McKeon unless otherwise indicated.
4. If we were to treat these in the standard manner of intellectual taxonomy, understanding them as 'ontological commitments' or merely part of a lexicon, an hermeneutic device, or simple constructs, then Aristotle's thought would be utterly lost on us.
5. In synthesis, this is how Aristotle arrives at this conclusion. Our common sense grasp tells us that a change is a coming to be of what was not: it is the coming to be of A from *non-A*. In this sense the principles of the coming to be of A involve A and its contrary, *non-A*. Now, if nature (and, consequently, change) is to be intelligible, there must not be an infinite number of principles. The question thus arises: Is a *pair* of contrary principles enough? Earlier thinkers like Heraclitus and Parmenides thought so. Aristotle, however, thought otherwise. He notes that contraries (such as love and hate) do not act on each other, but rather on some third element, a substratum; and in addition, no substance is made up simply of a contrary, nor can it be composed of contraries (which would run afoul of the principle of non-contradiction). So, Aristotle concludes that there must be three, and three suffices for intelligibility, and his thought proceeds as follows. All change proceeds from a supposite and an opposite, involving (1) the supposite x, and contraries (2) *non-A* and (3) A. He terms these three elements (1) 'matter' (*hypokeimenon* or *hyle*); (2) 'privation' (*antikeimenon* or *steresis*); and (3) 'form' (*morphe, eidos*, or 'the principle which forms the object of definition'). (1) and (2) or (1) and (3) together make up a substance (*ousia* or *tode ti*). Now, A does not arise from its opposite simply, for in nature, far from seeking each other, opposites are mutually eliminatory. Nor will Aristotle admit that A arises from nothing — *ek me ontos* (*ex nihilo*). A arises from a concurrence of A with the composite of x + *non-A*; the *non-A* yields its hold, as it were, on the pure potentiality of x to become A.

6. Scholasticism would call this 'prime matter' (*materia prima*) to distinguish it from what we normally understand to be 'matter' in its quantified and tangible state (*materia signata quantitate*). It is crucial to here understand that the underlying metaphysical dimension of interest here is the former; and it is the former, prime matter, pure potential to become, which is the basis for makes possible the latter 'signed matter.'
7. 'Real distinction' is to be contrasted with 'logical distinction' which is exclusively attributable to the activity of the mind and has no ontological footing outside of the activity of logical analysis. For example, only a logical distinction holds between the use of the English, four character proper name 'Mark' as used in the following two instances: 'Mark is my brother' and 'Mark is a proper noun.'
8. Aquinas' understanding of the *intensity of this union* is such that, were he alive today, he would not be surprised in the least by the tight correlation between mental events (characterised by consciousness, subjectivity and intentionality) and neurological events. This also helps him to articulate and come to a deeper appreciation of the Christian dogma of the resurrection of the body:

    In its own right, the soul is suited to be united to a body, just as a lightweight body is suited, in its own right, to be up high. And just as a light body remains light even after it has been separated from its proper place, and retains its readiness and inclination for that proper place, so the human soul continues in its existence even after it has been separated from its body, and it maintains its natural readiness and inclination for union with its body (*ST*, q. 76, a. 1 ad 6; Pasnau translation).

9. '[C]*um materia sit propter formam, hoc modo forma dat esse et speciem materiae, secundum quod congruit suae operationi*' (Thomas Aquinas, *QD de Anima*, Proem., 10 ad 2). In other words, at that basis of the act/potency paradigm is the *primacy of act* as the starting point of the dynamism. The momentum of that dynamism between ontological principles rests in the actuality component. That dynamism is metaphysically at the basis of physical objects: a determinable potency (matter) informed by the actuality (form).
10. In view of the foregoing, it is easy to grasp how any human existence, on the Aristotelian-Thomistic view, is richly teleological. The human person lives in dramatic tension toward

the great goal of full human flourishing and the full realisation of all that he or she can become. But this great human adventure is fraught with hazards, many of them internal to the human individual, particularly the disorder in which he finds his own passions. Thus in this view, central to attaining that human 'telos' will be (1) an account of morality, and accompanying it (2) an account of virtue and vice. The linear progression of the human individual toward his full flourishing will necessarily engage him in the interior exercise of moral reasoning and prudence whereby he strives to choose and act in ways that his own human reason perceives to be harmonious with the attainment of the uniquely human 'telos.'

11. This is, in fact, the meaning of the original Greek order, arrangement, regularity.
12. Human beings, according to Aristotle, share a common form or human nature. We are distinct and superior in kind with respect to all other corporeal and animate objects in the cosmos, enthroned, as it were, atop a hierarchy of natural kinds of such beings. Though we share a number of attributes with other types of beings, we remain unique and in sole possession of others. With inanimate objects, for instance, we too are subject to the forces of the cosmos. With plant-life, we share the functions of nutrition, growth, and reproduction; with animal-life, those of sensation and locomotion. What separates us from the rest of creation, according to Aristotle, is intelligence and will which are the soul's most significant and distinguishing operations.
13. 'If there is one belief Greek thinkers shared, it must be the conviction that both the essence of the real and our knowledge of it consists ultimately of form. Basically this means that it belongs to the essence of the real to appear, rather than to hide, and to appear in an orderly way' (Louis Dupré, *Passage to Modernity*, 18).
14. See Dupré, *op cit*, 17.
15. This development also has to be understood in light of what we might call two predominant tendencies (perhaps 'passions' is a better word) within Western thought. On the one hand, the growing predominance of autonomous self-assertion; on the other, the growing propensity over this period of time to separate, reduce, and fragmentise the holistic conception of reality we just elucidated: separation of 'object' from 'whole', 'meaning' (logos) from being, theology from ontology.

16. The entire passage from the Fourth Meditation, reads as follows:
    For in the first place, knowing that my nature is extremely feeble and limited, and that the nature of God is on the contrary immense, incomprehensible, and infinite, I have no further difficulty in recognising that there is an infinitude of matter in His power, the causes of which transcend my knowledge; an this reason suffices to convince me *that the species of cause termed final, finds no useful employment in physical or natural things*; for it does not appear to me that I can without temerity seek to investigate the inscrutable ends of God ('Meditations on the First Philosophy' in *The Philosophical Works of Descartes*, 173, emphasis my own).
17. 'Discourse on the Method', in *The Philosophical Works of Descartes*, 101.
18. Occasionalism held that all relations between physical bodies, or between human minds and physical bodies, which intuitively appear to be causal, are in fact not. Instead, the relations are the consequence of God's will. What we perceive of as a 'cause' is in reality only the 'occasion' for God to exercise his efficacious will and conjoin two bodies (or a mind and a physical body) in some proximate relation as conjoined events.
19. The following seem to be the most prominent theories within the discipline: Property dualists, while not countenancing anything like a soul, assert the ontological independence of mental properties from physical properties (for example, epiphenomenalism), but without acknowledging any causal role for mental properties in human experience; reductive materialists, while granting mental realism and acknowledging its causal role in human existence, will reduce mental events to the material realm by identifying them with physical events in the organism; eliminative materialists deny the possibility of reducing the mental to the physical, but this embodies the premise that mental events have no ontological status to begin with; they account for mental events as a cultural phenomenon of conceptual and linguistic confusion; finally, we can identify the stance of non-reductive materialism which seeks both to grant mental realism while maintaining the physical monism of the materialist school—in other words, this theory would grant the reality of mental events, yet attempt to account for them in a manner which neither undercuts the preeminence of biochemical activity nor, in accounting for mental phenomena, reduces the latter to the former.

20. Searle's theory *is* reductivist in a lesser sense that so-called 'non-reductivists' will tolerate. It can be termed a non-ontological causal reduction. Consciousness can be explained in terms of a *causal* reduction to neurobiological processes of the brain. Such a reduction, however, withstands the further *ontological* reduction (by redefinition) which holds of things such as electrical current, genes and temperature: electrical current in the wire is not caused by moving electrons, it *is* moving electrons; genes are not caused by chunks of base pairs of DNA, they *are* chunks of base pairs; temperature is not caused by molecular kinetic energy, it *is* molecular kinetic energy. On Searle's view, consciousness resists this latter kind of reduction for a simple reason: 'Part of the point of the reductions was to carve off the subjective experiences and exclude them from the definition of the real phenomena, which are now defined in terms of those features that interest us most. But where the phenomena that interests us most are the subjective experiences themselves, there is no way to carve anything off' (*Rediscovery*, 121).

21. 'Once we *see* that consciousness, with all its inner, qualitative, subjective, touchy-feely qualities, is just an ordinary property of the brain in the way that digestion is a property of the stomach, then the philosophical part of the problem is fairly easy to resolve' (*Consciousness and Language*, 2; emphasis my own). This seems to contradict a less ambitious statement of the same idea: 'We are at present very far from having an adequate theory of the neurophysiology of consciousness; but until we do, we have to keep an open mind about its possible chemical bases' (*Rediscovery*, 91). Also: 'The facts are that biological processes produce conscious mental phenomena and these are irreducibly subjective' (98).

22. 'Consciousness is a higher-level or emergent property of the brain in the utterly harmless sense of "higher-level" or "emergent" in which solidity is a higher-level emergent property of H20 molecules when they are in a lattice-structure (ice) . . .' (*Rediscovery*, 14).

23. *On the Soul*, II, 412a20.

24. *Ibid*, 412a 10; 412a 21.

25. *Ibid*, 412b 5.

26. *Contra Gentiles*, IV, c. 44, n.5.

27. See for example, *Contra Gentiles* II, c72, n2; II, c89, n3; *ST* I, q76, a8 ad 2; *De Pot*., q3 a1 2c.

28. *On the Soul*, II, 412a 22-26.
29. See Aristotle, *On the Soul* II, 414a4-18, and Aquinas, *ST*, I, q 76, a. 1c
30. *On the Soul*, 412b5.
31. 'Illud quod est tantum actus corporis viventis, animam vocamus' (In *II Sent*, 17, 2c); 'Anima autem secundum suam essentiam est actus corporis'(*De Spir Creaturis, Proemium*, a 11, obj 12); '*Ipsa essentia animae est actus corporis*' (*De principio individuationis*).
32. 'It is likewise impossible for [the intellective principle] to operate through a bodily organ, because the determinate nature even of that bodily organ would prevent the cognition of all bodies . . . . Therefore, this intellectual principle, which is called mind or intellect, has an operation on its own (*per se*) that the body does not share in' (*ST* I, q 75, a 2c, Pasnau translation).
33. *ST* I, q 75, a 2 ad 3. (Pasnau translation).
34. *ST*, q 75, a 2c (Robert Pasnau translation).
35. It therefore follows for Aquinas (here differing with his great teacher, Aristotle) that the human soul is incorruptible. In other words, once brought into existence, the human soul will continue to exist in perpetuity. This is so by definition as Aquinas understands soul to be pure actuality of an intellective type, that is, intrinsically independent of the body. In other words, the human soul is not only actuality of itself (like any form), but it possesses that actuality in and of itself, unlike the souls of brute animals (non-intellective) whose operation is intrinsically dependent on the organism (Cf *ST* I, q 75, a 3c). In other words, as pure actuality (like any form), the human soul contains no element of pure potential ('primer matter'), but rather is meant to be the actuality of matter and to give being to the whole composed of form/matter. In organisms, the cessation of existence is the result of the corruption (separation) of form from matter. Now since (a), there is no question of form being separated from itself since it is pure act, and (b) the human soul possesses that actuality per se, in and of itself intrinsically, Aquinas concludes that it is impossible for this kind of soul, namely a subsistent form, to cease to exist (*ST*, I, q 75, a 6.).
36. 'For the nature of a species consists in what its definition signifies. But in the case of natural things the definition signifies not the form alone, but the form *and* the matter' (*ST*, I, q 75, a 4c, Pasnau translation).

37. *On the Soul*, 412b9.
38. *Rediscovery*, 72.
39. *Ibid*, 72–3. I follow Searle's lead who offers as an example the recent discovery that some birds navigate by detecting the earth's magnetic field. See Thomas Nagel, 'What Is It Like to Be a Bat?', *The Philosophical Review*, LXXXIII, 4 (October, 1974): 435–50.
40. John Searle has no need for anything like a 'soul' in his account of the mind. He affirms: But nowadays, as far as I can tell, no one believes in the existence of immortal spiritual substances except on religious grounds. To my knowledge there are no purely philosophical or scientific motivations for accepting the existence of immortal mental substances (*Rediscovery*, 27).

Contributors

Teresa Wong Yai-Chow is Professor and Chair of the Department of Religious Studies, Fu Jen Catholic University, Taiwan.

Wen Hsiang Chen is a post-doctoral fellow in the Center for the Study of Science and Religion, Fu Jen Catholic University.

Frank Budenholzer is a Catholic Priest, Professor of Chemistry and Academic Coordinator of the Center for the Study of Science and Religion of Fu Jen Catholic University.

John F Haught is Professor Emeritus, Department of Theology, Georgetown University, Washington, DC.

Cheng, Chi-ming is a Professor in the Department of Religious Studies, Fu Jen Catholic University, Taiwan.

Kang, Phee-Seng is a Professor in the Department of Religion and Philosophy of Hong Kong Baptist University. He is also the director of the Center for Sino-Christian Studies of Hong Kong Baptist University.

Shih Chao-hwei is a Buddhist nun and Professor in the Department of Religious Studies of Hsuan Chuang University in Hsinchu, Taiwan and Head of Applied Ethics Research Center.

John B Chuang is a Professor in the Department of Religious Studies, Fu Jen Catholic University, Taiwan.

Thomas Berg a Catholic Priest and Senior Fellow of the Westchester Institute for Ethics and the Human Person, Thornwood, New York.

Glossary

Action 業

Aduhkhasukha-vedana 不苦不樂

Aharah（benefit and grow）食

Antara-bhava 中有

Anusaya 隨眠

Apatrapya 愧

Arbuda 遏部曇位

Arhat (demigod) 阿羅漢

Arupyadhatu (formless realm) 無色界

Asvabhava (non-inherent existence) 無自性

Atma-drsti (self view) 我見

Atma-mana (self pride) 我慢

Atma-moha (self ignorance) 我癡

Atma-sneha (ego desire) 我愛

Avidya 無明

Bagua 八卦

Bei Dou Jing 《北斗經》

Chang Kuang-chih 張光直

Chen Jun 陳鈞

Cheng Chih-Ming 鄭志明

Chu Ci (Poetry of the South) 《楚辭》

Daoism 道教

Divine Bird Clan 鳥族系

Divine Dragon Clan 神龍族系

Divine Fish Clan 神魚族系

Divine Goat Clan 神羊族系

Duyi Zhi《獨異記》

Fengsu Tongyi (Comprehensive Meanings of Customs and Habits) 《風俗通義》

Five aggregates 五蘊

Five migrators 五趣

Fu Xi 伏羲

Gao (jiao) mei 高（郊）禖

Ghana 鍵南位

Gui shen 鬼神

Guo Yu (Discourses of the States) 《國語》

'Gong Sun Chou' 《孟子》〈公孫丑〉篇

Han 漢

He Xin 何新

Hri 慚

Huang Di 黃帝

Hu Zhongshi 胡仲實

Huai Nan Zi (Book of the Prince of *Huai Nan*) 《淮南子》

Hun 魂

Jing 精

Jing (invisible space) 境

Jing qi 精氣

John B. Chuang 莊慶信

Kalala 羯羅藍位

kamadhatu (desire realm) 欲界

"King Zhao" 《左傳》〈昭公〉篇

Lao Zi 《老子》

Lao Zi Xiang Er Zhu 《老子想爾注》

Li Feng-mao 李豐楙

Li Ji (*The Classic of Rites*) 《禮記》

Lion's roar 獅子吼

Li Rong 李冗

Liu An 劉安

"Lu Yu" 《論語》〈魯語〉篇

Lie Zi 《列子》

Maharatnakuta Sutra 《大寶積經》

Mama-kara-sneha (attachment to what I have) 我所愛

Manas (consciousness or mind) 意

Man as a copy of heaven 天人相副

Mano sajcetanakarahara (food of mental thought) 意思食

Master Yin Shun 印順導師

Middle course 中道

Ming-tang (bright hall) 明堂

Muulasavraastivaada Vinaya 根本說一切有部毗奈耶雜事

Mythical thinking 神話思維

Nan Bei Dou Jing 《南北斗經》

Nan Dou Jing 《南斗經》

Nigantha Nataputta 尼乾子 （今之耆那教）

Nirvana 涅槃

Nivrtavyakrta 有覆無記

Nu Wa 女媧

Pan Gu 盤古

Peshi 閉尸位

Phassakarahara （food of touch） 細觸食

Po 魄

Prashakha 鉢羅賒佉位

Pratisamdhi samtati (to feel an embryo and continue) 結生相續

Pratitya-samutpada （dependent-arising） 緣起

Primitive thinking 原始思維

Protection for living beings 護生

Punar-bhava-sneha (attachment to one's life after death) 後有愛

Qi（the first ancestor of Zhou）棄（周朝始組）

Qin 秦

Qi Xue 《氣學》

Rupa-dhatu (form realm) 色界

Rupa-skandha (form) 色蘊

Sahaloka-dhatu 娑婆世界

Samjja-skandha (discrimination) 想蘊

Samskara-skandha (compositional factors) 行蘊

Samyuttanikaya 《雜阿含經》

Sattva（a passion for life）薩埵

Severing earth from heaven 絕地天通

Shan Hai Jing (Book of Mountain and Sea) 《山海經》

Shen (spirit of the heart) 神

Shih Chao-hwei 釋昭慧

Shijie 尸解

Shijie xian 尸解仙

'Shu Er' 《論語》〈述而〉篇

Shuo Wen Jie Zi (*A Character Dictionary*) 《說文解字》

Six migrators 六道

Soadanasya vijjana 有趣識

Suffering 苦

Tai Ping Jing 《太平經》

Taiping Yulan 《太平御覽》

Tian Di (emperor of heaven) 天帝

'Tian Wen' 《楚辭》〈天問〉篇

Three *hun* 魂

Trayo dhatavah （three realms）界

Tung Fang-yuan 董芳苑

Vedana-skandha (feeling) 受蘊

Vexation 惑

Vijjana-karahara （food of consciousness）識食

Vijjana-skandha (consciousness) 識蘊

Vijnaptimatratasiddhi-sastra 《成唯識論》

Wang Tzung-yu 王宗昱

"Xian Jin" 《論語》〈先進〉篇

Xiao Bing 蕭兵

Xing （body）形

Xing hai 形骸

Xu Shen 許慎

Xu Zheng 徐整

Ying Shao 應邵

Ying-yang 陰陽

Yi Zhuan 《易傳》

Yogacarya Bhumi Sastra 《瑜伽師地經》

Yuan qi (primordial vital energy) 元氣

Yuanshi Tianzun 元始天尊

"Ze Yang" 《莊子》〈則陽〉篇

Zhang Daoling 張道陵

Zhi（material）質

Zhou 周

Zhu Zi Yu Lei 《朱子語類》

Zi Chan 子產

Zunya (void) 空

Zuo Zhuan 《左傳》